THE HALIFAX EXPLOSION AND THE ROYAL CANADIAN NAVY

Studies in Canadian Military History

The Canadian War Museum, Canada's national museum of military history, has a threefold mandate: to remember, to preserve, and to educate. It does so through an interlocking and mutually supporting combination of exhibitions, public programs, and electronic outreach. Military history, military historical scholarship, and the ways in which Canadians see and understand themselves have always been closely intertwined. Studies in Canadian Military History builds on a record of success in forging those links by regular and innovative contributions based on the best modern scholarship. Published by the University of British Columbia Press in association with the Museum, the series will especially encourage the work of new generations of scholars and the investigation of important gaps in the existing historiography, pursuits not always well served by traditional sources of academic support. The results produced feed immediately into future exhibitions, programs, and outreach efforts by the Canadian War Museum. It is a modest goal that they feed into a deeper understanding of our nation's common past as well.

1   John Griffith Armstrong, *The Halifax Explosion and the Royal Canadian Navy: Inquiry and Intrigue*
2   Andrew Richter, *Avoiding Armageddon: Canadian Military Strategy and Nuclear Weapons, 1950-63*

John Griffith Armstrong

THE HALIFAX EXPLOSION AND THE ROYAL CANADIAN NAVY

Inquiry and Intrigue

UBC Press · Vancouver · Toronto

09   08   07   06   05   04   03   5   4   3

Printed in Canada on acid-free paper ∞

National Library of Canada Cataloguing in Publication Data

Armstrong, John Griffith, 1942-
    The Halifax explosion and the Royal Canadian Navy

    (Studies in Canadian military history, ISSN 1499-6251)
    Includes bibliographical references and index.
    ISBN 0-7748-0890-x (bound); ISBN 0-7748-0891-8 (pbk)

    1. Halifax (N.S.) – History – Explosion, 1917.2. Canada.
Royal Canadian Navy – History. I. Title.

FC2346.4.A75 2002   971.6 225   C2001-911556-3   F1039.5.H17A75 2002

Canadä

UBC Press gratefully acknowledges the financial support for our publishing program of the Government of Canada through the Book Publishing Industry Development Program (BPIDP), and of the Canada Council for the Arts, and the British Columbia Arts Council.

Publication of this book has been financially supported by the Canadian War Museum.

Printed and bound in Canada by Friesens
Set in Minion and Franklin Gothic by Neil and Brenda West, Typographics West
Editor: Barbara Tessman
Proofreader: Kate Baltais
Indexer: Annette Lorek
Cartographer: Eric Leinberger

UBC Press
The University of British Columbia
2029 West Mall
Vancouver, BC V6T 1Z2
604-822-5959 / Fax: 604-822-6083
www.ubcpress.ca

Contents

Illustrations / vi

Foreword / vii
J.L. Granatstein

Acknowledgments / ix

Introduction: Through Sailors' Eyes / 3

1 The RCN in Halifax – December 1917 / 9

2 Towards the Unthinkable / 25

3 Halifax Tide / 41

4 Through the Grim Day / 53

5 Reaction and Recovery / 82

6 Of Sailors, Lawyers, Goats, and Newspapers / 112

7 Goats to the Slaughter / 140

8 Covering the Tracks / 186

Notes / 211

Bibliography / 237

Index / 239

Illustrations

Maps

12   Approaches to Halifax Harbour

13   Halifax inner harbour

15   HMC Dockyard and Wellington Barracks, 1917

Photographs

73   Members of the RNCVR, c. 1916, including Able Seaman Bert Griffith. *Author's collection*

74   Admiral C.E. Kingsmill, director of the naval service. *National Archives of Canada PA-108013*

75   HMCS *Lady Evelyn*. *Department of National Defence CN-3274*

75   Minesweeping trawler *PV-II*. *Department of National Defence CN-6906*

76   HMCS *Grilse* at Halifax, 1915. *National Archives of Canada PA-209547*

76   HMCS *Canada*. *Department of National Defence CN-3793*

77   The officers and men of the RNCVR who carried out patrols of the St Lawrence and Atlantic on RCN trawlers and drifters. *Photographer: R. Montminy, National Archives of Canada PA-115373*

77   HMC submarines *CC-1* and *CC-2* at Halifax, c. 1918. *National Archives of Canada PA-113256*

78   HMCS *Niobe*, 1914. *Photographer: J. McLaughlan, National Archives of Canada PA-112438*

78   Trawler and drifter flotilla in Halifax Harbour. *National Archives of Canada PA-167307*

79   Damage to torpedo shops, with *CD-74* docked at left foreground. *National Archives of Canada C-147491*

79   The damaged victualling stores and YMCA building. *National Archives of Canada C-147487*

80   HMCS *Acadia*. *Department of National Defence CN-3278*

80   Damage to the married quarters, Wellington Barracks. *National Archives of Canada C-147480*

81   Shoreline view south from Wellington Barracks to dockyard. *National Archives of Canada C-147481*

81   Snow partially conceals the damage to the dry dock, SS *Hovland* and HMS *Highflyer* visible. *National Archives of Canada C-147485*

Foreword

The Canadian War Museum has always been the Cinderella of Canada's national museums. Although it has existed in various forms for more than a century, although its collections of art, military vehicles, weapons, primary documents, photographs, military clothing, and medals are truly extraordinary, the Museum suffered from substandard accommodation in Ottawa and a long tradition of weakly researched exhibits. For too long, the War Museum's exhibits were a heap of artifacts rather than a researched, coherent, and historically sound approach to Canada's long military history. The government's decision in 2000 to build a new museum at last will bring the War Museum to the forefront of Canada's national museums.

One area, however, was not neglected in the past: scholarship. In the dark days, the Museum staff created a Historical Publications series that helped greatly to encourage scholarly publication in Canadian military history. But this series, which was issued by many publishers, eventually succumbed under the weight of budget cuts. When I went to the CWM as Director and CEO on 1 July 1998, one of my primary goals was to establish the Museum's place as a research institution and to restore its role as an encourager of scholarly research and publication in military history. This volume, the first in what I trust will be a long association with the University of British Columbia Press, genuinely marks a new beginning.

Full scholarly standards, including peer review, have been scrupulously followed in the publication of John Armstrong's manuscript – and will be followed in the future. The Canadian War Museum Studies in Canadian Military History, I am happy to say, is well and truly launched.

Armstrong's book, the first, complete scholarly examination of the Halifax explosion, is a splendid beginning to the series. His research is extraordinarily thorough, most particularly in government records, his perspective is very different from those of earlier accounts, and his shrewd and careful exploration of naval, military, and social questions guarantees that no one will ever again be able to discuss the terrible events of December 1917 in Halifax in the same way. And, happily, Armstrong keeps the personal dimension of the catastrophe to the fore. This is no dry-as-dust institutional history, in other words. Ordinary people died, and ordinary people struggled to deal with the extraordinary disaster that fell upon them, and Armstrong has not forgotten this.

Armstrong is also especially interesting in the way he demonstrates how the young Royal Canadian Navy, less than a decade old in 1917, was vilified by Haligonians and blamed for the disaster. This was most unfair – Armstrong even suggests that the long memory of the navy may have helped contribute to the V-E Day riots of 1945 – and the author makes a signal contribution by carefully detailing the proceedings and results of the inquiry that tried to determine what had gone wrong. He also is careful to note the ways in which politicians predictably tried to pass the buck and ensure that no blame fell on them. The book is a model of careful judgment founded on a full command of the sources.

From my restored status as a civilian, I congratulate John Armstrong for writing a fine monograph, the CWM staff, notably Roger Sarty and Dean Oliver, who worked to ensure that this series would proceed, and UBC Press for being such a willing and helpful collaborator.

J.L. Granatstein

Acknowledgments

As I acknowledge the individuals and institutions that were instrumental in the completion of this project, I must begin on a personal note. If this book seeks to view the tragedy of the Halifax explosion through sailors' eyes, it is because one set of those eyes belonged to my grandfather, Lambert ("Bert") Barron Griffith. He was a thirty-five-year-old naval reservist from Red Deer, Alberta, serving aboard HMCS *Niobe*, the Royal Canadian Navy's depot ship, which was moored at the naval dockyard half a mile from the blast. Although he survived the blast, he was severely disabled – it marked his life forever. Letters he wrote to his wife in the days that followed the explosion are the reason I wrote this book.

On a more general level, this work would not have been possible without the active support of the Directorate of History and Heritage (DHH) at National Defence Headquarters; the director, Dr Serge Bernier; and, most particularly, the senior historian, Roger F. Sarty (now of the Canadian War Museum). Indeed, the project began under Dr Sarty's direction as a source list to support the directorate's project for a new official history of the RCN's early years. Dr Sarty is co-author of the best account of the RCN in the First World War, and I am deeply indebted to him for sharing his research and his sage knowledge. I am also very grateful that my former colleagues at DHH continue to treat me as such in my retirement and make me feel welcome. Despite brutal reductions in numbers and resources, they nobly carry on. I must name Owen Cooke, now retired, who was the first to urge publication of my grandfather's letters, and Donna Porter, who aided me in obtaining the Admiralty's subject file on the Halifax explosion from the Public Records Office in London. Isabel Campbell and Gabrielle Nishiguchi were also especially helpful in supporting my research, and the Canadian Forces Photo Unit kindly provided a number of rare photos from their outstanding collection.

It is always a pleasure to visit the Nova Scotia Archives and Records Service. It provides a warm and comfortable atmosphere consistent with its home province, and always ensured smooth access to the records I wanted to view.

The National Archives of Canada was my full-time home for six months and a regular destination for the next four years. It is truly a national treasure. Despite the frustrations of cutbacks and inadequate resources, its dedicated staff were unfailingly interested and helpful. There are too many individuals to name at the archives, but I must remark upon the particular role played by Timothy Dubé. His almost daily lunchtime presence in the archives' cafeteria has for some years provided a meeting and mingling point for almost every visiting known or budding military historian in Canada. Such informal points of contact add a remarkably human dimension, which makes the NAC an immensely agreeable place to work. I even excuse his almost daily needling over my "explosive research."

There are many influences behind any historian. I particularly want to mention my former teachers, and later colleagues, in the history department of the Royal Military College of Canada. As the only history graduate student in the department, I enjoyed ready access to some of Canada's best military historians of the time. Donald M. Schurman and the late Barry D. Hunt taught me to love naval history. Although the seeds they planted took a long time to germinate, I take great pleasure in acknowledging their impact on an air force officer. More recently, Ronald G. Haycock, now retired as Dean of Arts, was a key influence in my decision to write this book. Norman Hillmer of Carleton University contributed unerring insight and support when the chips were down. I was also very fortunate to have anonymous academic referees who worked hard to help me make this a better book.

Wonderful staff at UBC Press taught me that writing books is a team effort. Emily Andrew, Barbara Tessman, Camilla Jenkins, Andrea Kwan, and Ron Phillips, thank you so much for your hard work, unfailing dedication, and good humour. Eric Leinberger, thank you for a striking series of maps. Many thanks also to the Canadian War Museum and to Dean Oliver, Head, Historical Research and Archives for selecting this work for the museum's *Studies in Canadian Military History* series.

Portions of the research for Chapters 1 to 4 were published as "Letters from Halifax: Reliving the Halifax Explosion through the Eyes of My Grandfather, A Sailor in the Royal Canadian Navy," *The Northern Mariner/Le Marin du nord* 8, 4 (1998): 55-74. I am most grateful for the support received from *Northern Mariner* editors Lewis R. Fischer, Olaf U. Janzen, and, more recently, William Glover.

Finally I wish to thank my wonderful wife, Gaetane, and my dear daughters, Christine and Linda, for their love and support. They are my greatest treasure.

Introduction: Through Sailors' Eyes

We must remember not to judge any public servant by any one act,
and especially should we beware of attacking the men who are
merely the occasions and not the causes of disaster.

Theodore Roosevelt
10 April 1899

The Halifax explosion of 6 December 1917 razed much of the city of Halifax, vilified the Canadian navy, polarized elements within the media and government, and became a definitive event in Canada's national consciousness.[1] On that day, the collision of the ships *Mont Blanc* and *Imo* in Halifax Harbour triggered an eruption of almost 3,000 tons of picric acid, TNT, and gun cotton. The largest man-made explosion in the world to that time, it killed over 1,600 people and wounded some 9,000 others.

Yet despite the magnitude of the explosion and the tragedy and controversy in its wake, the event is curiously underrepresented in the country's political and military histories. Some national histories make no mention of the disaster, and even the definitive biography of the prime minister of the time remarks on it only in passing.[2] The response of the military history community has been similarly underwhelming. The vast majority of First World War studies have concentrated almost entirely on events overseas and on the politics and policies that directed them. Indeed, from the standpoint of Canadian soldiery, only Sir Andrew MacPhail's official army medical history of the Great War (1925) comments on the explosion and its aftermath. His observations, while brief, emphasize that the disaster was the "supreme test" of the army medical service in Canada.[3] Desmond Morton's widely used survey text on Canadian military history recognizes the threat that the disaster posed to the critical role played by the port of Halifax – and the nascent naval force it sheltered – in the war effort.[4] Gilbert Tucker's official history of the naval service provides a brief sketch of the local naval dimensions of the disaster but does not go much beyond generalities.[5] Much more recently, in their landmark study of the Royal Canadian Navy (RCN) during the First World War, Michael L. Hadley and Roger Sarty recognize the Halifax explosion as a "new datum in Canada's consciousness," but suggest that, owing to good fortune, it only briefly disrupted the operations of the navy and the port. Although coverage of the explosion is merely a digression in their study, they are the first historians to make the important point that the explosion turned public opinion against the navy.[6] Yet if this argument is accurate, it is puzzling that the most recent general history of the RCN makes no mention of the catastrophe.[7]

Although all but ignored by military and political historians, the Halifax explosion represents a significant benchmark in the field of disaster research. Indeed, the 1920 work of Samuel Henry Prince on forms of social change experienced during this catastrophe is still admired as a pioneering work in the genre.[8] More recently, analysts of disaster such as Russell R. Dynes, E.L. Quarantelli, and T. Joseph Scanlon have made additional contributions to a respectable body of scientific literature on the subject.[9]

These studies notwithstanding, most of what has been written about events in Halifax on and after 6 December 1917 is popular history and literature focusing on the local dimension. Many of these works convey a rich sense of the immensity of the tragedy, the sufferings of the population, and the endurance of the human spirit. Classic books such as Hugh MacLennan's *Barometer Rising* (1941) and Michael J. Bird's *The Town That Died* (1962) have particularly sharpened our appreciation of the event. For succeeding generations, books by Janet Kitz (1989) and by Robert MacNeil (1992) have continued the tradition.[10] These and other works, while all local in their viewpoint, range widely in style (from literary expressions to historical and scientific examinations) and subject (from relief and medical responses to legal issues and reconstruction). Most are worthy (and often very moving), but few are without errors. They suffer from lack of access to all the available sources. Some of the popular histories, perhaps inspired by MacLennan or MacNeil, cross into the novelist's realm of invented dialogue, which blurs their usefulness as credible history. Most seriously, the *national* perspective on the disaster is lacking because research has been confined largely to local sources.

If one examines all the political, military, disaster-analysis, and local accounts of the explosion, the common thread is that national context is ignored. Neither the Royal Canadian Navy, the Canadian Militia, nor any other government agency figures prominently in accounts of the disaster, despite their direct and immediate involvement. This is a striking omission for an event long regarded as one of our national touchstones. As part of the national war effort, the port of Halifax had been brought under federal control: Halifax, more than any other Canadian city, had become a garrison town. The French ship *Mont Blanc* was in the harbour solely because of Halifax's important role in the war effort. The administration that controlled the movements of *Mont Blanc* and other ships in the harbour was federal. Moreover, after the explosion, federal agencies were responsible for getting the port back into operation, for calling a public inquiry into the event, and for determining what lessons should be drawn from the disaster. Everyone in Halifax – from outraged municipal politicians to the citizens themselves – fully understood the federal context, and all looked to Ottawa when laying the blame or looking for relief.

Beyond these considerations, the national context is crucial in revealing the role and experience of Canadian sailors and soldiers in the disaster. No published study suggests that these men were other than bit players in the tragedy, but such a suggestion is misleading. Halifax was the principal base of Canada's tiny navy. With unforeseen events in the war at sea threatening the east coast of North America, the size of the naval force in the harbour quickly multiplied. At the same time, the city housed the most important army garrison in the country. Both soldiers and sailors were particularly well placed to witness and understand the events that unfolded in Halifax Harbour. Thus, like federal agencies, these military and naval men are an important part of the wider context of this study. Yet because it was ultimately the naval service that was responsible for the port of Halifax, it is the eyes of the "sailors" that provide the central focus.

This book is not a history of the Halifax explosion per se. It does not detail the civilian loss of life or damage to the city at large, nor does it review citizens' efforts at relief and reconstruction. It concentrates on local events only to the extent that they affected or were affected by the navy. Thus, the chapters that follow recount events from the point of view of individual officers, enlisted personnel, civilian employees, and officials of the navy, whether afloat or ashore, and whether in Halifax, Ottawa, or elsewhere. They include, as well, the perspectives of personnel in the allied Royal Navy and United States Navy. Such accounts provide the bases on which to revisit and revise the known sequence of events.

Such revision is made possible by the wealth of detailed information in the records of the armed services in Ottawa, which reflects the centrality of the armed forces to the life and economy of wartime Halifax as well as the forces' responsibility for the federal government's response to the disaster. The records of other federal departments and agencies that had a presence in Halifax are also rich sources: the political leadership and senior officials in Ottawa needed, demanded, and received a constant flow of information. Together, these sources not only clear up myths and misconceptions in earlier accounts but also bring new dimensions to the story. One of the notable new dimensions is the perspective of leaders in Ottawa – the people who, within a few days of the explosion, made most of the key decisions that affected subsequent events. Because they were in a position to make a somewhat detached assessment of local events and personalities, their perspectives frequently differ markedly from those of people closer to the disaster. Related to this consideration, federal personnel and institutional records are also invaluable for analyzing people and institutions under stress, one of the fascinating aspects of any disaster, and one of the most profitable areas of study.

Equally importantly, federal sources explain why the regional perspective has so completely dominated the record from 1917 to the present day. In the face of understandable outrage in Halifax about the apparent failure of federal officials and national institutions, the response of authorities in Ottawa – surprisingly well documented in the National Archives – was political damage control from which a more balanced assessment has never emerged.

Once the operation of the port had been restored, the Canadian Army publicly received some belated credit for its role in the wake of the disaster, although this acknowledgment greatly understated its crucially important, efficient, and effective part in all phases of the recovery. The navy's reputation, by contrast, had no chance.

In the aftermath of the tragedy, Haligonians searched for answers. Why had this awful thing happened? Who was responsible? A public inquiry established to address those questions rapidly became controversial: given the emotionally charged atmosphere in the city, it was rather too much to expect otherwise. A growing sense of public outrage accompanied the proceedings. The movements of ships and the orders given by masters and the pilots charged to bring the ships safely into port were scrutinized. The navy (and by implication the government of Canada) was responsible for traffic control in Halifax Harbour. Had it failed in its duty? That possibility became the subject of much debate, and a swelling wave of public vilification was directed towards the RCN. The navy was caught in what became a nasty search for people to punish. As the process played out, it was accompanied by what some would today call a media feeding-frenzy. Meanwhile, lawyers argued and postured, and politicians and officials struggled with appearances, issues, and outcomes while practising damage control. Despite an apparent array of circumstantial evidence against the navy, the Crown counsel to the inquiry, who had become convinced that the naval service was blameless in the matter, courageously tried to argue against the weight of intense public opinion. He failed. In a symbolic censure of the entire navy, Frederick E. Wyatt, the middle-ranking officer in charge of naval examination of shipping at the port, joined an equally unfortunate ship's captain and a pilot accused of manslaughter. Ultimately, the focus on Wyatt served as a useful foil to prevent other information from becoming public and to help the government weather the crisis. It is one of the goals of this book to redress this injustice.

The first chapters of this book offer an examination of the navy's physical presence in the port of Halifax and a reconstruction, from a naval point of view, of the sequence of events leading up to the disaster. Similarly, the explosion and its immediate aftermath will be addressed in terms of ships, facilities, and personnel. The focus then shifts outward in time and space through the day of the explosion as sailors and soldiers from three nations struggled to deal with the disaster. The account continues with an assessment of reaction and recovery efforts in still wider terms, including an Ottawa perspective, and the complex interactions by which damage was assessed and repaired and by which the port was brought back into operation as a vital cog in the ongoing war effort. Two chapters explore the difficult visible and behind-the-scenes processes that sought to determine blame, absorb lessons, and affect public policy. In concluding, some additional evidence will be considered to expand our understanding of how the affair played out and how it affected the Royal Canadian Navy.

Finally, it should be noted that Canadian military historians have long studied the difficulties between senior military officers and politicians. Such issues are not the focus of this work. Rather, this is a tale of an institution in crisis. It was composed of a "family" of politicians, civil servants, and uniformed personnel who shared certain values and objectives, interacted with and affected each other, and generally understood their place in the system. Despite the changed times, they were not unlike such institutions that exist today. Herein lie the modest lessons to be learned.

1

The Royal Canadian Navy in Halifax – December 1917

On 6 December 1917, a motley little navy was in charge of the port of Halifax. Although the British Royal Navy (RN) had inhabited Halifax Harbour for more than a century, it had relinquished direct control of the port to Ottawa in 1905. With the onset of the Great War, the White Ensign had returned as a very visible presence, yet the Royal Navy was no longer in charge. That responsibility fell to an utterly inadequate collection of Canadian vessels, which had only recently been cobbled together.

The Royal Canadian Navy (RCN) had been born in 1910 in almost farcical circumstances. It had begun the war with only two elderly cruisers. By the last month of 1917, minesweepers, armed tugboats, patrol ships (even a torpedo boat destroyer of doubtful lineage), and two antiquated submarines had been added. These vessels had been gathered at the Halifax naval dockyard to guard against the recent, and potentially serious, threat of enemy attack at sea and to ensure both clear access to the harbour and the safety of ships off Canada's coasts. These responsibilities were beyond the means and priorities of the overburdened Royal Navy, yet the ragtag flotillas of Canadian ships were hardly adequate for the task. By early December 1917, however, a steady trickle of newly constructed armed trawlers and drifters had begun to arrive from the interior. The RCN had little time to prepare for the distinct possibility that German submarines would be operating off the Canadian coast by the spring.

Halifax had been a garrison town and naval base since its inception in 1749, and had been a site of varying importance in the military security of the British Empire. Its importance was again highlighted as the war in Europe dragged on. Despite the priorities and demands of the overseas forces, the former imperial fortress possessed a substantial garrison, and the sea approaches to the harbour were shielded by a considerable network of coastal artillery and searchlights.[1]

The city of Halifax sits on a peninsula that juts into the west side of Halifax Harbour. From its narrow southern tip, Point Pleasant Park, the peninsula widens, and the harbour passage correspondingly narrows – indeed, the passage is called the Narrows – before expanding again into Bedford Basin north of the city. By the time of the Great War, the city's eastern shore, which faces Dartmouth across the harbour, was lined with port facilities. At the northern end were the railway wharves, the dry dock, and HMC Dockyard.

With its population of some 50,000 souls, Halifax had become an increasingly vigorous and vital port, serving the war effort of the British Empire and its allies. Indeed, the strategic position of Halifax on the Great Circle route to Europe and its status as the most important Canadian ice-free port had kept it at the forefront of the North Atlantic war effort. With the recent entry of the United States into the war, that country's northeastern ports were growing in importance, but Halifax continued as a key centre. Wartime shipping from Halifax was limited only by the capacity of the single-track rail line that connected the port with Canada's interior. Nearly two thousand commercial vessels passed through the port in 1917, not including the considerable coastal and fishing traffic. The city also remained the preferred port of embarkation and debarkation for Canadian soldiers.[2]

Unlike the unseasoned and generally untested RCN, the Canadian Militia had long been a significant presence in Halifax's social and cultural fabric. Although, as a national force, the Canadian Militia was inadequate in numbers, equipment, and training, its local importance was enormous. Its status within Halifax had been reinforced when the British garrison left the city in 1905 and Canada had assumed full responsibility for the protection of the port. Since that time, Ottawa had been obliged to maintain an operationally ready garrison to guarantee the security of the base as a safe haven for imperial fleets and commerce; indeed, the base had become the Canadian Army's premier peacetime defence commitment. To meet it, a relatively well-trained and balanced all-arms force – including garrison artillery, infantry, engineers, ordnance, service corps, and medical troops – much of it made up of full-time soldiers, was in place even prior to the outbreak of war. Their presence was pervasive, with military facilities scattered throughout the area.

By 1917, the 3,300 soldiers responsible for the defence of Halifax were largely older, married with families, or suffering from minor disabilities, which made them less eligible for service overseas with the Canadian Expeditionary Force (CEF). In addition to these men, the city housed many members of the CEF itself – mostly depot units and drafts of recruits awaiting transport overseas. Counting the 323 British Army recruits in the city, nearly 5,000 soldiers found themselves in Halifax at the end of 1917, representing about 10 percent of the population of the city. This number included over 600 medical troops – doctors, nurses, and medical orderlies – some of whom served in local military hospitals such as Cogswell Street, Rockhead General, and Camp Hill. Others were employed with No. 6 Casualty Unit, which received wounded at the Pier 2 Casualty Depot in the Deepwater Terminals. Two hundred more were to be found at the Army Medical Corps Training Depot, which was also in the city. With such a garrison in residence, surely Halifax enjoyed the dubious honour of being better prepared than any city in Canada to deal with a major disaster.[3]

If the war led to a significant increase in the number of troops in Halifax, the city's role as a naval centre of operations also expanded greatly with the appearance of the first German submarines in the western Atlantic, the German declaration of unrestricted submarine warfare, and America's entry into the war. From the onset of the war, the dockyard facilities, much neglected since the departure of the British, had been repaired and refurbished. Although not entirely modern, by the final months of 1917 they had become a busy, even overcrowded, complex of offices, residences, workshops, slipways, wharves, and storehouses. Among the more recent developments was the establishment of a new wireless school to train "wireless learners" for employment at naval radio stations, on Canadian ships, and in the dockyard wireless office.[4] Admiralty House, long the residence of senior Royal Navy

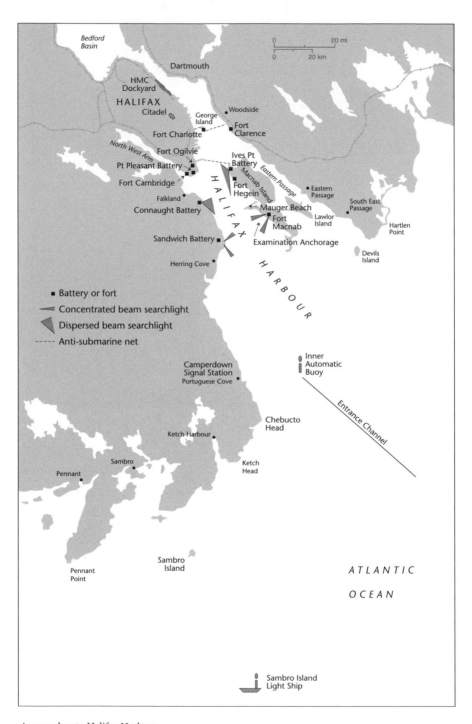

Approaches to Halifax Harbour

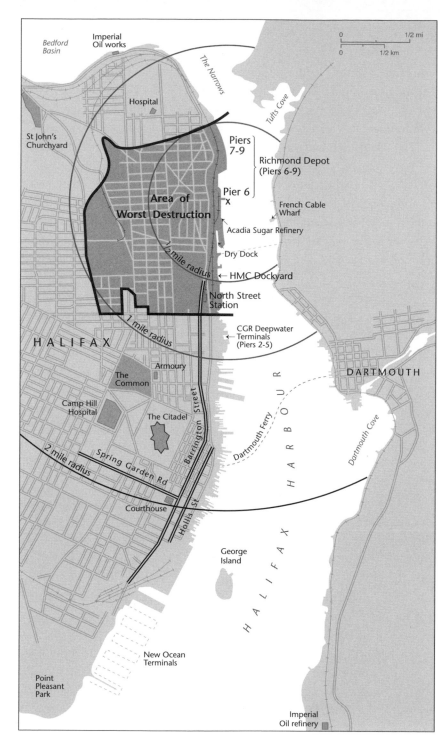

Halifax inner harbour

commanders in the North Atlantic and West Indies, and today the site of the Maritime Command Museum, was in use as the dockyard hospital. With a staff of three surgeons, two nurses, and ten attendants, the facility could accommodate fifty patients – more than sufficient for anticipated needs.[5]

The dockyard's civilian and military staff – and private companies as well – were under constant pressure to meet the mounting demands of repair, refit, and maintenance for both the varied collection of Canadian vessels and passing units of the RN.[6] On 18 November, the dockyard's efficiency suffered a setback when the office block that housed its headquarters was gutted by a fire that destroyed many records. The offices were transferred temporarily to the Marine and Fisheries Building, which was adjacent to the dockyard property.[7]

At the extreme north end of the dockyard, a building that the Royal Navy had constructed as a hospital housed the Royal Naval College of Canada. With thirty-eight cadets in residence, the college offered instruction comparable to that at Britain's two naval training colleges. The institution's small professional and academic staff was supervised by the much revered Commander E.A.E. Nixon, RN. Four members of the college's first graduating class had been the first RCN casualties of the war, having been appointed to the ill-fated HMS *Good Hope,* sunk off Coronel (Chile) in 1914. The names of Malcolm Cann, John Hathaway, William Palmer, and Arthur Silver are the first of the hundreds that now grace the Sailors' Memorial at Halifax's Point Pleasant Park and attest to Canadian sacrifice at sea.

Command over HMC Dockyard was exercised by a captain superintendent, Captain Edward H. Martin, RCN, who was also charged with responsibility for the naval defence of the port and its immediate approaches. The fifty-eight-year-old Martin had retired from the Royal Navy in 1909 after more than thirty-six years of service and had joined the RCN on its formation the following year. By late 1917, he had overseen the affairs of the dockyard for more than seven years.[8] At the end of November, however, he was not present in Halifax. Admiral Charles. E. Kingsmill, director of the naval service, had sent him off to the Admiralty as principal delegate in a mission to sort out continuing difficulties between the Admiralty and the Canadian navy. As Michael Hadley and Roger Sarty have noted, Kingsmill had earlier "telegraphed Admiralty over the [Naval Service] minister's signature and asked three pointed questions. What was the precise scale of attack that Canada faced? What defences were required? And what assistance might

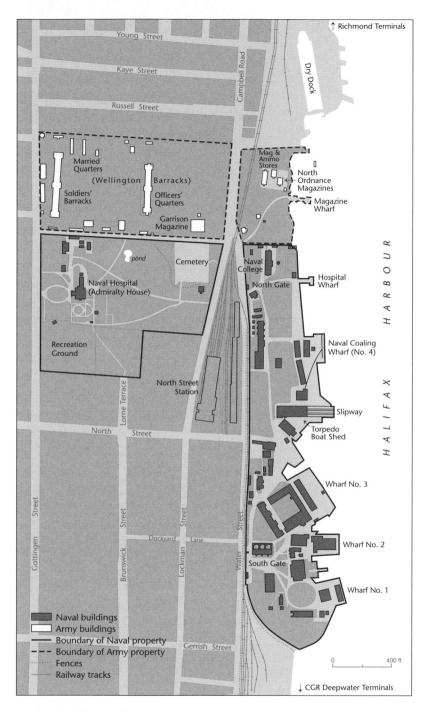

↑ Richmond Terminals

Young Street

Kaye Street

Russell Street

Campbell Road

Dry Dock

Married Quarters

(Wellington Barracks)

Soldiers' Barracks

Officers' Quarters

Garrison Magazine

Mag & Ammo Stores

North Ordnance Magazines

Magazine Wharf

pond

Cemetery

Naval College

Hospital Wharf

Naval Hospital (Admiralty House)

North Gate

Recreation Ground

Naval Coaling Wharf (No. 4)

Lorne Terrace

North Street Station

Slipway

Torpedo Boat Shed

North Street

Wharf No. 3

Gottingen Street

Brunswick Street

Lockman Street

Water Street

Wharf No. 2

Dockyard Lane

South Gate

Wharf No. 1

Gerrish Street

HARBOUR

HALIFAX

Naval buildings
Army buildings
Boundary of Naval property
Boundary of Army property
Fences
Railway tracks

0   400 ft

↓ CGR Deepwater Terminals

HMC Dockyard and Wellington Barracks, 1917
Source: Adapted from *H.M. Naval Yard, Hospital & Admiralty House, Halifax* (1904), NAC, National Map Collection, NMC 0034329.

15

Canada expect from the Royal Navy? Kingsmill followed the telegram with a lengthy memorandum that documented the difficulties that Admiralty's erratic advice had caused since 1916 ... an already too-familiar pattern of half-baked and misleading advice."[9]

Martin looked a good choice to plead the Canadian cause in London, and Kingsmill allowed he could be spared for a few weeks during the winter months. Only later would he confidentially reveal to the minister responsible for the navy that he had had other reasons for wishing the dockyard superintendent away from Halifax.[10] In Martin's absence, the post would be filled by the gruff but benevolent Captain Fred C.C. Pasco, another former RN officer of long service and experience, who had retired from the RN and joined the Canadian force in 1915. Free from his usual responsibilities as senior officer in the port of Sydney, Pasco took up temporary residence in Martin's house in the dockyard.

The captain superintendent was responsible for the naval defence of the port, although the reality was that the Militia Department's coastal defence guns were the port's premier insurance against warships operating on the surface. They provided small comfort in the face of potential submarine incursions, however. Thus, as early as mid-1915 the first anti-submarine net had been placed across the inner harbour from either side of George Island. By July 1917 a second net was established farther down the harbour between Ives Point and the breakwater off Point Pleasant.[11] Joint orders had also been issued by the local army and navy commanders in late 1916 to douse all lights ashore and afloat that might be viewed from seaward.[12] These orders had been reaffirmed and enforced with new zeal in October 1917. The virtual blackout made Halifax unique among Canadian cities and served as a constant reminder of the growing danger off the coast.[13]

Attacks on shipping were not the only reason to fear submarines. Concern mounted that the U-boats might lay mines in the approaches to Halifax and other harbours. Thus, outside the nets, a flotilla of ten minesweeping craft was moored at two buoys in the North West Arm, just above Chain Rock. A continuously manned telephone hut on the fore shore in Point Pleasant Park provided necessary communications with the dockyard, and the minesweepers normally proceeded into the inner harbour only for repairs.[14] Seven of the craft were converted menhaden (herring) trawlers commissioned (in distinctive Roman numerals) as *PV-I* through *PV-VII*. The other three – *Baleine*, *Musquash*, and *Gopher* – were ocean-going tugboats operated by civilian crews under charter. Four of the sweepers were radio equipped. A motor boat, *W.H. Lee,* attended the flotilla and conveyed stores back and forth into Halifax Harbour.[15] Early every morning, weather permitting, the vessels would sortie in pairs more than twenty miles to sea to ensure clear channels into and out of the harbour for warships, convoys, and coastal traffic.[16]

Tugs such as *Nereid* and the *Wilfrid C.,* armed with six-pounder guns, provided a measure of protection for the boom nets and acted as gate vessels. Beyond these, the captain superintendent had few armed resources to deal with potential threats outside the range of the militia's coastal defence guns. The fast, low-slung HMCS *Grilse* was an exception. A converted yacht permanently assigned to the port, she bore the perhaps optimistic designation "TBD" (torpedo boat destroyer) because she carried a torpedo tube in addition to her two twelve-pounder guns. Almost alone among the tinpot fleet of the Canadian navy, she bore at least some physical resemblance to a modern warship.[17]

Although the long-feared but still shocking appearance of German U-boats in North American waters had occurred in 1916, there were no major incursions the following year. The growing fleet of German submarines had at least temporarily found better hunting and easier access closer to home. Indeed, overall shipping losses had grown astronomically, and in July 1917 a reluctant Royal Navy had been forced to adopt a convoy system if shipping routes to Britain were to be kept open at all. Convoys from Sydney escorted by RN warships and armed merchant cruisers had begun in September of that year. With the freeze-up of the St Lawrence River by December, convoys had to be organized from Halifax instead. This move also brought about the relocation to HMC Dockyard, Halifax, of the RCN Patrol Service from its usual base at Sydney. Thus, on the eve of disaster, the importance of the Halifax naval base had been vastly increased and the challenges multiplied.

The arrival of the patrol fleet brought the competent and respected (Acting Captain) Walter Hose to Halifax. The Captain of Patrols was another former RN officer who had found the prospect of transfer to the newly formed RCN attractive, possibly due to his marrying into a family in St John's. Still relatively young, at age forty-two, he had a number of impressive successes to his credit and was one of the few truly able professionals available to the RCN with clear potential for senior command.[18]

The eight auxiliary patrol vessels that constituted the core of Hose's

Patrol Service were still a rather sundry assemblage, despite the replacement of some of the least suitable components. They ranged in displacement from 700 to 1,050 tons and had been turned over to the RCN from a variety of sources – mostly other government departments – and fitted with modest armament, usually one or two twelve-pounder guns.[19] Two of the ships, *Hochelaga* and *Stadacona,* were large yachts purchased earlier in the war and adapted to naval service. Another vessel, the former *King Edward* of Canada Steamship Lines, had been purchased by the navy in May 1917 and been given the name *Laurentian. Lady Evelyn,* acquired by the Post Office to transfer mail to and from passing transatlantic steamers, had entered naval service in June. *Margaret's* RCN service dated back to February 1915, when she had been commandeered from the Customs Service. *Cartier* and *Acadia* – the latter today preserved on the Halifax waterfront – were hydrographic survey ships. Of the eight, only *Canada,* built in 1904 and nominally intended for fisheries patrol, had been designed "along warship lines" in order to provide a foundation for training sailors for the future RCN.[20]

Only five of these patrol ships were considered fit for deep-sea work and the sometimes difficult conditions off Saint John in the Bay of Fundy, and all would have to be cycled through refit at some point during the winter season. *Laurentian* and *Lady Evelyn* were regarded as less seaworthy in heavy winter conditions and therefore were restricted to work close off Halifax and escorting warships.[21] *Acadia* also required repairs and, until these could be completed, she was to be anchored in Bedford Basin for the winter to be used as a guard ship and a base for Royal Navy staff assigned to control the movement of neutral shipping.[22]

Other new arrivals at Halifax were intended to beef up the Patrol Service. Although delayed by frustrating debates with the Royal Navy over numbers and allocations, and plagued by technical and manufacturing problems, by late 1917 the long-awaited Canadian-built trawlers and drifters had finally begun to make their way down the St Lawrence and across the gulf into Nova Scotia waters. By the time deteriorating ice conditions closed the route in early December, three of the new battle-class trawlers (*St Julien, Messines,* and *Ypres*) and thirty-nine of the drifters had been despatched.[23] All but one arrived safely in Halifax, although some of the voyages were not without mishap.[24]

The arrival of these new vessels in Halifax immediately improved the navy's ability to patrol the approaches to Halifax, including the routes taken by convoys from outside the mineswept channel a farther 130 miles to sea.[25] As well, the additional resources contributed to a more effective minesweeping program for the port, allowing vessels to be dedicated exclusively to that purpose.[26]

Not all of the new arrivals in Halifax were surface vessels. On 14 October, HMCS *Shearwater* had sailed into the dockyard accompanied by the RCN's two submarines. This sloop, brought into the RCN at the beginning of the war as the submarines' tender, was a remnant of the Royal Navy squadron that had once cruised from Canada's Pacific coast. The submarines, *CC-1* and *CC-2*, had been purchased early in the war by the premier of British Columbia, Sir Richard McBride, as a counter to a German cruiser squadron in the Pacific.[27] If it had ever existed, the need for the subs to remain on the west coast had long since passed. Under the mistaken impression that the already obsolete boats, with their finicky two-cylinder engines, would be of use in European waters, the British Admiralty had asked for them to be made available at Halifax. An epic voyage ensued. The vessels were en route from June, their 8,000-mile passage marred by frequent breakdowns and long stays in a series of ports. Although a dedicated but overworked crew constantly cleaned and overhauled the engines, cylinders and piston heads cracked, and fuel pump crankshafts broke. Without the enthusiastic assistance of the US Navy, including frequent towing, during the subs' passage through the Panama Canal and up the eastern seaboard, it is doubtful that the hapless little flotilla would have found its way to Halifax.[28] Once they arrived in that city, it was painfully clear that the boats would never make it across the Atlantic. Consequently, the Admiralty opined that the boats should remain in Halifax, where they might be of use should enemy U-boats threaten the Canadian coast.[29] First, however, an extensive refit would be required. Thus, in December 1917 the two hard-used boats were based at Pier 1 in the dockyard, with their own crews carrying out much of the labour from improvised workshops.[30] *Shearwater*, temporarily free from her onerous responsibilities, was detached to Bermuda in company with four drifters for delivery to the Royal Navy.[31]

The largest Canadian ship in the port of Halifax was no longer an effective part of the order of battle but was still very much a useful presence. HMCS *Niobe* was the 11,000-ton heavy cruiser that had been obtained from Britain at the RCN's inception. Outdated even then, the cruiser was to serve as a training ship for naval personnel on the East Coast. The fate of the vessel – damaged in a grounding in 1911, slowly repaired, and then left along-side with a skeleton crew – symbolized the fortunes of the RCN in the years immediately before the First World War. Although *Niobe* had been placed on a war footing in 1914 – and indeed was well used in the early part of the war for RN cruiser patrols in the western Atlantic – by mid-1915 the much-worn ship was no longer economical to maintain on active service. Given its size, the ship was also a severe drain on the RCN's limited manpower for anti-submarine patrol. Smaller, more manoeuvrable vessels better met the requirements of that job.

Yet recommissioned as a depot ship at Halifax, *Niobe* filled a vital need. Naval accommodation and office space were in very short supply, and the 450-foot "Hotel Niobe" could house and victual a thousand sailors while pro-viding space for training, classrooms, and communications. Her various operational and technical departments provided practical training for novice seaman. As one old hand remembered, the same routine, rules and regula-tions, and discipline were maintained aboard just as if she were on active ser-vice at sea. There were even Royal Marines aboard, employed by the RCN to enforce the traditional standards and as armed sentries. *Niobe* was moored at the extreme north end of HMC Dockyard, with her wide gangplank (near the stern) at what was then still known as the Hospital Wharf, directly opposite the Royal Naval College of Canada, and with her bow pointing directly up the harbour and into the frontage of the adjacent militia prop-erty, Wellington Barracks.[32] Her commanding officer was Acting Commander Percy F. Newcombe, once executive officer of HMS *Shearwater* on the Cana-dian west coast, a physical training enthusiast who had been lent to the Canadian service some months after having been seriously wounded at Gal-lipoli.[33] In addition to her other functions, *Niobe* provided a floating head-quarters for the RCN in the port of Halifax and provided a home for naval, transport, intelligence, and communications staff.[34]

Another essential function coordinated from offices aboard *Niobe* was the RCN's Examination Service, which controlled traffic into and out of the port of Halifax. Each arriving ship was met by a number of small boats at the Examination Anchorage off Macnab Island. There, the ship's legitimacy was verified before it was allowed into port. Thus, in wartime, the chief examin-ing officer (CXO) essentially supplanted the role of harbour-master.[35]

The CXO was Acting Commander Frederick Evan Wyatt, age forty. In addition to his experience as master of mail and passenger steamers, and as a navigator and pilot, Wyatt had also served in the Royal Naval Reserve until 1906.[36] At the outset of the war, his commission had been reactivated and he was accepted for service as a lieutenant aboard *Niobe*. After that ship was decommissioned, Wyatt's commanding officer recommended him for further service with the RCN as "a thorough competent and efficient Officer." Wyatt was appointed CXO for Halifax and was also placed in charge of the port's anti-submarine defence, with the rank of lieutenant-commander.[37] In March 1916 Admiral Kingsmill asked the Admiralty to promote Wyatt again, citing the zealous and able manner in which he had carried out his increasingly demanding duties.[38]

Towards the end of 1917, the dockyard had become so busy and crowded that not even *Niobe*'s considerable space was sufficient to accommodate the RCN's mounting needs. With the addition of the Patrol Service personnel and vessels, and with new men to staff the rapidly accumulating new trawlers and drifters, Walter Hose was urgently seeking additional space to establish a depot and base for his vessels and to provide for their laying up and repair. The Captain of Patrols felt the solution to the problem lay just north beyond the dry dock in the substantial adjoining waterfront property and wharfage of the Acadia Sugar Refinery. In addition to its towering building, a landmark on the Halifax waterfront, the refinery had some 900 feet of wharfage. The navy particularly coveted the 412-foot section immediately adjacent to the refinery's massive storage shed. With extensive renovations, the large storage shed would make an ideal barracks, with space left over for refitting, repairing, and stores. Negotiations with the refinery's owners, who had demanded the exorbitant sum of $36,000 per annum to rent the property, had lagged on into the autumn of 1917. With the situation becoming increasingly more urgent, a frustrated Admiral Kingsmill finally demanded that the government immediately appropriate the property.[39]

As this action suggests, from his office in Ottawa, Kingsmill was very much involved in the supervision of ship and dockyard affairs. Both Edward Martin, the captain superintendent who controlled the residents of the dockyard and the naval defence of the port, and Walter Hose, head of the Patrol Service, reported independently to Kingsmill. The immediate past had been marked by unseemly disputes regarding how best to manage meagre resources – the retired RN officer who had been Hose's predecessor had launched a vociferous campaign for overall command. By comparison, the chain of command in late 1917 represented a largely workable compromise.[40]

Yet not all of the naval and marine functions carried out at Halifax were in Canadian hands. Organization of the convoys and travel clearance of neutral vessels were the responsibility of the Royal Navy. An efficient and highly visible rear-admiral, Bertram M. Chambers, directed the RN's functions in Halifax. Although most of his staff were British, his second assistant was a Canadian from Quebec City, Lieutenant-Commander James A. Murray, Royal Naval Reserve (RNR).[41]

Chambers was an inspired choice for service at Halifax. During his long career he had distinguished himself in hydrographic work and operational theory. He had served as a flag captain with the Home Fleet and on the staff of the Royal Navy's War College. Then, from 1911, he had served under the Australian government to organize a training college for their navy and to act temporarily as a member of their Naval Board. Acting for Australia in a number of other high positions until May 1914, he was thus well grounded in the challenges of organizing and working with new navies in the dominions.[42]

Despite such experience, his arrival in Halifax had caused considerable consternation among Canadian naval authorities, because he ranked over the Canadians stationed there. Admiral Kingsmill considered it a problem that Canadian officers tended to defer automatically to their British seniors. Such a tendency undermined the autonomy and credibility of the Canadian service and the authority and jurisdiction of the government in Ottawa.[43] Thus, Kingsmill reacted with alarm when in November the Admiralty had somewhat blandly suggested that Chambers be described as senior Naval Officer Afloat, Halifax, "in order that his position may not conflict with that of Officers of the Canadian Naval Establishments at Halifax and at the same time to provide necessary authority and continuity of control in regard to convoy work."[44] Indeed, as he fussed to G.J. Desbarats, deputy minister for the naval service, Kingsmill could not see how such action could lead to anything but "unutterable confusion at Halifax," nor would it serve any advantage. The term held wide significance across the imperial navy: "The Senior Naval Officer Afloat has charge of everything that is afloat in Halifax, including minesweepers and patrol vessels outside the Port, or the title means nothing. It is most undesirable to have an Officer coming from England to take charge over the heads of our Officers who have been in Halifax and on the Coast since the War and are cognizant of all local conditions."[45]

Kingsmill's civil service and political superiors agreed with him, and the British were advised that the Canadians saw "no advantage" in such nomenclature.[46] Inexplicably, the correspondence on this picayune point was still going on two days after the tragedy of 6 December. Admiralty officials, acknowledging the possibility of "misconception," proposed the alternative title of Port Convoy Officer and Senior Officer of Escorts Halifax to describe Chambers's responsibilities, which included "control of any Imperial vessels visiting port in connection with escort work."[47] Kingsmill had won his point, but, under the circumstances, his victory would ring hollow.

Chambers's charges – the sleek and efficient British cruisers that appeared frequently in the port for replenishment and to escort the vital convoys across the Atlantic – were the most visible manifestations in the harbour of the naval side of the war. Halifax society warmly welcomed the visitors and, even more so, the prosperity they symbolized. The war economy contributed to what the business community characterized as a "banner year" for Halifax. Exports amounted to $140 million dollars, with 15 million tons of shipping passing through the port.[48] Haligonians attributed the vibrant economy to the war and the presence of the British and other foreign vessels, not to the RCN, who were still viewed as interlopers in the former imperial port. The aversion of Admiral Kingsmill for traditional political patronage in purchasing and in granting Canadian contracts did little to improve local opinion.[49]

Lack of respect for the RCN's "tinpot navy" was by no means limited to Halifax. Even the redoubtable Bob Edwards of Calgary's widely circulated and satiric *Eye Opener* found cause for comment on the RCN:

> Our dear old friend H.M.C.S. Niobe is still shedding tears in Halifax harbor. She is weeping over the 47 skippers and 35 mates who are undergoing a course of comic-opera training on her historic decks. Her anguish is especially keen over the pathetic activities of one of these ancient mariners who celebrated his 76th birthday last month and is reputed to be an orphan ... Occasionally they sally forth in a small gunboat to practice naval warfare outside the harbor. But it is well known that all they do on these occasions is fish. We should dearly love to see their booze account, because it is contrary to every known ethic to go fishing without booze.[50]

This barb aroused much indignation at naval service headquarters, where it was felt that, although such a comment might be "suitable in peace time ... it is highly objectionable at the present time."

Burdened by an unappealing image and negative expectations, the unsung Canadian navy nevertheless carried on with what it had. Although the RCN was being prepared for daunting challenges, it was as yet largely untested. That situation was to change quickly in early December 1917, and in a way that further jeopardized both its morale and credibility and had grave implications for the future of the Royal Canadian Navy.

2

Towards the Unthinkable

The fate of ships and shore facilities was determined by their positions in relation to the epicentre of the great Halifax explosion. Some of the ships had been specifically deployed to their position; others, through sheer bad luck, arrived on the eve of the disaster. Naval records and surviving logs shed much light on the location of traffic in Halifax Harbour on the eve of the disaster. As the routine day of 5 December wore on, the port sheltered more than the usual number of ships. Some thirty to forty merchant vessels being assembled for convoys that were scheduled to depart on 7 and 10 December were anchored in Bedford Basin. Other commercial shipping was berthed at various piers along the shore of the busy port, in the dry dock, and in the Narrows. Ships with names such as *Calonne, Curaca, Hovland, Middleham Castle,* and *Picton* were in the most vulnerable locations; thus, their sufferings are the most familiar from the various accounts of the disaster. But there are no detailed accounts of the RCN. This silence has left the impression that the Canadian navy in Halifax was little more than the dockyard and depot ship. As we now know, however, most of the RCN's little fleet was in port and had an integral part to play.[1]

Not all of the principal ships of Walter Hose's patrol flotilla were to be found in their new home at HMC Dockyard the day before the disaster. *Laurentian* was in Saint John discharging cargo and personnel from Sydney. She would sail for Halifax at 3:20 p.m.[2] *Stadacona* had just come back to Sydney from a six-day patrol of the Gulf of St Lawrence and would not sail again until 7 December.[3] *Hochelaga* was in Halifax, however; only that morning, she had dropped anchor in the stream, or channel, of the harbour after returning from offshore patrol. She would remain there until a place could be found for her at Pier 4 in the dockyard later that day. Pier 4 was immediately south of *Niobe*'s hulking presence and housed the dockyard coal sheds that replenished ships' fuel.[4] Farther south at Jetty 3, the minesweeping trawler *PV-V* was in "usual refit"; the dockyard navvies had been working along with the vessels crew for the last two days. The preceding day her main boiler had been shut down, temporarily crippling the boat.[5]

Farther south, *Margaret* had also been host to various dockyard working parties since the beginning of November; one such group had mounted two new twelve-pounder guns. The ship's entire port watch had been sent on three weeks' leave until 17 December. On the morning of 5 December, one of the dockyard tugs had helped move *Margaret* to Jetty 2 to await further dockyard work.[6] This space had just been vacated by *Acadia* following her new assignment in Bedford Basin. These moves had briefly displaced the torpedo boat *Grilse* so that she could be brought back outboard of *Margaret*. The dockyard superintendent's "special patrol" vessel had to be kept in a position where she could quickly get to sea if necessary.[7]

Pier 1, with its two resident RCN submarines and their workshop, bounded the southern limits of the naval dockyard. The new 130-foot-long battle-class steel trawler *Messines*, carrying a twelve-pounder gun and a crew of eighteen, also occupied a berth at the pier.[8] Two other newly arrived trawlers, *St Julien* and *Ypres*, almost certainly shared space nearby as well.[9] Given the numerous technical difficulties and delays that had plagued the construction program, it is highly probable that these three vessels, even if in operational use, were not yet ready to carry their weight in the Patrol Service.[10]

Determining the operational state and precise placement of the diminutive coastal drifters present at Halifax is extremely difficult. Of the thirty-seven that had so far arrived, at least four (and probably more than that number) had by 5 December already been sent away to the Royal Navy.[11] Only a handful of mostly cursory logs remain in existence today for ascertaining the presence of the smaller vessels, and the identity of only a small number more can be confirmed from occasional references in the logs of larger ships and other sources, for a total of fourteen.[12] There were almost certainly more present at the time.[13] Most of the drifters were either anchored along the harbour's northern face at Dartmouth Cove, at Mill Cove at the far northwest of Bedford Basin, or out in the North West Arm.[14]

The master of drifter *CD-53* faithfully maintained a detailed record from the arrival of the crew of eleven in Sorel, Quebec, on 14 November to claim the boat from her builder, throughout her fitting out and working up, and until the end of the war. This valuable document provides a wealth of information about the busy first weeks of the vessel. The nine-knot drifter had arrived in Halifax on 1 December after an eventful voyage down the St Lawrence and into the gulf. The next day, marines from *Niobe* came to the drifter to arrest Stoker Campbell, whose debauched behaviour at Quebec City had delayed the boat's departure for Halifax. Although now a man short, *CD-53* was anchored in Mill Cove on the 5th, and the dockyard carpenters had just completed building a gun stand for the six-pounder that would eventually constitute her only armament.[15]

Two more drifters arrived on 5 December to join the growing fleet of small patrol craft. *CD-26* and *CD-27* had left Quebec on 24 November, and despite challenging weather conditions and technical difficulties had passed through the Examination Anchorage off Macnab Island just before 3 p.m. Shortly thereafter, they were safely anchored in Dartmouth Cove. Liberty men were landed for a well-earned evening ashore, and the crews as a whole were undoubtedly looking forward to a few days of less stressful living.[16]

The other major presence along the shores was, of course, *Niobe*. That vessel had been taking on coal since 9:30 that morning. Some among the hard-worked sailors would later remember grumbling about having to complete the onerous outside task that day. By 4:45 p.m., 364 tons had been taken aboard; the starboard watch would shortly enjoy leave for the night.[17]

Out in the harbour, three more of Captain Hose's larger patrol ships were anchored in the stream. *Cartier* had been shifted from Jetty 4 early that morning, after having completed coaling, to a position off Jetty 3.[18] *Canada* had been anchored off the dockyard since returning from a patrol on 1

December in a position noted in her log as "flag staff at steps & chimney at workshop in line" (roughly opposite Jetty 2). The men of her port watch were looking forward to overnight leave, which would start at 5:15 p.m. and continue to 6:30 in the morning.[19] There would be no leave ashore for the crew of *Lady Evelyn,* however. Preparations were under way for her turn at patrol duty outside the harbour; she would have to sail before sunset when the "booms" would be closed.[20]

Visitors from other navies were also on the scene. Among them were two armed merchant cruisers in Royal Navy service. HMS *Knight Templar* and HMS *Changuinola* were representative of the dozen or more converted liners or fast steamships that were fitted with enough weaponry to ward off attacks by surfaced submarines – the type of attack preferred by U-boat commanders. On the surface, a submarine's diesel-powered engine enabled it to patrol widely and to maintain pace with passing convoys. It could carry many more gun shells than torpedoes, and the former were far more effective at sinking ships. Yet in any encounter with a resolute foe, even one hit on a U-boat could be crippling; thus, commanders had to be extremely cautious. Once submerged and under battery power, subs became slow and blind and were very limited in their operating radius and attack power: they were, therefore, far less able to locate and attack their prey. Accordingly, some merchant ships carried a gun with a naval crew. Armed merchant cruisers were a more powerful innovation along the same lines: ships under naval command providing more powerful ocean escort for merchant shipping while carrying additional cargo as well.[21] Such a cruiser, *Changuinola* had just arrived in Halifax and was expected to remain until the 12th, when she was assigned as escort to a fast convoy.[22] In the meantime, she was anchored in the stream roughly abreast of *Niobe.* Below her was another RN visitor on convoy duty, the nimble light cruiser *Highflyer.* She and *Knight Templar* were waiting for the slow convoy that would set out across the Atlantic on 7 December.[23]

With the United States now among the Allied powers, American ships were also present on 5 December. One was the USS *Old Colony,* a recently built steamer of 3,800 tons displacement, which the United States Navy (USN) had classified as a "passenger patrol boat," although she was slow, had an inexperienced crew, and did not carry a gun.[24] She was commanded by a United States Naval Reserve (USNR) captain, Lieutenant Commander W. McKay, and carried a crew of 270. The ship had been on her way to Britain to be turned over to the Royal Navy but had limped into Halifax on 22

November requiring repairs.[25] Her arrival created something of a problem for Canadian naval authorities. The Admiralty was pressing for her to be despatched with the next fast convoy, but the Canadian dockyard navvies had declared that her boilers would require a complete retubing and that she was in no state to join a convoy. Now she sat in limbo, waiting for authorities in Washington, London, and Ottawa to decide what to do with her and who should pay for her repairs.[26]

Another American visitor had arrived on the afternoon of 5 December and, with no dockyard berthing available, had been directed to anchor in Dartmouth Cove to take on fuel and water. There she found herself in the company of several of the recently arrived Canadian drifters. Like many of the Canadian drifters, the US Coast Guard revenue cutter *Morrill*, built in 1889, had just completed the difficult passage down the St Lawrence. Transferred to the US Navy Department, she was en route from Detroit to Philadelphia, where she was to augment the resources of the 4th Naval District.[27]

Late in the afternoon, the configuration of the harbour changed somewhat, with the departure of *Lady Evelyn* and the arrival of some new vessels. At about 4:30, as daylight faded into dusk, *Lady Evelyn* passed the gate vessel securing the channel between Ives Point and the Point Pleasant breakwater. At the same time, she logged the steamer *Wagland* "bound in" just before the nightfall deadline.

As evening approached and *Lady Evelyn* moved into the wider passage past Macnab Island and the Examination Anchorage, another arrival was probably noticed by some of the crew, although it passed unremarked in the patrol ship's log.[28] The arrival of the 3,121-ton SS *Mont Blanc* off the Examination Anchorage was not particularly unusual, although the French ship appeared hard-used and looked to lack the speed needed in a transatlantic convoy. Under orders issued by the French government marine services, Captain Aimé Le Médec had brought the French vessel up from New York along the eastern seaboard and across the mouth of the Bay of Fundy at about seven knots. The ship had then hugged the South Shore of Nova Scotia until she steamed into the Halifax approaches.

As was the case in most major ports, arriving ships were met by a pilot boat from which a master mariner possessing a detailed knowledge of local waters and peculiarities of navigation would come aboard to guide the visitor safely into the harbour. Thus, off Chebucto Head, Captain Le Médec was now joined at his helm by Pilot Francis Mackey of Halifax.[29]

At 4:36 p.m., an examining officer, Mate Terrence Freeman, RNCVR, boarded *Mont Blanc* from one of the armed tugs used by the Examination Service.[30] He was somewhat surprised to discover that the ship's cargo was almost exclusively explosives. French authorities had assigned her to carry a mix of almost three thousand tons of wet and dry picric acid, TNT, and gun cotton. Metal drums of benzol, which was desperately needed in France, were stacked three or four high on the fore and after decks. Freeman later recalled that he had no special instructions for dealing with ships that had such unusual – and dangerous – cargoes. Nor was there any "special procedure ... in force for munition ships" in federal Public Traffic Regulations for the port.[31] After the fact, this lack of special procedures for munitions ships might seem a glaring lack of foresight. Yet Halifax had not long been a gathering point for convoys, and there might not yet have been a full sense of what was usual and what was not for ships directed into the port under the convoy scheme. In the event, under his instructions, Freeman had no prerogative to treat the arrival of *Mont Blanc* as other than routine.

Since the decision about whether *Mont Blanc* was too slow for convoy was a matter for Rear-Admiral Chambers's staff inside the port, the ship had to make its way into the harbour. Le Médec was directed to remain in the Examination Anchorage until morning brought sufficient light to navigate into Bedford Basin. Freeman's boat would signal that *Mont Blanc* might proceed up the harbour, at which point she would be expected to display the identity signal Freeman had given her.[32] The formalities concluded, the examining officer returned to his vessel and reported details of the new arrival and cargo to *Niobe,* where the information was acknowledged by Commander Frederick Wyatt, the chief examining officer.[33]

Mont Blanc was not the only ship awaiting clearance to proceed through the Halifax Harbour channel. At its far end, in Bedford Basin, the Norwegian-registered SS *Imo* had fretted away the afternoon of 5 December awaiting the promised load of coal she needed to fuel her passage to New York. The former White Star liner (then called *Runic*) was one of a number of steamers of mostly neutral registry that had been chartered by the Commission for Relief in Belgium in an effort to alleviate the desperate state of the civilian population in the German-occupied nation. Due to the urgency of the situation, British authorities expedited these shipments by allowing the vessels to proceed directly into the English Channel without the normal requirement of first stopping at a British port for inspection. *Imo* had already completed eight such voyages and was on its way to New York in ballast – that is, empty – to load cargo for a ninth, and was expected to reach Belgium in January. She would not clear Halifax on 5 December, however. The harbour boom closed for the night before the coal could be loaded.[34] Darkness settled over the harbour. At sea, *Lady Evelyn* had reached her cruising station in the outer approaches by 10 p.m.[35]

THE NIGHT WAS COLD, BUT NOT UNTYPICAL for Halifax at that time of year. By midnight the temperature had fallen to 28°F. The thermometer would dip only a few more degrees before the warmth of the rising sun in an almost cloudless sky promised to raise the day's temperature above the freezing mark. There was no wind, and the barometer slowly rose through the night.[36] While most sailors slept, the normal naval routine of the ships and the dock-yard carried on, with duty watches awake and alert and the "rounds correct" annotations found in some ships' logs reflecting that officers of the watch had done their duty.[37] Aboard *Niobe,* intelligence and transport staff burned the midnight oil to complete their paperwork, and junior personnel manned the phones and communications centres. The night was not marked by any unusual occurrences; the arrival of two recruits from New York at 1:30 a.m. was the only event considered weighty enough to merit an entry in the ship's deck log.[38]

It was still dark when the men aboard *Niobe* were roused from their sleep at 6:00. Indeed, other ships allowed their sailors up to another half-hour of rest.[39] In a salty memoir he left with the RCN Historical Branch in 1955, A.H. Wickens, a veteran of the RNCVR's original west coast contingent, recalled the typical morning routine aboard the ship:

> Lash up and stowing of hammocks, hands to the galley for cocoa 6.20 [sic] day men fall in the front battery for scrubbing down and brass polishing and clean-ing of steel stauntions which supported top decks ... Whilst the activities were in progress two hands were preparing for breakfast. Two men were told off each day to look after their particular mess, get the grub, set the table and draw the stores, these were known as the cooks ... 7.a.m. [sic] Cooks to the galley was piped and the hands would go to breakfast after the scrubbing down and clean-ing was completed. The sooner the hands scoffed their bacon and fried toma-toes bread butter and jam and tea that you could stand a knife up in the longer they would have to smoke before divisions.[40]

Not unlike aboard *Niobe,* cadets at the Royal Naval College of Canada began their daily routine at 6:15, "cleaned into flannels" (the light clothing for boat work or gymnastics) and with a quick cup of cocoa. After an exercise period, they washed, changed, and had breakfast. Divisions were normally held at 9:00 in the newly completed wing on the north side of the college building. On 6 December, however, the senior class was using every spare moment to cram for the end-of-term examinations scheduled for that day, and Commander Nixon had decided that the morning inspection would be delayed for fifteen minutes.[41]

As the first traces of light began to penetrate the darkness, activity increased in the North West Arm among the minesweeping trawlers and CDs in the anchorage. At 7:00 a.m., *PV-VII* and *Baleine* began to move gingerly away from their moorings and down the neck towards Point Pleasant and the wider harbour channel. The two vessels were to conduct the daily sweep to ensure a safe passageway from the inner harbour to sea past Chebucto Head. This essential but monotonous task would occupy them well into the afternoon.

As the predawn light continued to build, the outbound sweepers moved past the Examination Anchorage, where *Mont Blanc* awaited the signal authorizing her passage through Halifax Harbour into Bedford Basin.[42] The signal from the examination tugboat came at 7:30, some nine minutes before the sun would rise over the horizon into the clear sky. An American "tramp steamer" had been the first vessel allowed into the port of Halifax that morning.[43] Now *Mont Blanc* weighed anchor and began to creep out of the Examination Anchorage and into the clear channel towards the outer boom. At four knots, she was under the five-knot speed limit for traffic in the harbour, and she would not expect to arrive in Bedford Basin much before 9:00 a.m.[44]

As *Mont Blanc* moved up the passage with its explosive cargo, more and more of the city was awakening, and both the civilian and military populations were beginning to prepare for the day ahead. While the naval ships were well into their daily routine, the work day at HMC Dockyard would not begin until about 9:00 a.m, the same time that the naval officers ashore – including the dockyard superintendent, Captain Pasco – would start work. *Mont Blanc*'s progress up the harbour coincided with the progress through breakfast of most Canadian and British naval officers.[45]

Imo began her passage out of Bedford Basin at 8:10, guided by Pilot William Hayes. Initially, she had been obliged to pick her way very deliberately through the crowded shipping in the basin, but as she moved clear Hayes rang the engine room for more speed, bringing her up to seven knots. Her speed seemed to increase even more as she came around to starboard out of the basin and into the Narrows, with the Dartmouth shore fairly close to her port side.[46]

The wrecking tugboat *Stella Maris*, which was owned by the Southern Salvage Company of Liverpool but was under charter to the RCN at fifty dollars a day, "owner paying crew,"[47] had just left the dry dock north of the naval dockyard. With two scows in tow, the tug was moving up the Halifax side of the channel towards Bedford Basin when her crew saw the *Imo* turning into the passage and noted the foam at her bow. The Captain of *Stella Maris*, Horatio H. Brannen, was heard to comment that *Imo* was "going as fast as any ship he ever saw" in the channel.[48]

Meanwhile, *Mont Blanc*'s slow progress through the two booms and into the harbour had brought her abreast of HMS *Highflyer*. Because the British cruiser was "partly swung across the harbour," the French ship had to pass close to shore, dipping her French ensign in salute as she did so.[49] Lieutenant Richard Woolams, officer of the watch on board *Highflyer*, had come on deck at 8:30 and was walking up and down the quarter deck on the starboard side. The heavily laden cargo ship held his interest for only a moment. He then "crossed over to the port side and continued walking up and down."[50]

A more interested spectator stood aboard the Canadian naval tug resting in the dockyard somewhat off Pier 4 towards *Niobe*. The fifty-foot tugboat *Nereid* had been chartered in August 1917 from J. Willard Smith of Saint John, for $35 a day, and had been armed with a six-pounder gun for patrol of the Halifax net defences. As was the case with many vessels chartered by the RCN, like *Stella Maris*, the tug had come with her own crew. Although the men aboard *Stella Maris* remained civilians, *Nereid*'s crew had been enrolled into the navy. John L. Makiny, her captain, was enrolled with the rank of mate, RNCVR.[51] *Nereid* was under the orders of Commander Wyatt of the Examination Service, but the CXO had not yet arrived at the dockyard. Makiny himself normally came aboard his tug about 7:00 a.m., but on 6 December he was "a little early on duty." While he was in the wheelhouse, an approaching ship caught his attention: "I am always looking around, looking to see what is going out or coming in; I took my little glasses and I seen this loaded ship coming up."[52]

Makiny watched *Mont Blanc* bearing up between Piers 1 and 2, still below the position of *Highflyer,* on the Dartmouth side of the channel, slowly making to pass to the east of the warship. As he later observed, "She was I should positively swear not four knots; very slow." Then, he saw *Imo,* "somewheres about Tufts Cove; quite a little ways above the wharf there in the Narrows." Raising his glasses again for a closer look, he could see the words "Belgian Relief" on the side of *Imo,* red letters on a white background. He could also see that "there was quite a foam at her bow"; indeed, he later added, "there was quite a little fuss at her bow; quite a little ruffle," although he wouldn't hazard a guess at her exact speed. The approach of the two ships, both holding the eastern shore, now had Makiny's full attention, and he remained in his wheelhouse watching what should have been a simple and easily solvable traffic problem quickly reach catastrophic proportions. The two ships were closing on the Dartmouth side of the channel in sight of each other. Makiny called his crew up from below to join his powerless vigil.[53]

By normal rules of manoeuvre in harbours or narrow channels, ships pass to their own right – that is, port side to port side. If special circumstances require them to manoeuvre otherwise, they are required to signal their intentions by whistle, horn, or siren. One short blast indicates intent to pass steering starboard, and two whistles to port. Having blasted a short, sharp signal to claim her right to pass on the Dartmouth side, *Mont Blanc* eased her speed to "dead slow" and directed her course even closer to the shore and increasingly shallow water. Incredibly, *Imo* responded with two blasts and held to her path. At this point, the whistles would have attracted few glances from other than the expert or the idle. *Mont Blanc* indicated the same intentions a second time, steering to starboard into shallower water. The answer was another two blasts from *Imo,* indicating she was still set on her course. Suddenly, the danger was palpable, and heads began to turn.[54]

The drifter *CD-73,* commanded by Mate Herbert Whitehead, RNCVR, was the day's duty boat on behalf of her sisters anchored in Mill and Dartmouth coves and the North West Arm. Whitehead had manoeuvred his craft away from the small Flagstaff Dock between Piers 2 and 3 at about 8:35, and was moving up the dockyard shore towards *Niobe* to load the provisions for delivery to the rest of the drifter flotilla. While he was still backing away from the wharf, he had noticed *Mont Blanc* moving past *Highflyer*'s position, but the freighter had not as yet caught his full attention. As he approached *Niobe* he found that the previous day's coal hulk was still alongside, blocking the drifter's access to the depot ship's gangway. Moving closer to the hulk, with a view to resolving the difficulty, Whitehead "heard a lot of whistling out in the stream and on my starboard side." His helmsman pointed up the stream and said, "It looks like some trouble coming there." Whitehead saw that *Mont Blanc* was now abreast of the dry dock and still on the Dartmouth side. He also saw *Imo* apparently head on.[55]

The two ships were now perilously close. Simultaneously, both took emergency action. Either manoeuvre would almost certainly have averted a collision had the other vessel maintained its original course. *Mont Blanc* elected to go hard to port, changing her path diagonally towards the Halifax shore. Although the sluggish, heavily laden explosives ship had already stopped her engines, she had sufficient speed and time to answer her helm and escape in safety to pass *Imo,* wrong side or no. Yet at the instant that *Mont Blanc*'s helm began to respond to the now irreversible order, three whistles erupted from *Imo,* signalling that she had reversed her engines.

Imo's stratagem would have been a feat of cagey seamanship had it not been cancelled out by the coincident manoeuvre of *Mont Blanc.* In addition to reducing closing speed and thereby providing desperately needed time to manoeuvre, the rotary movement of *Imo*'s propellers produced a transverse thrust, altering the lightly laden ship's course strongly to starboard. All other things being equal, this should have brought her safely on to *Mont Blanc*'s wrong side. Instead, *Imo*'s still advancing bow swung to meet the new path taken by *Mont Blanc.* A collision was now inevitable. With no hope but to soften the impact, and perhaps direct it closer to his ship's bow, Aimé Le Médec ordered full speed astern. The ships were both near midchannel between the cable wharf on the Dartmouth shore and Halifax Harbour Pier 6. It was 8:45 a.m.[56]

Agonizing seconds passed in surreal slow motion as the physical laws of impetus and thrust wielded their effect. At slightly less than a right angle, the *Imo*'s bow sliced deeply into *Mont Blanc*'s starboard side over her No. 1 cargo hold and near her fore hatch. Herbert Whitehead had by this time brought *CD-73* slow ahead a little north of the *Niobe* and midpoint to the dry dock. From this position, he and his crew witnessed the collision from a distance of one hundred yards. Whitehead remembered "a crashing, rending sound; I can hardly describe it; as though – well you can imagine how iron will crash iron with a rending sound." It lasted long enough to give the impression that "one ship had gone into the other a certain distance."[57]

Had the *Mont Blanc* been carrying a less hazardous cargo, this relatively minor collision would have been quickly forgotten in the routine of the busy port, a matter of interest only to marine insurance assessors and the dominion wreck commissioner. Instead, it was inevitable that at least some of the 494 barrels of benzol stored on her decks would be ruptured. The brief coupling of the ships ended with *Imo*'s rasping and sluggish withdrawal from the deep wound she had created, as she twisted away and the two began to drift apart. Friction and heat did the rest. The thick black smoke pouring from *Mont Blanc*'s No. 1 hold already told the tale.

Le Médec knew almost at once that his ship was lost. The only decision left to him was whether to sacrifice his forty-man crew in a vain effort to quell the flames. Aware that the vessel's pumping apparatus was already crippled by the heat and choking smoke, he issued the order to stop the engines and abandon ship. The crew moved to the port and starboard boat stations near their ship's stern. The captain himself intended to remain on board but was dissuaded by his first mate. Such a heroic gesture would make no difference at this point.[58]

Two junior RCN ratings in a passing despatch boat found themselves fairly close by *Mont Blanc*'s bow just after the collision. George Abbott, who was in charge, was bringing the morning mail down from *Acadia* to *Niobe*. He later testified that he saw the gash in the ship extending from the water line "right up into her deck, enough so it showed two tiers of metal casks." At the top, the wound appeared to be five or six feet wide. Abbott stopped his engine for a minute or so to survey the damage.[59]

CD-73 had also moved in closer to the scene of the accident. As Herbert Whitehead later testified, "I saw the fire break out on the Mont Blanc, saw that there was a ship on fire with a crew aboard and needed assistance; as I got alongside her the crew of the Mont Blanc were lowering their boats and I got my megaphone and shouted through the wheel-house window, 'jump into my boat, and I would take them to Bedford Basin if there was any danger;' I din't [sic] think they understood; they got into boats and pulled to the Dartmouth side."[60]

After he saw the boats leaving *Mont Blanc*, George Abbott restarted his engine and headed down to the dockyard. Abbott's despatch boat and *Mont Blanc*'s lifeboats passed within hailing distance.[61] Herbert Whitehead's *CD-73*, however, passed around the stern of *Mont Blanc* as she began to drift towards Pier 6. At one point Whitehead was only twenty feet from the two lifeboats.

He noted some commotion among the French sailors, including one man waving his arms, but he had no sense that they were trying to warn him of serious danger. Although one of the stokers of *CD-73* was a French Canadian on lookout at the bow, Whitehead claimed that the man said "he never heard any warning given in French and I never heard any in English."[62] It is impossible not to speculate on what lives might have been saved had the *Mont Blanc* sailors managed to convey warnings to Whitehead's vessel. That opportunity missed, the French boats made the Dartmouth shore, and *Mont Blanc*'s crew disappeared into the cover of a wooded area. Meanwhile, *Imo* drifted towards the Dartmouth shore broad on. By the time the ships had drifted about fifty yards apart, Whitehead noted that many of *Imo*'s crew had rushed on to the forecastle head and were looking over the side to survey the damage done to their own ship.[63]

While *CD-73* and her inexperienced crew stood off impotently from *Mont Blanc,* Horatio Brannen on the chartered tug *Stella Maris* had dropped off the scows he was towing and had headed back towards the burning ship with the tug's fire hose coupled. Although unaware of the explosive cargo, Captain H.N. Garnett of HMS *Highflyer* was cognizant of the dangers of an abandoned ship ablaze in a crowded port, and he ordered his "Number One" (executive officer), Commander T.K. Triggs, to send an officer over in the ship's whaler to deal with the situation. Triggs decided to take the job himself. By the time the whaler with its five-man crew and additional junior officer had rowed three-quarters of a mile up the stream, *Mont Blanc* had drifted in, her starboard side parallel to Pier 6. She ground to a complete halt close enough to the pier to ignite its wooden pilings.[64]

Help was also on the way from another quarter. Acting Boatswain John Mitchell, the officer of the day aboard *Niobe,* had reported the fire to the captain, who gave orders for the ship's steam pinnace "to go and see what could be done." Acting Boatswain Albert Mattison volunteered to lead the six-man crew.[65] Carpenter Rodney O. Burnett did not go on the steamboat, but got off *Niobe* and rushed to the site in an automobile. They would all share the same fate.[66]

Stella Maris was first to arrive alongside *Mont Blanc,* and, by the time the whaler from *Highflyer* pulled in against the tug, her crew were directing a puny stream of water from her hose at the blaze above. Commander Tom Triggs leapt aboard the tug to speak with Brannen and take charge of the situation. The best approach seemed to be to get the ship away from the pier, both to assist the approaching Halifax Fire Department in safeguarding the dock and buildings nearby and to provide more room for manoeuvre for the other tugs that they hoped would soon be arriving to attack the shipboard fire. As Mattison and the crew of *Niobe*'s steam pinnace arrived, Triggs and Brannen had decided to rig a tow, and the commander ordered the Canadians to secure a five-inch hawser to *Mont Blanc*'s stern. In his famous account of the disaster, Michael Bird reliably recorded what followed: "They climbed slowly up the port ladder amidships, left dangling when the ship was abandoned, arching themselves away from the metal plates which were now so hot from the fire raging within ... When all was ready the tug, with Triggs still aboard, went ahead gently to take up the slack while the whaler from *High-flyer* stood off a yard or so. The towline snapped taut but the freighter did not move and it was obvious to everyone that the hawser was not strong enough to stand the strain and Brannen took the *Stella Maris* back in alongside."[67]

Brannen thought they should try again with a hawser of double the thickness. Triggs agreed. Believing that things were reasonably under control, the commander left Mattison and Brannen to get the job done and ordered his oarsmen to head towards the apparently lifeless *Imo* so that he could determine her situation.[68]

CD-73 had moved slightly away from the scene and was now off the dry dock. Three distinct explosions – "minor ones" – appeared to come out of the fore hatch of *Mont Blanc*, according to Herbert Whitehead: "I came to the conclusion from the dense black smoke that was sent up by these three explosions ... [that] the vessel was loaded with oil and I thought I had better get out of the way."[69] Through the thick smoke, Whitehead saw the movements of the steam pinnace and the whaler. He could not see the *Stella Maris*, although he did catch a glimpse of two men on the deck of *Mont Blanc* calmly making their way along the fore and aft bridge from the amidship bridge to the stern. One of them was wearing a red sweater. It was not regulation dress, but a lot of the men did not always conform to such rules, especially on cold mornings.[70]

When the collision had occurred, Frederick Wyatt, the CXO, was crossing the railway tracks to go into the dockyard's north gate. One of his assistants had come running "half way up the hill" to inform him of the accident. Wyatt responded by hurrying to the coaling wharf south of *Niobe*, where he had expected to find the motor boat *W.H. Lee*, which he could take out to investigate the accident. As it turned out, the boat was on the other side of the slip, and as *Mont Blanc* burned at Pier 6, Wyatt waited for the motor boat to arrive.[71]

The spectacle of intense smoke and flame emanating from the abandoned ship and the efforts to deal with the accident drew a wide audience from surrounding craft of all sizes in the harbour as well as from the windows and roofs of buildings on the surrounding slopes. Able Seaman L.B. "Bert" Griffith, a naval reservist from Red Deer, Alberta, was one of the men aboard *Niobe* who witnessed the *Mont Blanc* in flames: "She put in to shore about 500 yards from the stern of the *Niobe*. A lot of us boys went up on deck to see the sight. It did not look very bad. There were three pretty loud explosions & everyone just imagined that it was the oil blowing up."[72]

At the Naval College, the collision and fire had caused some commotion. Many cadets had watched spellbound until the *Mont Blanc* had drifted out of view on the other side of the massive sugar refinery. Generally, however, the cadets were preoccupied with making themselves presentable for divisions and, in the case of the seniors, with their examinations. The morning warning gong had already sounded, and Commander Nixon had arrived, ready to conduct the day's business. As Captain H. Kingsley, RCN (Ret.) was to remark more than thirty years later, "We had no reason to be unduly alarmed and we had not observed the collision." Most had therefore turned their attention to what appeared to be more important matters. For those not so preoccupied, the large window in the college's chemistry and mechanics laboratory afforded an excellent view of events, and Chief Petty Officer (CPO) William King of the school staff and Cadet Mackenzie of the senior class watched as avidly as the numerous Haligonians who occupied similar vantage points. At least one of the college's instructor lieutenants, Bill Robinson, was pleasantly oblivious to the spectacle. He was in his bath.[73]

Others in the Canadian naval dockyard were also oblivious to the impending disaster and carried on their normal routine. Below *Niobe*'s mass and the more distant sugar refinery to the north, not much could be seen at shoreline level, although before *Mont Blanc* drifted inshore, ships below would have had a view of the initial fire. In her log *Margaret* recorded the sighting from her berth at Pier 2.[74] Just astern of *Niobe*, a naval diving party under the supervision of John T. Gammon, acting gunner, was busily engaged working on the concrete foundations of a crane bed. One diver was already under the water and a second was descending the ladder to the surface. Four seamen worked at the hand-operated two-cylinder divers' air pump that fed oxygen to the men; two more kept the connecting lines clear.[75] *Canada,* anchored in the stream, had a better view of the fire but still ordered hands to physical drill at 9:00 a.m. Farther south, down the dockyard shore, some of the submariners at Pier 1 were doing morning exercises under the direction of one of the officers, while others were at work in and about the two hard-used submarines.[76]

Captain Fred Pasco, the dockyard's acting superintendent, was at his breakfast in the yard at the house of the absent Captain Martin. At 8:40 (twenty minutes before dockyard staff were due at work), the telephone rang to report a signal from *Highflyer* through *Niobe* reporting two ships in collision in the Narrows, one on fire. Like Wyatt, Pasco thought of the *W.H. Lee.* Wanting to order it to the scene because of the salvage appliances and pumps it carried, Pasco telephoned Acting Commander Graham Holloway, Royal Naval Reserve (RNR). Holloway was the principal naval transport officer but, more important, was also the man in charge of Fleet Auxiliaries at Halifax. Pasco found Holloway's line busy. As Pasco later recalled,

> I was getting impatient and I said to Captain Martin's servant ... take the telephone and try and get the transport office; I must try and see what is going on outside. He said you can see it from the upper window – and there was a telephone up there – I went straight up, leaving him at the telephone and I looked out of the window and I saw the *Imo* motionless apparently across the harbour blocking the whole harbour right across and I didn't see the other vessel and the *Imo* ... had apparently a certain amount of smoke coming from the fiddleys [sic]. I thought there is not much fire and I was craning to see if I could see the other ship, and thought she had gone in the Basin, when I heard a man's voice down below at the telephone and I went to the telephone in the bedroom and got hold of the transport officer's No. 2 man, Lieut. Poole, and I told him to send the Lee and the Gopher and the Musquash, anything he had, with pumps in case the fire was serious, and he understood and I put the thing on the hook, and I suppose I was half way across the room when ...[77]

It was 09:04:35 Atlantic Standard Time.[78]

3

Halifax Tide

A shrill whistle and a ring of a bell
There's a fire among us and we're blown to hell
I wish we could roll back, could roll back the tide.[1]

Folk song

The blast that obliterated *Mont Blanc* killed more than sixteen hundred souls outright, wounded nearly six times that number, and rendered twenty thousand homeless. Thousands of stories of individual tragedy, suffering, and escape ensued. For most who survived, the calamity would be a permanently etched memory, even a defining moment in their lives.

In one of the first scientific analyses of the explosion, Professor Howard L. Bronson of Dalhousie University informed the Royal Society of Canada in May 1918 that the blast had the power equivalent to some 2.4 million kilograms of high explosive. It "undoubtedly far surpassed all previous explosions both in its destructive effects and in the quantities of explosives involved." In describing the damage done he observed that

> in a general way it can be said that the buildings within a radius of half a mile of the explosion were totally destroyed and that up to one mile they were very largely rendered uninhabitable and dangerous. No section of Halifax city escaped serious damage to doors, windows and plaster … More or less severe damage was caused as far away as Sackville and Windsor Junction, 9 or 10 miles N.E. of the explosion, and for a similar distance in the opposite direction. At Truro, 62 miles, and New Glasgow, 78 miles, the shock was sufficient to jar buildings very appreciably, and even to shake articles from shelves. Even as far away as Charlottetown, 135 miles, and North Cape Breton, 225 miles, the explosion was distinctly felt or heard.[2]

Aside from those very close to the blast, the vast majority of deaths and injuries resulted from people being caught on the wrong side of window glass or trapped in burning buildings as tipped coal stoves and broken gas lines ignited hundreds of individual fires. The blast and shock waves flattened much of the adjacent Richmond shore, the railway terminals, docks, and the residential districts above. The damage was only slightly less severe on the less heavily inhabited Dartmouth shore opposite. There, the explosion had thrust *Imo* hard aground, her upper works shattered, and many of her crew dead, including her captain and pilot. Merchant shipping unlucky enough to be berthed near *Mont Blanc* suffered heavy damage and casualties.[3] Among them was the RCN tug/minesweeping trawler *Musquash,* set afire at its berth near Pier 8. The Acadia Sugar Refinery was reduced to a pile of rubble, and the blast smashed through the adjacent dry dock facilities and on into the Militia Department's Wellington Barracks just north of the dockyard.

On the water, the steam pinnace from HMCS *Niobe* disappeared in the same instant as the *Mont Blanc.* The bodies of Albert Mattison and the six-man crew were never found, "presumed blown to pieces."[4] The more distant whaler from HMS *Highflyer,* moving towards *Imo,* was also shattered, but it left several survivors floundering in the water, only one of whom was eventually rescued.[5] The wrecking tug *Stella Maris,* which had been moving head on towards the doomed ship as her crew brought up the heavier ten-inch hawser for the second towing attempt, was blasted away and left ablaze on the Dartmouth shore. Horatio Brannen and twenty of his civilian crew died.

Of the five injured survivors, two had been below; the mate, Brannen's son Walter, was blown into the hold from on deck; the two others were working on fresh-water tanks aft of the funnel, which provided shelter sufficient to save their lives.[6]

In the wheelhouse on *CD-73*, Herbert Whitehead was knocked unconscious by the force of the blast, which perforated the starboard hull with pieces of metal both above and below the water line. He awoke as the boat heaved in a "serious disturbance" and one of the stokers from below put his hands on the wheelhouse windows and pulled himself up. Whitehead recalled hearing the stoker call, "Captain are you alive? Come and jump; we are gone." Despite his state of shock, Whitehead opined that it was best to stay with the boat. He observed his wheelman unconscious and seriously wounded on the deck. Taking the wheel, Whitehead realized that the boat still had headway, despite the engine being knocked out of action, and had been thrown close enough to *Niobe* by the explosion that he was able to bring her neatly in alongside the coal hulk. Despite sustaining burns after being thrown on top of the cylinders in the engine room, the engineer had stood by. He was subsequently able to restart the engines, although *CD-73* would later be listed among vessels badly damaged in the explosion. Remarkably, Whitehead himself received "no serious injuries at all; minor cuts about the head and face ... and bruises about the body."[7]

The northern boundary of HMC Dockyard was just on the edge of the half-mile radius described in Professor Bronson's dissertation. First in the path of the blast were HMCS *Niobe* and the Royal Naval College of Canada. Able Seaman Bert Griffith, who had been among a considerable group crowded at the depot ship's bow, wrote to his wife two days later:

> All at once there was a most hideous noise & I saw the whole boat vanish, a moment after I saw something coming can't describe it. I was hurled on the deck & there was an awful noise going on. I got to my feet & ran with a whole lot of fellows. My one fixed idea was to get below. We all tried to get down the one ladder without any success. I had presence of mind enough to dig my head in between all kinds of legs & etc. After that I ran along the deck & heard all kinds of things falling. It was shrapnel & bits of the side of the ship. I did not know this at the time.[8]

The blast was followed by a powerful tsunami, doubtlessly Herbert Whitehead's understated "disturbance," which smashed against *Niobe* between one and two minutes after the blast.[9] By this time, as Griffith later recorded, "I managed to get to the gangway unhurt & found that the ship had broken her big cable & the gangway gone. As she crashed in to the jetty I jumped off & got ashore just before she shoved the jetty over."[10]

In the general pandemonium of bodies rushing for shelter or escape, a number of sailors were either blown overboard or fell. Flying glass and debris accounted for several deaths and serious injuries.[11] *Niobe*'s ship's office, which was located in a wooden superstructure that had been rigged above the main deck, was particularly hard hit. The roof was torn off and the glass windows blown in, cutting the writers working on their quarters' ledgers and scattering their files all about the ship's deck. The head writer, Chief Petty Officer William Morgan, subsequently died in hospital.[12]

Bert Griffith, who found himself safe on shore, started to assist the wounded. His first task was pulling a wounded man out of the water.[13] A number of sailors who had reached the gangway after Griffith's narrow escape had leapt into the harbour. More lives would certainly have been lost in this way had not one of the depot ship's senior ratings, Gunner William O'Reilly, acted promptly to check the panic. Also under his direction, *Niobe*'s cutter was manned in time to fish a number of ratings from the frigid water.[14]

Niobe looked as if she had been through a battle. Two of her four funnels were down, and there were gaping holes in her superstructure and stanchions. Lines, blast bags (protecting gun positions), broken glass, and other debris were strewn everywhere. Her anchor and cable were lost, along with canopies, lifebuoys, telescopes, signal flags, and other paraphernalia. Despite the obvious damage, the ship was structurally intact. Still, the job of putting her back in order would be a daunting challenge: clearing wreckage from the deck alone would occupy two full days.[15] As one survivor, Fred Longland, later described the scene, the main deck was "an unholy mess." He recalled that "19 men lay dead without a mark of any kind on them," although undoubtedly many of those thought dead were merely unconscious. Longland also remembered that the sick bay was crowded with wounded men seeking attention.[16] Remarkably, however, the majority of *Niobe*'s complement escaped crippling injury and, despite cuts and wounds, were able to carry out their duties in the short term. Others were suffering from apparent shock.[17] *Niobe*'s captain, Percy Newcombe, was among those rendered "practically out of action" for a time.[18]

Astern of the depot ship, the blast had scattered John Gammon's diving party in all directions. The second diver had been thrown into the water with the first, who had been submerged when the explosion hit. When Gammon, who had been knocked over but was uninjured, recovered his senses, his first thought was for the men trapped below. No one was at the air pump. He rushed to the ladder with a view to bringing the divers up before the air in their hoses was exhausted. One other survivor had not fled in panic from the shock and the subsequent rain of falling metal. The blast had blown Able Seaman W.G. Critch back some twenty feet from his station at the pump. Gammon saw Critch making his way back towards the diving shed and shouted for him to man the pump, a task that normally required four men. The roof of the shed had been blown onto the pump, and Critch had to brace what remained of the roof with his left arm while frantically trying to work the pump with his right. His struggle to push air to the stranded divers was successful enough to give Gammon sufficient time to raise the terrified men and remove their face plates. As *Niobe*'s commander later remarked: "Though this may appear to have been only their duty I think, taking into consideration the natural panic which prevailed immediately after the Catastrophe, the debris falling in all directions, the unexpected suddenness of the whole affair, and the fact that under normal conditions four men are required to start the pump, the action of the Warrant Officer and Able Seaman was gallant and undoubtedly saved these men's lives."[19]

At the Royal Naval College the orderly scenario of earnest preparation was instantly transformed into chaos: there would be no divisions or examinations. Thirty-four years later, retired Captain Harry Kingsley still remembered with great clarity the moment when, as a cadet, he turned towards his locker:

> A terrific concussion with ear-shattering roar closely following it, struck us. This was followed almost immediately by a second. The windows all came in, the inside walls collapsed and leaned against each other, but the main floors held. There was a rain of chimney bricks, bits of steel, and worst of all, flying glass. The floor in the parade hall in the north wing caved in, and a piece of steel weighing 150 pounds, passed through the roof of the north wing, and landed plunk ... where the officer invigilating the examination would have been sitting a few minutes later.[20]

Kingsley indirectly highlights the significance of the fifteen-minute delay Commander Nixon had authorized earlier that morning. Had the school been running according to schedule, the cadet corps would have been in the parade hall. Thus, Nixon's small concession probably spared the lives of a number of RCN cadets, some destined for senior command in the Second World War and later.

Rear-Admiral P. Willet Brock remembered one cadet being driven through the gunroom window while the rest staggered outside through a shower of plaster and rubble. "We cowered there with rivets and pieces of iron plate falling all around us ... A gigantic cloud of smoke, visible for miles, rose over the harbour."[21] Occasionally, memories of even the greatest tragedies can be laced with humour. As the mass of struggling cadets made their way out of the ruined building, some found themselves "flung aside by a wild figure, naked but for a towel it was clutching, madly fighting its way back inside." It was Lieutenant Bill Robinson, unceremoniously hurled outside onto the grass in front of the building from the refuge of his bath.[22]

As in much of the rest of the city, many of the injuries at the Naval College resulted from flying glass and other debris. Several cadets suffered deep lacerations, but ultimately, only three – Orde, Pentelow, and Mackenzie – were reported as seriously injured, all of them about the face and eyes.[23] Cadet Mackenzie and instructor CPO William King, both of whom had been watching the burning *Mont Blanc* from the college's laboratory, were cut down when the lab's large windows burst into countless fragments. Mackenzie briefly recovered consciousness to hear screams from King. In terrible pain, Mackenzie managed to render some rudimentary first aid before again fainting away.[24] He would awake in the Cogswell Street Military Hospital at the end of Gottingen Street. Eventually, he would lose an eye and be forced to leave the RCN. King's apparently lifeless body ended up in the morgue, where, to everyone's surprise, he awoke two days later.[25]

Besides King, several others among the college staff were also seriously injured. Commander Nixon remembered being "thrown against an ordinary wooden door which was shut, and door and I came down together." He later recalled that his head was the only part of him that was damaged.[26] That was something of an understatement. His medical case history, while somewhat gruesome, was not uncommon among the more serious injuries suffered in the disaster:

Scalp wounds – one T shaped one over forehead on left side extending from eyebrow three inches upwards joining a transcersr [sic] wound at upper end of this one four inches long. This wound gaping widely exposing the bare bone of skull and the wound having splinters of wood in it. The undermining of this wound extended widely and down to the bridge of nose between the eyes.

Other scalp wounds over left side of head and above and below the left ear with glass embedded in them.

There was a deep ragged wound of left cheek four inches long extending upwards into the left eye separating left eye lid. Another wound of upper eye lid two inches long across and an inch deep. There was a deep wound of left side of chin from lower lip extending into neck about four inches long.

There was a punctured wound of right eye with iris protruding this wound being in the middle of the lower edge of pupil. Besides the above there were small minor wounds pitted about the face and nose, especially the left side. There was marked headache and interference of sight from the concussion.[27]

Similar destruction and injuries were sustained throughout the dockyard. Most of the buildings were damaged to some degree, and several were completely destroyed. Windows and doors were blown out; trusses, partitions, and woodwork collapsed; and roofs and walls were ripped away. Valuable naval stores were laid open to the elements.[28] The Torpedo Boat Shed was nearly demolished. So was the newly constructed YMCA, which had briefly provided the Canadian sailors with a place of rest and refuge away from their ships.[29]

The Wireless Office at the yard was "badly shaken," although the fleet wireless officer hoped to have things back in shape within the week. The Wireless School building fared much worse. It had been smashed, and one of the wireless learners, George Veals, had been killed. Four others were seriously hurt from cuts and bruises but were able to continue with their duties.[30]

The dockyard's civilian staff did not escape injury. Two stores labourers lost their lives when part of the roof collapsed in one of the new victualling stores buildings. Several office workers were seriously hurt, and one of the ledger clerks was blinded. Mr Laurie, the stores officer, escaped with small cuts to his head, but two other office workers were killed: Miss Vaughan, who was Commander Graham Holloway's stenographer, and Mr Burnette, who was his assistant. Those civilians who survived the carnage at the dockyard faced the added strain of the impact of the explosion on their homes and families. Most of the dockyard staff lived in the city's devastated North End. Several of these people saw their homes ruined and their families almost wiped out.[31] Unbowed, many of these civilians performed beyond the call of duty. As a Canadian Press despatch distributed across the country later reported, "Miss Jean Groves was the operator at the private branch telephone exchange at the dock yard. Though the building was badly damaged, she remained at her post, as she knew there must have been many killed and badly injured. She sent out calls for help, for doctors, fire department and other aid. Everybody was ordered out of the building, but she remained until she was carried out. Less than an hour later she was at the Lorne Exchange reporting for duty."[32]

Such extraordinary devotion was also in evidence at the Naval Hospital at Admiralty House. Although the building's solid construction had provided a measure of protection, the roof had crashed in among the staff and patients, adding to the chaos caused by smashed windows and fixtures. Staff Surgeon Joseph A. Rousseau suffered cuts to the head, face, chest, and arms, including one to his jugular vein. Nursing Sister Alice M. Boutin, RCN, had her face cut and shoulder injured. Despite their injuries, Rousseau, Boutin, and a second nurse set about checking on the safety of their patients and attending to their injuries, until the doctor collapsed from loss of blood. The two nurses carried on, also treating the injured who were being brought to the hospital. Boutin remained until late that evening, when she was carried off exhausted. She was later found to have a fractured rib and a dislocated shoulder.[33] Thanks to such dedication, all of the patients survived. Without a roof, however, the hospital building had to be evacuated. It would not reopen for some months.[34]

Captain Fred Pasco, the dockyard's acting superintendent, had been walking through an upstairs room in Captain Martin's home when the explosion took place. The force knocked him down, and flying glass nicked him around his eyes and on his hand. Although his facial cuts were superficial, the blood got into his eyes and affected his sight. Finding the front door of the residence blocked with debris, Pasco and the frightened housekeeper escaped through the back into the midst of the ruined dockyard. He wanted to get out in the open

> to see what was going on, where the explosion was. I had it in my mind, seeing this fire was so small on the Imo, the impression in my mind was ... I thought the cruiser Highflyer had gone up. I then went around to see what was going on and tried to formulate matters as to what to do; I got down as far as No. 3 wharf

but there quite a lot of people were hurt; they tried to pull me on board one of these trawlers for first aid and I told them there was nothing the matter, but I was a nasty sight covered with blood. I told one or two skippers on going there to carry people straight out to the hospital if there was any in sight.[35]

No deck log entries identify the trawler crew who hauled Pasco "willy nilly on board" for first aid despite his protests. After being "washed down" with a bucket of water and having his hand tied, he headed south as far as the office building, noting that things did not look as bad as they did to the north. As yet, he did not know the source of the explosion, noting that the men at the south end of the yard believed that an oil tanker had blown up. While surveying the damage, Pasco encountered Captain Hose, and the two men set up a rudimentary station where ships' companies could report and receive orders.[36]

With the blast causing such damage and injury ashore, its impact on the motley collection of RCN vessels huddled south of *Niobe* and on the opposite shore must have been equally serious. And indeed, the effects were similar to those on land, both within and beyond the half-mile radius of devastation. Vessels had been subjected to an intense shaking, with larger ships faring better than the smaller ones. As onshore, most of the injuries were due to flying glass. Some shelter from the blast had been afforded by the now demolished sugar refinery and the bulk of *Niobe*'s hull. The tsunami, however, wreaked havoc with moorings and anchor cables.

Aboard the tug *Nereid*, John Makiny had been watching the *Imo*, which was across the channel, from his berth at Jetty 4: "I didn't see her doing anything else; just seemed to lay there; it was not very long when the big one knocked us all out; when I came to myself we were all knocked to pieces."[37] *Nereid* had received what Makiny described as "the full force of the Explosion." The deckhouse was severely strained, the doors were blown out, and wooden bulkheads were broken. The cooking stove in the galley had been broken by fallen material. Yet the damage was not severe enough to render the tug beyond useful service. Her dedicated master kept her in harness through the aftermath of the explosion with improvised mends. Later, rather than quibble over the terms of the tug's charter and whether the blast had been an "accident" or an "act of war," the RCN authorized dockyard repairs at government expense to the privately owned tugboat to compensate "this most willing, conscientious Captain."[38]

At No. 3 Jetty, the minesweeping trawler *PV-V* was also fiercely shaken, with "all windows blown out and some doors and sashes and damages done to housework." With her boilers already out of action because of repairs, the crew, though uninjured, was without heat as the weather deteriorated over the next two days, and the trawler itself was unable to move.[39] The three battle-class trawlers in the dockyard also sustained significant damage but, having their engines intact, remained serviceable.[40]

In her log, *Margaret,* the inboard ship at No. 2 Jetty, noted the "terrible explosion," which caused "terrible waves which broke ship away from moorings, windows and various doors in ship broke in, no one hurt." As in so many other cases, the crew responded with diligence and dedication: in only half an hour, the men had made the ship fast, and her captain and navigation officer were rendering first aid on the ship and then in the dockyard.[41] A lengthy entry in *Grilse*'s log, written rather after the fact, noted only five injuries among the crew, all of them slight. The log neglected to mention that one of the casualties was her captain, Lieutenant-Commander W.T. Walker, with cuts to the forehead and eyes. Despite the injuries onboard, by 10 a.m. the ship was declared secure and all spare hands were sent ashore on relief duties.[42]

The scene at No. 1 Jetty, where the two Canadian submarines were moored, was recorded by the cox'n of *CC-2* in a later undated account published in the *Victoria Colonist:*

> One petty officer, poking his head out of a hatch, was knocked upside down and hurled below. Pitts [Lieutenant A.C.S, RNCVR] was blown over but not hurt and Edwardes [Lieutenant G.H.S., RNCVR] was badly cut on his face after hitting a wall. Everyone on the jetty had to tumble for cover as pieces of metal rained down on them. Some pieces of shrapnel were small, but one rating saw the entire funnel of a ship sailing over his head ... A quick head count revealed that none of the submariners had been killed or badly injured.[43]

As had been the case with other vessels moored at the dockyard, the tsunami snapped the submarines adrift, but the crews had no difficulty securing them again. Because their hulls were mostly below the surface, neither sub sustained much damage. Their facilities ashore were unprotected, and the interior of the men's bunkhouse was badly wrecked.[44]

In the stream, HMS *Changuinola,* although roughly abeam of *Niobe,* miraculously sustained only minor damage. Below her, HMS *Highflyer* was not so lucky, possibly as a result of being anchored diagonally with part of her starboard beam directly exposed to the explosion. Like *Niobe,* the British light cruiser suffered considerable damage to her plating and upper works. Three of her crew were killed and another fifty were injured. Interestingly, the rumour among the men on *Niobe* was that forty-five had died on *Highflyer.*[45]

Neither of the two RCN patrol ships in the stream, *Hochelaga* and *Canada,* suffered major damage, although six of the former's crew were reported to have suffered slight injuries.[46] *Canada* reported only one injury, an engine-room artificer (ERA) who was paralysed as the result of spinal damage.[47] Yet, clearly, the crew of *Canada* had experienced a shock of considerable magnitude from the blast. The crew of the vessel later registered a claim in the amount of $23.16 for replacement of lost uniform items, most of them caps and ribbons emblazoned with the ship's name, that had been blown off in the explosion.[48] Nevertheless, the ship was quickly secured and, only seven minutes after the explosion, her captain, Lieutenant Woods, led a landing party in ships' boats to render aid in the dockyard.[49]

Farther away from the centre of the explosion, the coastal drifters in Dartmouth Cove rode out the explosion and tidal wave relatively unscathed. The greatest damage was sustained by *CD-53,* which had just sent a boat to the Dartmouth shore to retrieve her second engineer. The explosion took place while the boat was on the beach, leaving it with holes in its planking.[50] The log of *CD-26* merely noted a "heavy explosion bearing NWN"; amazingly, the log included no further entries until 29 January.[51] *CD-27* made even more casual reference to an "explosion in harbour," which the logkeeper wrongly recorded as having occurred at 8:45.[52] Such reticence is extraordinary. Even given their relatively sheltered position in Dartmouth Cove, the drifters must have been aware of the seriousness of the disaster.

Acadia, in her position as guard ship inside Bedford Basin, was also outside the ring of worst destruction and far enough back from the basin's entrance that the tsunami had somewhat dissipated by the time it reached her. Thus, her damage was negligible, although those aboard would have had a good scare. Behind her to the north, the shipping in the basin barely suffered at all. In contrast, the channel leading out from the basin through the Narrows – closer to the epicentre of the explosion – was "completely covered with wreckage of all kinds, principally the refuse of destroyed wharves."[53]

Farther out to sea from the shattered harbour, the ships patrolling the approaches were also aware that something terrible had happened. The minesweeping chores of *PV-VII* and *Baleine* had taken them twenty-one miles out, still some ten minutes short of the outer automatic buoy, when they were startled by the "terrific report of an explosion" astern. Whatever the source of the sound, the minesweeper's mission remained her priority – indeed, perhaps the more so should the port be under any form of coordinated attack. With the outer buoy abeam at 9:25, the little trawlers turned to the south southeast and continued their sweeping.[54]

Lady Evelyn's initial early hours out from Halifax had been the usual routine. She had passed in HMCS *Lansdowne,* a former patrol ship now being used for supply purposes, and an oil steamer towing a barge. Then, the calm was shattered by the "terrific explosion" from the direction of the harbour. Preparing for the possibility that the explosion signalled an attack, the crew went to general quarters (action stations).[55] Despite the preponderance of Allied sea power elsewhere, *Lady Evelyn* with her puny twelve-pounder guns was suddenly alone at sea in the face of an unknown threat to Halifax. Although with hindsight, it was clear that the crew of *Lady Evelyn* were relative safe, their situation called for considerable courage. Although those aboard could not know the extent of the damage and suffering, it was immediately clear that something dramatic and deadly had occurred. They had to wonder who among their friends and loved ones had been affected, and whether worse was to follow.

Through the Grim Day

In the crisis following the explosion, most naval personnel and dockyard civilians alike shook off their personal fear and injury and rose to the challenges before them. But such heroic responses were not universal. Aboard *Niobe*, for example, officers were unable to maintain discipline among the full complement. Some men were overcome by shock and fear. The thoughts of local men naturally turned to their families ashore; several were disconcerted by the conflicting demands of naval and familial duty. A.H. Wickens, a veteran of the RNCVR, provided the following account that, although uncorroborated, has the ring of authenticity. Some of the men, he recalled,

> were about to make a break for it when some officer heavy on tradition, yelled thru a megaphone for all hands to stand fast, keep cool and everything will be alright, there's no immediate danger and to remember the *Birkenhead*. So someone yells back at him, to hell with you and the *Birkenhead* we got wives and kids ashore, so there was a general stampede for the gangplank which was somewhat

out of kilter, it was a good thing those ratings took the law into their own hands, they did a lot of good saving lives and putting out fires after which they were commended for their bravery and in helping the civic authorities who at the time did not know that they broke ship and had a charge of mass mutiny hanging over their heads but said charge was dropped.[1]

It is not clear whether this incident occurred as part of the first panicked rush to the gangway or somewhat later, when it became apparent to all that widespread fires were raging ashore. Subsequent reports of the day's events do record, however, that Captain Walter Hose later ordered *Niobe*'s captain, Commander Percy Newcombe, to take a motor car through the city to round up all naval ratings who had gone ashore and order them to return to the dockyard.[2] Despite such lapses, discipline held for the most part, and both individuals and those working in groups displayed remarkable dedication to duty.

The leadership of the men who had remained on *Niobe* was assumed by Temporary Lieutenant-Commander Allan Baddeley, *Niobe*'s executive officer, who was later cited by his captain for the "excellent manner" in which he carried out the many duties imposed on him immediately after the catastrophe:

> Being practically out of action myself the whole burden of a hundred and one details needing immediate attention fell on his shoulders, and very often no opportunity of referring more important matters for my approval.
>
> He carried out all these duties quietly, thoroughly and efficiently. I would especially point out the able manner in which he insured [sic] the securing of the ship from the time her cables first parted, throughout ... until she was properly secured, the congested state of the Quarterdeck rendering this work one of considerable difficulty.[3]

Serious crises tend to have a graduated pattern of response. The initial response of those caught up in the catastrophe is ascertaining their own well-being, after which individuals tend to their immediate environment. Having offered aid to those closest to them, they turn their attention further outwards to their vessel or building, and then its environs, working in more organized groups. The speed of the response depends partly on the challenges faced at each level. Thus, in the aftermath of the explosion, those ships that had sustained the least damage – such as *Canada* – were able to respond most quickly. Other Canadian vessels took somewhat longer, but, as their own immediate situations were brought under control, various parties began to land in boats or move into the devastated dockyard from their berths.

Foreign vessels responded to the crisis as well. Indeed, the presence of British and American naval vessels in the port was particularly fortunate. Unlike the diminutive Canadian vessels, all of the visitors carried doctors and medical staff. *Changuinola* and *Highflyer* sent parties ashore to assist, as did the US Coast Guard cutter *Morrill* and the USS *Old Colony.* The latter had secured itself to No. 4 Jetty, which was still intact.[4] With spreading fires threatening to cut the waterfront off from the interior of Halifax, more and more military and civilian casualties from nearby were being brought down to the shore, where they found a haven and medical help in the roomy vessel.

The dockyard, which was the heart of the RCN structure in Halifax, was a shambles, but ascertaining the extent of the damage was not the first order of business. Captain Pasco's immediate priority was the protection of life and property. All available men were employed searching the ruins for survivors and performing rescue work. As best they could, Pasco and Hose endeavoured to direct the arriving resources to that end.[5] Most of these ad hoc arrangements depended on the initiative of individuals and formed parties; these had soon reached out beyond the dockyard's limits and along the shoreline to the north. None had far to go before meeting someone crying out in need. Soon the mixed groups of ratings from three navies and all manner of civilians were reinforced by the first groups of soldiers from parts of the garrison less severely affected by the explosion.

Among the first soldiers to arrive at the waterfront was a contingent of mostly American recruits for the British Expeditionary Force who had been on parade inside the Armoury on Cunard Street. The blast had wrecked the Armoury, killing two and injuring dozens. Despite widespread shock and injury, 150 of the new soldiers had marched to the devastated waterfront. Captain J.A. Armitage, who led the party, had received medical attention for serious cuts about his head. Many of the soldiers worked all day, ignoring their own injuries. Among them was a sergeant major – his name was not recorded – who was later found to have suffered three broken ribs.[6] On the following day, one of the young recruits, Carl Moulton, described the experience when he wrote to a young woman he was courting in Connecticut. Despite the grim news his words contain a certain pride and exhilaration:

We lost two of our boys and a good many of them were cut up pretty bad. I caught quite a bit of glass but I looked a good deal worse than I felt. In fact I never realized how fast I could run before. You must wait until I get sight of you again and you will see. I intend to run after you tho.

You will probably read about this explosion here. We were marched down to the water front as soon as we could get the men together. Fires were raging all about, buildings all flat, glass all about and the people – the least said the better. We worked among the ruins for hours, had to improvise stretchers and take the injured to tugs and other boats to be carried to the hospital ships ... There was little confusion for the military took hold of the situation.

It's a fact that I have lived thru such a nightmare that I am not stuck on writing about it. Let me hear some cheerful news from home.[7]

Sailors, too, were sent ashore to deal with complications arising from the explosion. *Niobe*'s Temporary Lieutenant-Commander Baddeley despatched a party to rebury the ship's port bower anchor, which had been dragged from its concrete bed. Baddeley was also concerned that the spreading fires ashore might reach the partly demolished structures housing the North Ordnance Magazines on the Wellington Barracks property close to the shore. The results could be disastrous. He therefore decided to send Gunner William O'Reilly with a large working party of sailors – including Bert Griffith – to empty the magazines and try to hold off the fires.[8] One member of the group, Seaman Jack Stotesbury, recorded the experience the following day in a letter to his parents in Ottawa:

I had my new uniform on and dirtied it by the first job we had that of clearing the Niobe's decks of wreckage so that men could move about a bit. Then we went to the magazine on shore about two blocks away & carted boxes of shells, primers, fuses & detonators on our shoulders & dumped them all into the water off a jetty. We were asked to do this by our Commander as there was great danger of the fire getting to this magazine. When he told us all what he wanted us to do he asked, "is there anybody who doesn't want to do this?" Of course nobody answered him & we all went cheerfully to work and worked all morning at carrying this ammunition to the water's edge.[9]

Carl Moulton's group passed within twenty feet of the hard-working sailors. The American soldiers thought the sailors' job "did not look good," but they would later change their minds as they encountered the dead and dying in

Richmond.[10] Eventually, an army ordnance officer arrived on the scene and halted the destruction of the ammunition. Instead, the sailors began to distribute the remainder over as large an area as possible on land, until more soldiers could be spared to collect it.[11]

As was evidenced by the damage to the North Ordnance Magazines, the Halifax Garrison's Wellington Barracks were hit hard by the explosion and the wooden buildings – including quarters housing soldiers' families – were totally destroyed. Even the more solidly constructed brick structure housing the officers had suffered very material damage, taking the full force of the concussion. This building had acted as a buffer for the men's quarters, leaving that structure partially intact. Despite extensive damage to the barracks and a few other exceptions, most of the widespread garrison facilities around Halifax were relatively unharmed. The military chain of command took hold quickly and as the district commander, Major-General Thomas Benson, reported some days later:

> Immediately after the explosion all troops in the Garrison and outforts were ordered to stand to and as soon as the location and the nature of the disaster were determined, men stationed in the huts on the Common were marched up and put to work rescuing the imprisoned living from the ruins, extinguishing fires and rendering assistance generally. By one o'clock every available man who could be spared from the 63rd and 66th Regiments, and from the Artillery manning the forts was also in the city and placed at work, fighting fires, clearing streets, searching for wounded and the dead, patrolling the streets, furnishing guards and fatigue parties generally, and this work is still being carried on.[12]

The disaster presented a medical crisis of the first order. Until outside help could arrive, existing civil and military medical facilities and personnel had to bear the brunt. No. 6 Military District's senior medical officer, Lieutenant-Colonel Frank McKelvey Bell, was paramount in deploying and managing the local militia medical resources in Halifax, despite serious damage to the Cogswell Street military hospital and the destruction of both the Pier 2 Casualty Depot and Rockhead General Hospital. As the militia's official medical history of the war later remarked, "The Service in the field was never faced with a more desperate problem."[13] Bell's efforts provided an almost instant infrastructure, which made it possible to link and coordinate a united civilian-military struggle of rescue, treatment, and care. While overburdened facilities struggled to cope with the frightened and injured, Bell's medical troops distributed military medical stores and blankets, established emergency hospitals and neighbourhood dressing stations, and coordinated consignment of patients.

It took some time for troops from outside to reach the demolished Wellington Barracks, although two junior medical orderlies on the site set up a station to treat their wounded comrades and their wives and children.[14] In the meantime, the survivors had to avert potential disaster. Charles A. McLennan of the 76th (Colchester and Hants Rifles) militia regiment was a member of the composite battalion that had been put together for local guard duties and many of whose members were in residence on the Wellington property. He had survived the explosion to find the barracks orderly officer at his side, mortally wounded. Immediately assuming the orderly officer's place, McLennan had fallen in the physically able troops and had organized the dousing of fires caused by upset stoves within the remaining buildings. He found the garrison magazine (not to be confused with the North Ordnance facilities nearer the shore) damaged and wide open. He immediately posted three of his people to maintain a watch:

> I then found that a piece of steel had ripped a hole in the magazine fence. I went into the enclosure to investigate the magazine. The entrance was badly smashed: the entrance roof had collapsed and the doors were kindling wood. All the inner doors were forced open and the wooden gratings on the floor were all smashed. The temperature inside seemed to be excessive. All the buildings in the vicinity were burning and, as the wreckage lying around the magazine would catch fire very easily, I decided to clear it away.[15]

At this point a large party of sailors entered the barracks square. They were from HMS *Changuinola* and had been landed astern of *Niobe* to render aid.[16] About twenty of them commanded by RNR Lieutenant E.B. Thompson were detached to assist the soldiers, and they set to work clearing debris from the magazine. With no light inside the building, the work had to be done by touch, by men unfamiliar with the layout of the building. Once the work was under way, McLennan went over to check a small building attached to the lower side of the magazine. It was a heater house. "The door was blown in and smashed, the window frames were smashed on the floor, the roof were [sic] half off, the smoke pipe was blown from the heater. The hot-water heater itself had all its doors blown open and the coals scattered over the floor among the smashed woodwork. This was smouldering. From this building a duct about two feet square ran into the magazine. This condition, together with the excessive heat of the magazine, seemed to be very dangerous."[17]

McLennan hailed two sailors and directed them to dump the coals from the furnace into a bucket. He then ran out looking for water to douse them. In the meantime, the naval working party had cleaned the magazine out as far as its inner doors, which, luckily, were still on their hinges. Ordering the doors secured, McLennan directed the sailors to "get at the stuff lying at the entrance." He then rushed back to the heater house with a chemical extinguisher that he had found. The two sailors were bringing out the first bucket of coals. McLennan turned the extinguisher on the woodwork and on the coals in the furnace. The resulting cloud of steam shot up and through the damaged roof. One among "quite a crowd" of civilian bystanders attracted by the activity pointed at the roof and yelled that the magazine was on fire.

> When the alarm came the natural impulse was to run. [Like the bystanders] I started but when I reached the hole in the fence found that the entire Naval party were running out and had it blocked. I started back and passed one of my sentries who was running on the outside of the magazine fence. I asked him where the fire was and he said on the roof. I had thought it was inside because the sailors were running. I ran up the side of the roof. There was no sign of fire though it was badly damaged. From the roof I could see the crowd, that had been on the street, running in every direction.[18]

Cadet Edward Woollcombe of the Naval College told the *Ottawa Citizen* some days later that "hundreds of people passed him running as hard as they could for the common."[19] Indeed, many of the naval cadets joined the flight.[20] Despite the panic, a few of McLennan's soldiers remained, and he was able to gather others to re-establish the sentry beats and to place fire pickets. When Major-General Thomas Benson, the Nova Scotia district commander, arrived on the scene a few minutes later, McLennan was able to report the magazine secure, enabling the senior officer to turn his attention to other matters. McLennan expressed no malice towards those who had panicked in the face of the near disaster: "Regarding the action of the sentries, in running when the alarm came, that the magazine was on fire; I may say that everyone was shocked, nervous and on edge. Having, within an hour, experienced one terrific explosion, the fear of another one occurring, in the immediate vicinity, was enough to start anyone. Under the circumstances nothing else would be expected and I attach no blame to any of them, especially as they all returned to their beats."[21] The sailors from *Changuinola* also recovered order upon reaching the waterfront and continued to assist in the general rescue efforts. Nothing was made of the panic in subsequent reports by the RN personnel.[22]

The panic of both civilians and military personnel near Wellington Barracks was infectious. The fleeing crowd expanded and spread. These circumstances underlie later intense controversy over the "mysterious" origins of widespread expectation of a second explosion and the spontaneous flight from shelter of thousands of Haligonians to open areas and Point Pleasant Park.

The panic also found its way into HMC Dockyard. At the far end from Wellington Barracks, a work party of submariners under Lieutenant Arthur Pitts was just leaving No. 1 Jetty in search of wood to repair their ruined bunkhouse when the cry went up that "the ammunition dump was about to blow." The senior submariner, Lieutenant Francis Hanson, yelled for his people to take cover. Many of them, including Pitts's work party, jumped into the shallow water along a jetty wall. As the seconds and then minutes passed with no explosion, Hanson decided to move the boats to a safer location down the harbour. Eventually, when it became apparent that there would be no explosion, the submarines returned to the jetty and the sailors set out first to put their depot in order and later to join in the general rescue effort.[23]

Captain Pasco had been doing his best to defuse the countless crises affecting the dockyard. He had to try, simultaneously, to arrest the panic that spread from rumours of fire at the magazine and to organize precautions in case the rumours turned out to be true.[24] But mounting pain and the blood in his eyes took their toll: "Eventually I saw it was no use my taking a top hand because I could not rush about and see things, I could see on the ground but not horizontally; eventually I said to Captain Hose, I think about 11 or 12, I don't think it is any use my pretending to be in charge any longer you had better take charge."[25] Although Pasco, with the help of Hose, continued to struggle to get a grip on the situation, he was handicapped by his physical state. Moreover, his attention was, of necessity, focused on dangers in the immediate vicinity of the dockyard. He was largely unable to spare thought, energy, or attention to wider concerns.

Some of these wider concerns were taken up by Rear-Admiral Bertram Chambers. As director of convoy operations, the able and experienced rear-admiral of the Royal Navy had been further removed than those in the dockyard from the first shock of the explosion. Despite the handicaps posed by the sometimes baffling jurisdictional overlaps between the RN and the RCN, he was in a position to contribute intelligently and decisively to managing the crisis.

Just before nine o'clock that morning, Chambers, like other senior sailors in the port, had been enjoying breakfast in his well-appointed dining room, reflecting on the plenty of wartime rations on this side of the Atlantic. The home he shared with his wife and young son was in the genteel south area of the city and facing Citadel Hill. By nine, he had left his front dining room, with its large plate-glass window, and was saying a "leisurely good-bye" to his wife,

> when there came a thundering roar which shook the whole house. The day previously we had received a notice that firing would be carried out from the forts. As new-comers, and thinking that some gun existed much closer to the house than I had any idea of, I began to explain that there was no cause for alarm. Before I had finished speaking – an interval of possibly ten seconds – there came a second crash. This time the floor seemed to rise up and the room was filled with dust and soot, though luckily the windows, which were double and facing away from the explosion, stood. My wife cried out that it was a bomb in the garden, and made for the door. My own view was that it was a gas explosion in the kitchen and the whole side of the house must have gone. On reaching the hall I saw that the big double front doors had been burst wide open. I ran towards them, and there, right in front of the house ... was rising into the air a most wonderful cauliflower-like plume of white smoke, twisting and twirling and changing colour in the brilliant sunlight of a perfect Canadian early winter morning.[26]

Chambers had no idea of the explosion's cause and thought perhaps the Germans had blown up the Citadel. Whatever its source, he knew he would be required at the RN convoy offices on Hollis Street. Throwing on his naval greatcoat, he set off, leaving his wife to cope with the domestic disaster as best she could. As he walked, he noted the considerable damage: "The windows of every house had been shattered, and the side walks were a mass of glittering glass. Trees were twisted and splintered, telegraph posts bent and broken."[27]

Thanks to the willing driver of a passing commercial vehicle that Chambers hailed "in the name of the King," the admiral reached his office by 9:20,

Prior to the explosion, Chambers's office had already received signals from *Highflyer* reporting first the collision of *Mont Blanc* and *Imo* and then the fire onboard the French ship. At 9:04 the rear-admiral's deputy, Captain Turn-bull, had been on the telephone with Lieutenant-Commander Murray from Pier 9, receiving a report on the developing situation. When Chambers arrived at the office, Turnbull informed him only that he believed the explosion "had been caused by a burning ship," with no reference to either its name or cargo.[28] Chambers knew little more by the end of the day, when he prepared his initial report of the disaster to the Admiralty: in it, *Imo* was referred to as a "Belgian Relief Ship" and *Mont Blanc* as a "French Steamer." The report mentions a collision, a fire, and then "a tremendous explosion"; it does not mention or speculate as to cause or cargo.[29]

This documentation casts doubt on the accuracy of Michael Bird's colourful description of the last moments of Lieutenant-Commander Mur-ray's life and of the legendary heroism of train dispatcher Vincent Coleman of the Canadian Government Railway at the telegraph key. According to Bird's account, Murray knew the particular dangers of *Mont Blanc*'s cargo and sent a passing sailor to warn others in the vicinity of the urgency of the situation. When Coleman received the information, he remained at his sta-tion in the railway terminal, in disregard for his personal safety, and began tapping out a warning to approaching trains that a munitions ship was on fire in the harbour.[30] Despite the lack of documentation and the clouding effect of invented dialogue, the account could indeed be generally accurate in terms of Murray having sent a danger warning. Nonetheless, it is clear that Murray, like Chambers, did not know that a truly cataclysmic explosion was in the offing. Had he been aware that *Mont Blanc* was filled with such a deadly cocktail of high explosives, he would surely have reported this in the phone conversation with Captain Turnbull.

A more plausible explanation for the behaviour of Murray and Coleman, and one in keeping with the evidence, is simply that a fire on any ship, espe-cially one in a crowded seaport, is a very serious matter calling for prompt and effective action. In other words, Murray and Coleman did not need to have known the horrible truth about *Mont Blanc*'s cargo before spreading an alarm. Almost any experienced mariner would have appreciated the danger from the vessel's fuel or from chemicals and combustible cargo that could have been onboard. Moreover, during the war it was common for ships to carry armaments, and many included crates of ammunition in their cargo.

This did not necessarily render them "munitions ships," although the term was widely applied to any and all. The initial flare-ups and explosions witnessed before the destruction of *Mont Blanc* were typical of wartime dangers. Captain Garnett of *Highflyer* later reported that he had not known the nature of *Mont Blanc*'s cargo but had nonetheless reacted because he thought "a dangerous situation was arising."[31] Courageous men doing what they were trained to do died without knowing the full extent of the peril. This in no way diminishes their heroism.

Determined to inspect the extent of the disaster for himself, Admiral Chambers invited the new senior British officer in the port to accompany him. Vice-Admiral Evelyn R. Le Marchant was shortly due to hoist his pennant aboard *Knight Templar* as convoy admiral over the ships anchored in Bedford Basin. The two of them, with Captain Turnbull, went afloat immediately aboard one of their locally chartered tugs, the *Maggie*. The little vessel was mastered by her owner, Captain Gordon, a spry septuagenarian. Gordon already had her steam up, and Chambers later recalled that they were moving through the water by 9:30 [sic]. They headed for their own warships, stopping first at *Changuinola*, which was the nearest to the tug.

The admirals agreed that Chambers, while technically the junior in rank, held operational responsibility by virtue of his appointment as the RN's senior officer of escorts in the area. In effect, though, the two acted in consultation. Reaching *Changuinola*, Chambers ordered Captain Wilcox to signal the captain of *Highflyer*, who was senior officer afloat. *Highflyer*, however severe her apparent damage, had already raised signal flags calling for the landing of all available medical and relief parties. Now Chambers directed that she signal "that all vessels were to raise steam immediately, and be ready to leave wharves or get under way if necessity arose."[32] He then waited a few minutes for *Changuinola*'s relief party to board Gordon's tug so they could be brought ashore. During this brief time, he was able to gauge something of the magnitude of the disaster from a perspective less confined than that of the Canadian officers in the dockyard:

> The district from Royal Canadian Dockyard to Pier 9, at Richmond, was a complete wreck, and even as we watched fires were springing up in all directions, and increasing with amazing speed. First a puff of white smoke, like a tuft of cotton wool, then a bright spark, and then a raging furnace. One wondered when the flames would stop as they burrowed further and further into the

comparatively intact part of the town. Fortunately the day was an extremely fine one, and such wind as there was blowing took the flames away from the better part of the town; but even so the progress was truly alarming, and one wondered if anything could escape. Round the wharves the flames flickered and threatened to take hold on the piles themselves, most of the wharves being timber construction, and in many cases the ships alongside some of which were laden with explosives, were also threatened.[33]

In addition to *Changuinola*'s relief party, part of which Chambers held in reserve, *Maggie* also landed a surgeon, Horace G. Brown, and a stretcher party at the dockyard. Surgeon Brown found the dockyard hospital's staff surgeon Joseph A. Rousseau lying wounded in a ruined basement and had him evacuated to the *Old Colony.* Brown was also present at No. 3 Jetty to render first aid to what he characterized as the "severe lacerations" on Captain Pasco's face.[34] Admiral Le Marchant was also landed, to interview the Canadian senior naval officer and formulate a report for Chambers on conditions in the dockyard.[35] He found Pasco and Hose "ably controlling the affairs in the Dockyard," despite the wounds to the former. But if the Canadians were having any difficulty coping, they were not going to acknowledge it to the admiral. They told Le Marchant that the situation was sufficiently well in hand that they did not require additional assistance from the Royal Navy people, who were released for general relief work.[36]

Maggie set off for *Highflyer,* where the rear-admiral viewed the damage and conferred with Captain Garnett. A large party from the cruiser was already ashore in Dartmouth, providing whatever help they could. Chambers now directed the remaining surgical party from *Changuinola* to the assistance of the wrecked merchantmen lying outside the dry dock, where the survivors appeared "much shaken by the explosion." In order that his passenger could view the wreckage at Piers 8 and 9 and in Tufts Cove, Captain Gordon was asked to steer his little tug into the floating wreckage that nearly choked the Narrows. On the way, they saw *Hilford,* the other small tug chartered by the Port Convoy office (and also owned by Captain Gordon), which had carried Lieutenant-Commander Murray to Pier 9. Thrown on top of the wharf by the blast, it was lying a complete wreck on a pile of jumbled timber thirty feet above the water.[37]

Preoccupied by the safety of the ships awaiting convoy in Bedford Basin, Chambers directed *Maggie* on up the cluttered stream to close on the guard ship *Acadia*. Once assured that all was well, the tug turned back towards the worst-hit part of the shore, around the Richmond Depot of the Intercolonial Railway. Chambers recalls:

> In passing this point on my return I observed a person making signals to attract our attention, and on closing I found it was a survivor from the Hilford, one of my own vessels. We landed to see what could be done. Around was confusion beyond description. The stacks of timber, the debris of the piers and railway sheds, the ties and lines of the sidings which had been torn up by the wave were inextricably mixed up and piled in heaps ... Amidst the ruins wandered a few dazed creatures, blood-stained and in rags. They were the remains of the military guard stationed on the pier. Many of the guard were in a dying condition, others had been pinned to the ground by the flying masses of timber. Beneath one of the largest piles I could distinguish the body of my very capable second assistant, Lieut.-Commander T.A. Murray, RNCVR, who had been making a telephonic report to the convoy office at the time the explosion took place. It was a terrible business getting the dying and badly injured men across such a terrain and down to the boat, but the route shorewards was even more impassable, and Captain Turnbull and the crew of the Maggie accomplished wonders.[38]

Because his cargo of seriously wounded men required immediate attention, Chambers took them back to *Highflyer*. By this time, other vessels were aiding in rescue efforts. Commander Graham Holloway, the naval transport officer in charge of the fleet auxiliaries, had despatched several small naval craft for general rescue work and to assist vessels in distress.[39] Holloway himself went afloat in *W.H. Lee*, taking her from vessel to vessel to fight fires with her hoses. He was later credited with "especially noteworthy" efforts in rescuing the RCN's tug *Musquash*, quelling the fire aboard and bringing her to safety.[40] Another ship in particular trouble was the SS *Picton*. Anchored at the sugar refinery at the time of the blast, the vessel had sustained considerable damage, with many of her crew killed or missing. She still carried part of a cargo of shells that the men had been unloading when the explosion occurred. With the fire in the refinery area pressing close, naval tugs moved in to pull her out into the stream, where she was safely anchored.[41]

Chambers decided to leave further rescue work to Holloway and others. Now that he had a sense of the magnitude of the disaster from a naval perspective, Chambers felt it was vital for him to get some word to the Admiralty and to main ports along the coast. No wireless capability was at hand, all aerials were down, and no radio messages through the navy's coastal radio system would be possible until the delicate equipment could be restored to service. Chambers decided to visit Captain George Eldridge, RN (Ret.), the senior naval staff officer aboard *Niobe* – who was also responsible for naval intelligence – to confer on how best to proceed.

On his way to *Niobe*, Chambers found Walter Hose in the tumult and turmoil of the dockyard, dealing with matters as best he could in the place of the now incapacitated Pasco. Chambers, who quickly realized that his Canadian colleague had his hands full, offered his services in dealing with the wider situation "from a naval point of view, such as organisation of patrols and piquets." Recognizing that this was no time for fretting over the niceties of chain of command, Hose not only readily accepted Chambers offer but agreed that the admiral should represent the RCN locally in making the immediate arrangements necessary with civil authorities and with Major-General Benson's command. Hose, in turn, would organize soundings in the Narrows to determine if the channel were navigable. The two officers parted, Chambers heading for *Niobe* with a view to getting the word out. At the ship at noon, he drafted a brief cable to the Admiralty and commander in chief North America and West Indies: "At 9 a.m., as result of collision, the French munition vessel Mont Blanc blew up in Narrows. Radius quarter-mile complete wreck, and town badly damaged. Fear loss of life considerable. Fires raging, but getting under control – difficult to exaggerate damage. Ships in basin safe, also armed vessels. Highflyer slightly injured. Fear loss of three officers and about 40 men – officers Triggs, Murray, and Ruffles. Hope to sail convoy shortly, but please notify all centres Halifax out of action for some time."[42]

Chambers left the depot ship with assurances from George Eldridge that he would get the message out if at all possible. The staff officer handled the matter wisely. With no assurance that commercial telegraph connections would be in any better state than the local wireless, he had the message taken by motor car out into the countryside until an operational telegraph terminal was found. This proved to be the only communication received that day by frantic officials in Ottawa.[43]

By early afternoon, additional help was arriving from an unexpected source. The USS *Tacoma* was an ageing 3,200-ton protected cruiser (*Denver* class) built in 1900. It had a principal armament of ten five-inch guns and a complement of 309 officers and men. One of the so-called peace cruisers that had represented Theodore Roosevelt's "big stick" off the coasts of Central America and in the Caribbean, the ship corresponded roughly to the British category of third-class cruiser. Because of her slow speed and limited armament, she had been near the end of her useful life by the time the United States entered the war. But, with an urgent need for ocean escorts, she had been kept in service and brought north out of her usual sailing waters. Now under the command of Captain Powers Symington, USN, she was returning to the United States after her third trip escorting troopships and convoys to Europe.[44] As later reported by her captain, at shortly after 9:00 that morning she had been fifty-two miles from Halifax "when a heavy concussion was felt, so strong that the officer of the Deck immediately went to quarters. A great column of smoke was seen to rise in the air in the direction of Halifax."[45] Symington immediately followed the sound, setting course for the port. At noon, *Tacoma* came up upon *Lady Evelyn,* still cleared for action and nervously patrolling the outside approaches. *Tacoma*'s proper response to the little patrol ship's flashed challenge must have been a great relief to the Canadians. Symington received the signal to proceed into the harbour at slow speed, with the Canadian vessel guiding the American cruiser as far as the inner automatic buoy.[46]

Only thirty minutes behind *Tacoma,* a second American cruiser was approaching Halifax Harbour. In her earlier incarnation as the German auxiliary cruiser *Kronprinz Wilhelm,* her approach would have caused much alarm, but the vessel had been interned in Philadelphia and then seized by the US government when that country entered the war. The 23,500-ton former passenger liner had been rechristened the USS *Von Steuben* and put into service with a complement of 975. Her captain, Stanford E. Moses, had also decided to proceed into the port after his lookouts had spotted "a great flame and a high column of smoke" followed by concussion.[47]

Tacoma passed through the outer defences and into the inner harbour, where she anchored in the stream at about 2:00 p.m. *Von Steuben* joined her half an hour later. Symington noted in passing that a "great fire" was still burning in north Halifax (most certainly the sugar refinery and dry dock area) and that none of the houses facing the harbour on either side had any windows or doors. He also noted that the sides of all the piers were burst open and that several ships were ashore and others looked badly battered.

As was naval custom, Symington proceeded on board HMS *Highflyer* to tender his services to the senior officer afloat. Probably upon Captain Garnett's information that the port was under the control of the RCN, the American officer went to the dockyard to look for the captain superintendent. Following a "considerable search," Symington found not Hose but Pasco, who, he later reported, was "badly wounded." Although the American reported that he "tendered his services to him and asked him if he would call on me for anything I could possibly do," no mention is made of Pasco's response. Symington records that he found *Old Colony* tied up at No. 4 Jetty, where he saw that his countrymen had "already started to do hospital work." Quick to seize upon this initiative as a course of effective assistance, he immediately returned to *Tacoma* and ordered his senior medical officer, R.M Hayes, to take his staff and equipment to assist on the *Old Colony*.[48]

When Dr Hayes and his party arrived aboard *Old Colony*, they found Assistant Surgeon J.J. Hardy of the US Coast Guard cutter *Morrill* in charge of the medical work. The ship's own surgeon, H.C. Petterson, was assisting with relief work ashore. As senior medical officer, Hayes took charge of the effort. Fifty-four injured had already been brought aboard ship. Eleven had died before receiving medical attention, but the balance had been given first aid and put to bed. *Old Colony*'s captain, Lieutenant Commander McKay, and non-medical crew were instrumental in coordinating the logistics of outfitting two operating rooms on *Old Colony* with equipment found on the American ships and from the ruined RCN hospital ashore as well as from the Victoria General Hospital. Working feverishly, they converted *Old Colony*'s staterooms into wards for 150 patients; ultimately, they were able to accommodate twice that number. Among those transferred in were the patients from the abandoned RCN hospital. With the addition of three graduate nurses from Halifax, *Old Colony* became a full-blown hospital within the growing network of medical aid facilities. Although these medical facilities were indispensable, one of the most appreciated aspects of *Old Colony*'s services were the hot meals that were "obtainable at all hours for both patients and attendants," something of a luxury in devastated Halifax over the next few days.[49]

At about 3:00 p.m., after Rear-Admiral Chambers had left the dockyard, he met with the Halifax area's senior soldier, Major-General Thomas Benson "and gave him a resume of the situation from the naval point of view." Chambers later remarked on the "very courteous reception" he received from Benson. The general officer commanding (GOC) asked the British admiral to accompany him to a meeting about to be convened by the Nova Scotia lieutenant governor, J. McCallum Grant, at Halifax City Hall. There, the two military men saw all the principals responsible for public safety, order, and government in the city striving to come to terms with the grim extent of the disaster. As Chambers recalled,

> The conference was a remarkable experience – held in the shattered town hall amidst splintered woodwork and floors covered with broken glass. In many cases those present had been at work since the explosion without even an opportunity to ascertain whether their nearest and dearest were in safety. Some showed traces of quick surgical attendance in the shape of plaster and bandages. I was much struck with the sane and business-like way in which the situation was faced. The difficulties were enormous, all telephonic communications were down and the roads blocked, but I left the building with the impression that order was already beginning to arise out of the chaos, and that what could be done would be done.[50]

This was the second such emergency meeting called that day. An ad hoc relief committee was formed on the spot to deal with the disaster, although General Benson would later report to the Militia Council that "the citizens did not organize for systematic relief till Sunday the 9th." Benson's report probably exaggerated the army's predominant role in the immediate aftermath, but it is true that the militia's organizational structure provided much of the necessary direction and coordination of the initial relief effort through the first days of the disaster. This ought not to be surprising. The garrison had an organizational structure and trained manpower on the spot, including medical services, engineers, transport, logistics, administration, security, and other services. While the point is hardly profound, neither is it necessarily obvious: soldiers train for war; war is a disaster. The Halifax explosion, too, was a disaster, and in the short term the militia organizational structure provided a template for effective reaction to the crisis. Yet the point must be added that martial law was not declared, and civil government and agencies acted to the best of their abilities within their normal areas of jurisdiction.[51]

When the meeting at city hall was over, Chambers returned to the Convoy Office, which had withstood the explosion "with much less than our fair share of damage." Nevertheless, his naval secretary had narrowly escaped the stilettos of plate glass that the blast had embedded in the door and walls. Chambers found the convoy admiral and Captain Garnett of *Highflyer* awaiting his return. After discussing the general situation, the officers agreed to send out an advisory suspending all convoy work at Halifax and asking all centres not to despatch vessels for convoy until further instruction.[52]

Chambers was about to leave his office again for discussions with Lieutenant Governor Grant when the American captains of *Tacoma* and *Von Steuben* appeared. Having failed to find the US consul general, Powers Symington now sought to tender his services to Chambers as senior British naval officer in the port. He no doubt was somewhat confused – perhaps even incredulous – when Chambers explained that, while he was in charge of convoy operations, he had "nothing to do with the dock yard or the Canadian authorities."[53] Once Chambers outlined the fuzzy local command structure and added his own endorsement of and encouragement to the American efforts at medical relief, he walked Symington over to the nearby Militia District Headquarters offices on Granville Street to meet Major-General Benson. The general instantly seized upon the American presence and manpower as a very welcome asset. According to Symington, Benson informed him that

> the situation was very much confused and that owing to the fact that the front of all stores and buildings were broken in, he was afraid there might be looting during the night and that as his men had been on duty all day, he would be very grateful if I would take over the patrol of the business portion of the city during the night so that his men could get some rest. I informed him at once that I would land two hundred men ... and in conjunction with Commander Moses of the *Von Steuben,* we organized a patrol force, which force went on duty at 8:00 p.m. and patrolled the city until 8:00 a.m., the following morning when the force was withdrawn.[54]

As evening fell, Acting Captain Walter Hose was aboard *Niobe.* The dockyard headquarters' temporary offices, so recently removed to the Marine and Fisheries building south of the dockyard, had suffered serious damage in the explosion, and the building could not be used until the roof was replaced. Thus, the dockyard would for some time be commanded from a portion of the smoking room, senior officers' mess, aboard *Niobe.*[55] It was probably in this location that at 8:30 p.m. the weary officer signed his own first official report of the disaster for naval service headquarters in Ottawa. The text was then converted into cypher for transmission along the commercial telegraph lines that carried the bulk of Canadian forces domestic message traffic: "Regret to report French munition ship MONT BLANC blew up at 9 a.m. after collision with Belgian Relief ship in Narrows leading to Basin. Most yard buildings practically wrecked, certain number of service casualties and deaths but unable at present to report numbers or names. Understand Rear-Admiral Chambers has already reported that no convoy work or other operations can be carried out from Halifax at present. I concur in this. Damage to city very extensive and it appears that the town to the North dockyard is destroyed."[56]

As THE LONG DAY DREW TO A CLOSE, no further fires were burning, although some observers were still fearful of further explosions or conflagrations. The circumstances of the accident and subsequent explosion were not well understood; concerns were raised that the disaster was the result of enemy action and that more of the same might be expected.[57]

It had been a grim day. Anyone surveying the area could not but be disheartened by the extent of the destruction and the tragic number of casualties. Yet those taking stock could find hopeful signs among the devastation. Although the railway facilities along the Richmond shore had been savaged, and the North Street Station completely demolished, another rail line had just been completed. It connected the main line from the north, which ended at Bedford Basin, with new Ocean Terminals in the city's South End. The new line, which was not damaged by the explosion, would provide access to the city for the trains that would soon be bringing in badly needed supplies from central Canada and New England.[58]

Restoration of communications had already begun. Before the end of the day, seven multiplex telegraph lines were functioning out of the city. The telephone system had been greatly damaged, and many operators were among the casualties. Nonetheless, some lines for emergency use were expected to be up the following day. Although the gas supply would be out for three days, electricity was still available in parts of the city, though it would take some time to repair and reconnect the rest.[59]

Despite the wreckage throughout the dockyard, most of the ships moored alongside afforded a degree of warmth and shelter. *Niobe*'s crew faced a massive clean-up, but the depot ship was able to spare some hands for a "sailors patrol" at 7:00 p.m. Indeed, from her CO's subsequent report, it would appear that the ship's officers and non-commissioned officers had been equal to the task of dealing with the immediate crisis. Among those commended for energy and devotion was the depot ship's head steward, who had managed to serve a proper dinner to the exhausted members of the ship's company at the regulation time.[60]

As Rear-Admiral Chambers would later remark, it was fortunate that the weather throughout the day of the disaster had remained fine for that time of year, making the task of those digging through the ruins and rendering aid to the survivors somewhat less difficult than it might have been. Among the RCN ships at rest in the harbour that night, the logkeeper aboard HMCS *Grilse* was unable to record the air pressure because the ship's barometer had been cracked in the explosion. Otherwise he might have noted a slight drop in the mercury. The skies over the harbour remained clear, however, and the winds were calm.[61] Out to sea, where the *Lady Evelyn* continued her distant vigil over the approaches to the port, all had been quiet since rounds at 9:00 p.m., when the winds had begun to swing from south to southeast and to increase from Force 1 to Force 2 (Beaufort scale). By midnight the barometer had dropped again, and the wind was blowing from the northeast at Force 3. The good weather had come to an end. A gale was beginning to blow.[62]

Members of the RNCVR, c. 1915. Able Seaman Ben Griffith is in second row at far left.

Admiral C.E. Kingsmill, director of the naval service. Born and educated in Canada, he served some thirty-eight years in the Royal Navy and retired in 1908 to become first commander of the Canadian naval service.

The auxiliary patrol ship (APS) HMCS *Lady Evelyn* was acquired from the Post Office in June 1917. On the eve of the Halifax explosion, the ship patrolled the approaches to Halifax Harbour.

Minesweeping trawler *PV-II*. One of seven converted menhaden (herring) trawlers used in daily patrols to ensure a clear channel into Halifax Harbour and numbered *PV-I* through *PV-VII*. The Roman numerals that distinguished them were unique in Canadian service.

HMCS *Grilse* at Halifax, 1915. Commissioned as a Torpedo Boat Destroyer (TBD), the ship was actually a speedy private yacht purchased in the United States by financier J.K.L. (Jack) Ross of Montreal, who placed the ship at the disposal of the RCN. Ross also served in the navy as the ship's first commanding officer.

HMCS *Canada* served before the First World War as a fisheries protection cruiser but was operated "along naval lines" to prepare for the formation of a Canadian Navy. The first class of the Royal Naval College of Canada trained aboard the ship.

Some officers and men of the RNCVR who carried out patrols of the St Lawrence and Atlantic on RCN trawlers and drifters.

HMC submarines *CC-1* and *CC-2* were purchased at the outbreak of war by British Columbia's premier, Sir Richard McBride, to meet a perceived threat to the west coast from German cruisers operating in the Pacific Ocean. The threat soon evaporated, and in 1917 the boats undertook a lengthy cruise through the Panama Canal to Halifax.

HMCS *Niobe* in 1914. Purchased in 1910 as the centrepiece for the newborn RCN, the already obsolete 11,000-ton heavy cruiser was used in a RN cruiser patrol force off North America in the first year of the war. By mid-1915, *Niobe* was beyond useful sea service but filled an essential function as a depot ship in Halifax Harbour.

Trawler and drifter flotilla in Halifax Harbour. Some of these newly built craft arrived in Halifax before 6 December 1917. With additional arrivals in the aftermath, they provided much-needed augmentation to the east coast patrols for 1918.

HMC Dockyard, Halifax, after the explosion. Damage to torpedo shops, with coastal drifter *CD-74* docked at left foreground.

HMC Dockyard, Halifax, after the explosion. The damaged victualling stores and YMCA building.

The auxiliary patrol ship (APS) HMCS *Acadia* in wartime service. Anchored in Bedford Basin as a guard ship, *Acadia* sustained minor damage in the Halifax explosion. After a fifty-six-year career as a hydrographic vessel, the ship is preserved at the Maritime Museum of the Atlantic in Halifax.

Damage to the married quarters, Wellington Barracks.

Shoreline view south from Wellington Barracks to HMC Dockyard. *Niobe* is at left. The snow cover suggests this photograph was taken on 7 December.

Snow partially conceals the damage to the dry dock. The ship with a smoke stack hanging over is the SS *Hovland*. HMS *Highflyer* can be seen at the centre of the photograph.

5

Reaction and Recovery

On Thursday morning, 6 December 1917, George Joseph Desbarats, the deputy minister responsible for the naval service and a long-serving mandarin noted for his capability and efficiency, walked to work through the crisp Ottawa air. From his home on Wilbrod Street, he passed l'Université d'Ottawa and the area that is now the site of the Rideau Centre, until he arrived at the A.E. Rea Company's department store, a structure now better known in local memory as the Daly Building. Naval service headquarters was on the fifth floor in the same space it had occupied at the onset of the war. With the conflict now in its fourth year, close to 350 staff were crowded into the ill-ventilated space. Efforts to obtain additional room had so far been fruitless in a national capital where every suitable building was crammed with expanded government operations.[1]

Official Ottawa and the nation were weary and preoccupied after more than three years of war. Continued losses at the front in 1917 – particularly the terrible battles at Vimy in April and Passchendaele in October – had heightened demands for conscription in some quarters and protest against compulsory service in others. Union government had been proclaimed in October, a coalition of the governing Conservatives of Sir Robert Borden with a substantial rump of conscriptionist Liberals, leaving an ageing and frail Sir Wilfrid Laurier isolated, his support largely limited to an angry and alienated Quebec and a few bastions in the Maritimes. In this bitter and emotionally charged political atmosphere, an election had been called for 17 December. The major campaign issue was conscription, which was ardently supported by patriots and by newly enfranchised military members and their families, opposed by many farmers and others who depended upon their sons to help support a family business, and violently resisted by most French-speaking Quebeckers.

With the House not in session, and an election in the offing, few politicians were in Ottawa on 6 December. The prime minister himself was in Prince Edward Island preparing to address an election meeting. Also absent was Charles Colquhoun Ballantyne, the new minister of marine and fisheries and the naval service, appointed only since the Union government had been proclaimed. A prominent and straightforward Montreal businessman and manufacturer, Ballantyne had been one of the first Liberals to mount the Unionist bandwagon.[2] Given Ballantyne's recent appointment and lack of background in naval matters, George Desbarats, his deputy minister, was almost certainly still in the early stages of that discreet tutelage and interplay traditional in government between men of action and those who must advise them not to be too impetuous.

Desbarats's mastery of his department was comprehensive and even extended to full subordination of Admiral Kingsmill, the director of the naval service, and the admiral's access to the minister. This situation presented a curious contrast to the easy collegial equality that existed between deputy minister and chief of the general staff (CGS) in the Militia Department, yet there is no reason to think that the arrangement was inefficient or reflected a lack of mutual respect among the participants. Indeed, Kingsmill was up for a knighthood on the New Year's honours list, a nomination that could not have been contemplated without Desbarats's approbation.[3]

This working relationship would be put to the test with news of the disaster in Halifax, which would soon begin to trickle into official Ottawa. Word of the catastrophe seemed to spread almost instantaneously. In far-off Esquimalt, British Columbia, for example, my grandmother – the wife of

Able Seaman Bert Griffith – had the news from a neighbour within five hours.[4] Yet the disruption in wireless and telegraph communications kept the details well hidden from those who most needed to know. Telegraph communications from Nova Scotia had been cut for some days following a sleet storm on 3 December that had destroyed six miles of line in the Tantramar marshes (the border area with New Brunswick).[5] Whether the backlog created by this interruption in service had been cleared by 6 December is not known.

The flood of cables and telegrams attempting to get into and out of Halifax following the explosion would have been a strain on the system at the best of times. The media along with thousands of anxious private individuals all had good cause to resort to this normally reliable means of communication. The navy and the militia also depended upon it for their message traffic – in cypher when necessary to ensure security. But the hub of operations for both the Great North Western and Canadian Pacific Railway telegraph services had been in the Richmond terminal area, which was devastated in the explosion. Indeed, the stratagem by which a copy of Rear-Admiral Chambers's first cable found its way to Ottawa became general practice for a time. A number of motor cars were procured to carry some of the outgoing telegrams to Truro for transmission. Some were later found to have been carried out by train and sent from various other points along the railway. All would have been delayed some hours. Other communications, including many of the first press reports, were transmitted from Halifax to North Sydney by land lines and then redirected by submarine cable to New York. Some others got through by submarine cable directly from Halifax to Rye Beach, New Hampshire, and then via Boston to Montreal and Ottawa. Even these tenuous channels would prove short-lived.[6]

Whether or not the first member of official Ottawa to hear of the Halifax disaster was the government's chief press censor, Lieutenant-Colonel Ernest J. Chambers, he was undoubtedly the first to act with a view to establishing a clear picture of the dimensions of the crisis. A respected public servant and littérateur, the well-connected Chambers was also a noted journalist, long-serving militia officer, and gentleman usher of the black rod of the Senate.[7] As chief press censor, his sweeping mandate was to prevent media and communications facilities from transmitting any information of use to the enemy or detrimental to the armed forces or the Canadian people. Although the moral authority inherent in his position was backed by powerful legislation, he generally chose to carry out his responsibilities collegially.[8] Indeed, at a time when the position of press secretary was unknown, Chambers worked with the journalistic community to get their stories out, although he counselled discretion when necessary. The disaster at Halifax had serious implications for Chambers's responsibilities. Journalistic interest was instant, massive, and worldwide, its intensity brushing aside even the continuing drama of the war. Chambers realized the importance of details of the disaster being made public as soon as possible, to avoid overly gruesome and exaggerated hearsay and rumour. Thus he moved quickly to urge the telegraph companies to do everything they could to facilitate transmission of journalists' reports from the scene.[9] At the same time, he had to try to protect details of the fortress garrison and disposition of transport and naval ships. Early in the day he approached the military and security authorities for information and guidance. Yet neither Major-General Willoughby Gwatkin, the CGS, nor Sir Percy Sherwood, commissioner of the Dominion Police, were able to provide Chambers with any solid specifics of the disaster. Indeed, by late that night the military headquarters – in the Woods Building on Slater Street – had still not received any reports from Halifax, and Gwatkin had to turn to Chambers for such information as was available in whatever press service reports had arrived from the scene.[10] Chambers also provided those same unverified stories to the governor general's staff.[11]

On the morning of the disaster, Chambers had contacted Admiral Kingsmill, only to discover that the naval service director was equally in the dark as to the details. Kingsmill must have found the lack of information particularly distressing. He had clear professional reasons for requiring news on the general safety of the people and installations at Halifax and the many operational aspects that might be affected. Yet for Kingsmill, as well as Desbarats, personal worries added to the hunger for information. Both men had sons who were cadets at the Naval College in Halifax.

Not realizing that the naval wireless facilities in Halifax were out of commission, Kingsmill told Chambers he would try to raise Halifax by the departmental service (which linked ships with a number of coastal stations) and pass on any definitive information received.[12] Several urgent signals intended for relay to Halifax or, failing that, any information known at the receiving station, went out through the afternoon, one of them via the three radio stations at North Sydney, Sable Island, and Camperdown, another to the Naval Transport staff at Saint John, and a third to the Camperdown station via Partridge Island and Barrington. The third provided a hint of Kingsmill's personal concerns: "Urgent. We are anxiously awaiting information re Halifax. No direct word from dockyard up to 2 p.m. Can you give us any news, can you advise if any Naval Cadets were injured. Rush reply."[13]

While the small naval staff at naval service headquarters fretted to no avail at the vague and indefinite news, the initiative for action in this informational vacuum came not from a military man but rather from the able and energetic civilian director of stores. John A. Wilson was an engineer and civil servant who had emigrated from Scotland in 1905. He is now best known for his work as secretary of the Air Board in the 1920s and as director of Air Services during the Second World War, but during the First World War he was responsible for stores and contracts, a position he had held since the inception of the RCN in 1910. Convinced that "the explosion had caused great havoc and considerable dislocation" in the work of the dockyard, he pressed Desbarats for permission to proceed immediately to Halifax. He left Ottawa by train at 3:30.[14] Kingsmill was unquestionably frustrated and anxious by this time. "Why do you not report fully what has happened to Naval College and Cadets," he chided the silent senior naval officer in Halifax over the obdurate air waves, "also casualties among officers of Department"?[15]

Into the evening the futile wait continued. The only fragment received through the naval radio system arrived at 6:10 p.m., a report from the station at North Sydney: "French Ammunition Ship MONT BLANC blown up result of collision considerable damage in dockyard and neighbourhood many fires in town considerable loss of life communications broken."[16] Later in the evening a more encouraging snippet arrived from the transport staff at Saint John, reporting that telegraphic communication from there had been re-established with Halifax and that headquarters' messages for the HMC Dockyard had been forwarded.[17] By midnight, however, there was still no reply from Halifax. No one could explain why no naval reports were coming through, in contrast to the growing flow of media reports. The only source of information for the naval staff was still the chief press censor, who sympathetically telephoned naval services with a synopsis of the still unsubstantiated press service reports.[18] Nonetheless, naval service headquarters continued overnight to prod for news from Halifax.[19]

As the calendar turned to a new day, an official response was beginning to be formulated, despite the continuing lack of specific information. The deputy minister of marine and fisheries, Alexander Johnston, sent a telegram for eventual delivery to the senior naval officer, Halifax. The minister of marine, fisheries, and naval services had ordered "a formal inquiry into the disaster." Arrangements were required to "detain such witnesses as may be able to give material evidence." The telegram instructed the senior naval officer to consult with W.A. Henry, a prominent Halifax lawyer Johnston intended to retain as counsel to the inquiry.[20]

Personnel at militia headquarters were also frustrated with the communications difficulties, but they took active measures to deal with the known situation and anticipated needs. Both the command structure and staff system contributed in positive ways to such arrangements. Willoughby Gwatkin's personal message despatched to the general officer commanding in Halifax that day did not demand a report but merely contained a query: "Is there any possible way in which Militia Council can assist?"[21] Gwatkin then sent messages to commanders in Saint John, Quebec City, and Montreal that they were "at liberty and expected to do anything" they could to relieve the situation at Halifax.[22] At some point the following day, Gwatkin's telegram got through to Major-General Benson. The district commander's reply was simple and straightforward: "Many thanks. Situation well in hand. Full report later."[23]

A full account of the Militia Department's performance in the Halifax explosion disaster awaits the telling. Yet it merits comment in this account as a contrast to that of the naval service. In fairness, the soldiers possessed more relevant experience than their comrades in the navy, and the Militia Department had massive resources at its disposal. More significantly, there would be no military micro-management from Ottawa: the situation was Benson's to deal with. Militia headquarters in Ottawa would despatch expert staff by train to assist and would coordinate the response of other military districts, including the significant resources based at Toronto. The department also placed medical, engineering, transport, and other troops on standby, and made preliminary arrangements to ship needed stores. Although, in the end, a number of specialist troops were sent – particularly military doctors and nurses, as well as carpenters, painters, and glaziers – the Halifax Garrison proved remarkably self-sufficient. Once the communications crisis passed, Gwatkin continued to provide staff support, and his adjutant general smoothly supplied the Prime Minister's Office with a daily résumé of ongoing events as well as all significant militia correspondence and activity.

No crisis is handled perfectly. Inevitably, various sorts of difficulties confronted the militia. By and large, however, the Canadian home army performed effectively and competently.[24]

First thing on the morning of 7 December Admiral Kingsmill tried to telegraph the local press censor in Halifax, again on the subject of naval casualties.[25] He was also on the phone to Ernest Chambers to report his growing anxiety that neither he nor his department had yet been able to secure "any information of any kind from any of the Naval establishments at Halifax." The chief press censor promised to use his good offices with the telegraph companies to give priority to military communications into and out of Halifax, an undertaking that he would also extend to press despatches.[26] Then, the anxious father/admiral sent an urgent wire "in plain" (uncyphered) to Rear-Admiral Chambers in Halifax: "Your messages are coming through but we have not received one word from Dockyard yet. Please give me any information you can relative to casualties of Officers and cadets."[27]

Later that day, naval services received the brief report that had been prepared by Walter Hose the previous night, but it only increased the admiral's exasperation. The frustration of Kingsmill, who had been trying to get word of his son for over twenty-four hours, was understandable, but the formal memorandum he signed in reply must have seemed both callous and unrealistic to those in devastated Halifax: "It is to be reported who actually compiled this telegram and under what conditions, observing that the information contained therein is practically useless. It gives no information as to such important matters as to which, if any, Dockyard buildings have collapsed, whether any H.M. Ships have been damaged, etc., etc."[28]

His anger mounting by the continuing lack of communication from naval sources in Halifax, on the afternoon of 7 December Kingsmill left Ottawa by rail to connect with the Ocean Limited express train out of Montreal and find out for himself what was going on in Halifax.[29] Two weeks later, he would return to sheepishly inform the chief press censor as to much of the cause of the communications difficulties: "I may say that the whole thing was the fault of the Officers of NIOBE in a way and of the G.N.W. [telegraph company]. NIOBE has a special wire and is the centre of Naval Intelligence of the whole coast. They were sending their telegrams out in ordinary course and never received any information from the distributing office that they could not be sent forward. However, in view of the fact that they must have expected everything to be down, I consider it was entirely the fault of NIOBE."[30] The initiative shown by Captain Eldridge on 6 December in getting Rear-Admiral Chambers's message out of Halifax seems to have been an exception that did not find its way down to the levels that routinely processed naval messages. Not much of this delayed traffic would get through before the flow halted completely for a time.

One of the few telegrams that arrived in Ottawa on the afternoon of 7 December was from the deputy minister's son. George Desbarats was safe, staying with friends at 62 Inglis Street.[31] There was as yet no word on Walter Kingsmill or the sons of many other anxious families. Nor was there any indication that the situation at Halifax had taken a new and ugly turn.

VERY EARLY ON THE MORNING OF 7 DECEMBER, *Lady Evelyn* was still cruising on station as the winds increased and the barometer continued to fall. By dawn, a fierce wind from the northeast was lashing the patrol boat with thick snow. *Lady Evelyn* made for shelter, anchoring with thirty-five fathoms chain in the lee of Mauger Beach off Macnab Island near the mouth of Halifax Harbour. Shortly before nine o'clock, with the wind increasing to between Force 6 and 7 (Beaufort scale), the patrol ship passed in her sister *Laurentian,* safely back from Saint John in time to shelter from the worst of the advancing storm.[32] Due to the worsening visibility, *Laurentian* had to move very slowly upwind through the outer and inner barriers and into the stream, and it was 10:30 before she tied up to Dockyard Jetty No. 3, where she was placed alongside the engineless *PV-V* with her shivering crew. The snow would have been too thick to allow the men aboard much sense of the surrounding devastation – that would begin to become apparent only after a work party was sent ashore that afternoon.[33]

Although the harbour initially offered some shelter from the conditions at sea, the weather continued to worsen through the day. The blinding snow and wind did not begin to abate until after midnight. The blizzard was later remarked upon to be one of the worst in memory. At its height, *Lady Evelyn* in her less sheltered position recorded the gale as Force 9 from the north, but the Force 6 noted by *Grilse* in the harbour was quite enough. By the time the storm ended the following morning, the snow was waist high in the dockyard, seriously hampering the rescue efforts.[34]

As it blew straight down the harbour, the storm wreaked havoc, particularly among merchant ships already rendered precarious by the explosion. Captain Walter Hose received reports through the evening that *Saranac* and

Clove were blown ashore on Macnab Island. *Picton, Middleham Castle,* and *Northwind* had all dragged their anchors; naval tugs and manpower had been "taking all possible steps ... to deal with them."[35] Hose requested help from the United States Navy, and Captain Symington detailed the Coast Guard's *Morrill* to go to the assistance of *Saranac. Northwind* ultimately drifted into collision with the USS *Von Steuben,* but the Americans managed to tie the merchant ship alongside and hold her there.[36] That evening, as the tempest persisted, there were reports in the logs of *Margaret* and *Canada* of unknown ships adrift in the harbour.[37]

One of the dragged anchors took out the submarine cable connection between Halifax and Rye Beach, thus cutting communication through Boston to the Canadian interior. Farther to the north and east on Cape Breton Island, the storm tore down the land lines to North Sydney, closing access to that submarine cable as well. With the Halifax-Truro land line still down from the explosion, Halifax was temporarily cut off from all communication. Gangs of men working through the harsh weather were able to restore the Truro connection by 11:00 p.m. on the night of the storm, but in the meantime, thousands more unsent telegrams – including responses to anxious inquiries from Ottawa headquarters – piled up at the terminals.[38]

Through the day of the storm and into the next, crews aboard *Niobe* and the patrol ships called their rolls to identify the missing, worked at securing and clearing wreckage from their ships, shovelled snow, and provided sentries for the dockyard. Early on the 7th, *Niobe's* divers again took to the water, although her log does not record whether the purpose was to continue the work interrupted by the explosion or to search for bodies of the missing. At 4:00 that afternoon, a pithy entry in the log recorded a decision fraught with individual poignancy – "leave to married men and natives."[39] Some would find their homes destroyed and loved ones dead or missing.

On the day of the explosion, Rear-Admiral Chambers had several times remarked it fortunate that the initial rescue efforts coincided with clear, calm weather. Now, he characterized the blizzard as a complication come "to complete the difficulties of the situation." As the weather worsened – "the snow being absolutely blinding and forming deep drifts" – visibility was reduced to a few yards. Under the circumstances, Chambers saw no point in going afloat that day but carried out such general organization as was possible from the Port Convoy office. The office was crowded through the day with people seeking directions and information and others desperately hoping to learn the fate of friends and relatives. The slow convoy that was to sail on 7 December with *Highflyer* as escort would remain in port, and not only due to the weather. Considerable work would be needed on the part of Captain Garnett and crew before the cruiser was in any condition for operations.[40]

Looking beyond local conditions, Chambers saw a pressing need to come to terms as quickly as possible with the impact of the disaster on the capability of the port. Could Halifax continue in its vital role as a shipping and convoy centre? Could it continue as a base of naval operations and a despatch and reception centre for the Canadian overseas forces? If not, urgent and massive action would be needed to assess and coordinate alternative ports, routes, and resources. It appears that such an undertaking was beyond the capacity and perhaps the rank and local stature of the Canadian naval officials in the dockyard. It was no time for such mean distinctions, however, and when Chambers took the initiative, he was careful, both at the time and later, to state that he was acting "at the request of the Captain Superintendent."[41]

> In view of the number of vessels lying in the port which had been injured, and the great damage which had been done to the repair shops, wharves and railways, it seemed to me that it would be desirable to take steps that a gathering of those representing the principal waterside interests at the port should be convened to decide how far the transport activities of Halifax would be interrupted and what reconstruction measures would be possible. Captain Hose, the CSNO (acting), who was very busy clearing the wreckage in the dockyard, asked me to take the initiative in the matter, and after consulting with the Lieut.-Governor and the military authorities, who warmly supported the idea, I agreed to preside at such a meeting on the evening of the 8th.[42]

The British admiral was in a daunting position. Time was short, and his knowledge of local conditions and personalities was much less than he would have liked. He wasted no time, however, and spent much of 7 December personally seeking out those who should attend and putting together a warning notice and an agenda for discussion. Wider questions coexisted with more immediate concerns. Damage overall to the vessels in port had not been terribly heavy, but the war effort needed every ship. What was to be done with the merchant vessels too damaged to go to sea? They would have to be surveyed, perhaps jury-rigged to enable movement in port, and then berthed and repaired within the as yet unknown capacity of the devastated port and dockyard facilities.[13]

Another immediate concern was the condition and safety of naval supplies and stores buildings. Initially, the stores officer, W. Laurie, thought his department might be able to carry on to some extent, but no civilian staff appeared for work on the 7th, or for several days thereafter. Most of the labour force resided in the devastated North End of the city. Their time and energy was understandably occupied with more pressing worries. Laurie and his wife, who had been seriously cut by flying glass, were among the tales of "marvellous escape." Their house in the dockyard was badly damaged, and they had been forced to find refuge with friends who had suffered less severely.[44]

After investigating the structural damage, the stores officer and his associates, Mr Gainings and Mr Phillips, found that the storehouses were "in dangerous condition and unfit for occupation without considerable danger." Thus, work could be carried out only temporarily and under dangerous conditions.[45] The continuing heavy snow caused further damage to the storehouses, and several roofs had fallen in by the 8th. Laurie was forced to relocate his office to *Hochelaga,* and he considered moving his family to Ottawa because of the impossibility of finding other affordable accommodation.[46] At the time, Laurie's superior, John Wilson, was still en route to Halifax. The weather had seriously delayed railroad operations, and Wilson's train would not reach the Halifax Ocean Terminal Station in the South End until 4:00 p.m. on Saturday the 8th, about double the normal time for the trip.

With no dockyard labour force available, not much could be done to remove the naval stores. Indeed, there was no place to put them better than the partial shelter still afforded by the semi-demolished buildings. All efforts concentrated on saving the more perishable clothing and victualling stores. The victualling assistant, Mr Townshend, and two devoted storehousemen were later credited with saving practically all of these stores, with a probable value at the time of over a quarter of a million dollars. As much as possible, the stores office made every effort to reduce stocks by providing maximum issue to visiting imperial ships. The physical labour was performed by already exhausted working parties from *Niobe,* who "performed the work under most arduous weather conditions and at considerable personal risk to themselves as the buildings are in a very shaky state, the roofs having collapsed in places and their structures being badly shaken throughout."[47]

Able Seaman Bert Griffith was among the dockyard working parties. He later reported that they had been "worked half dead" and had received no shore leave until 14 December, "and that only from five p.m."[48] His first letter, written with a stub of pencil to his frantic wife in Esquimalt from Mess #9 *Niobe,* was not composed until Saturday night, 8 December:

> Just a few lines to let you know that I am *alive* & have not received a single scratch. [He chose not to worry her with news that there were slivers of glass buried in his chest]. I wrote to you on Tues the last day I was ashore. This is Sat & I have not had my clothes off since the awful explosion. I have only had time to get one little wash so you can imagine how I look. I am alive but do not know why ... I got your telegram & just had time to rush to the ships office & get them to answer it. There is no shore leave, in fact the town is in absolute darkness & ruin.[49]

Clearly the exhausted Canadians were all but overwhelmed. In these circumstances, the US Navy ships at Halifax continued to be a valuable source of assistance and manpower ashore. Early on the 7th, as his overnight security patrols of central Halifax returned to their ships, Powers Symington again visited General Benson to see how the Americans might help further. "He informed me that mechanics were badly needed for putting up shelters for homeless people, so I organized gangs of five men each, headed by an artificer, supplied with tools for doing rough mechanical work. These men worked all day putting in windows and assisting anyone who was willing to work."[50]

Despite the ongoing confusion, the first attempts were made from the dockyard to report the names of the twelve known naval casualties, although the notice ended with the qualification "regret delay in reporting deaths and casualties but many ratings are missing who are probably in the city looking after their homes stop Names of those known definitely as killed or injured will be forwarded as soon as known."[51]

At the Naval College, everyone had been accounted for. Those without injuries had been sent out the day of the explosion to find billets for themselves with friends in safer areas. The injured were now safely in private hospitals. Christmas leave would come early; on the 7th, the cadets were being brought aboard *Niobe* with the intention of sending them home as soon as transportation was available. That would take some time, however, given the blizzard and difficult communications. The "in plain" telegram filed reporting these developments included specifics of each cadet and officer. It included the information that Cadet George Desbarats had slight cuts and Cadet Walter Kingsmill somewhat deeper ones.[52]

This news did not arrive in Ottawa until very late in the afternoon of the

7th, after Admiral Kingsmill had departed for Halifax. It was Mrs Kingsmill who received the news. She was reassured only after receiving the additional information that Walter was in Pine Hill (convalescent home) and that his injuries were not serious. Mrs Kingsmill wired the news on their son's condition to her husband, who was still on the train to Halifax. His relief was palpable when he wired back, care of the department: "Received message think that cadets will be sent almost at once that is if not requiring dressing you will be notified am sure if Walter is sent before I get down we have very heavy train probably late bad luck for poor Walter but we have much be thankful for."[53]

SHORTLY AFTER MIDNIGHT OF 7/8 DECEMBER, watchkeepers aboard *Lady Evelyn* at Macnab Island recorded that the confounding high winds and snow had begun to moderate.[54] The wind gradually diminished into occasional gusts as the barometer rose and the sky began to clear. Throughout the storm, HMCS *Canada,* had remained precariously anchored in the stream. At 4:00 a.m. her log recorded that the weather had become fine and clear.[55]

Lady Evelyn called her hands at 6:00 Saturday morning, and at 6:50 she hove in both anchors and was under way in the predawn twilight. Twenty minutes later, she had passed Mauger Point Lighthouse, where she observed the *Saranac* ashore under Fort Macnab, and spoke to another steamer, *Northern King*, which had dragged her anchor into a second ship, the *Ames*. The patrol ship flashed a message into Halifax for a tugboat to assist the two vessels. Then, at 7:35, a signal was passed from the examination boat to order *Lady Evelyn* in to Halifax. From a temporary anchor in the harbour off No. 1 Jetty she was moved shortly before noon into berth alongside *Niobe*. No one recorded the reaction of those aboard as she slipped up the harbour, but the effect must have seemed almost surreal, with the heavy blanket of snow concealing much of the destruction underneath. Later in the day, she was placed on standby to sail, but that order was cancelled some hours later: *Lady Evelyn*'s men were needed ashore, and the only leave granted that evening would be to those with families in Halifax.[56]

In the much improved weather, the energetic Rear-Admiral Chambers was finally able "to carry out a further inspection of matters afloat and arrange for the collection of the dead from the various vessels. I was also getting out details of the damage for transmission to the Admiralty. My assistant, Captain Turnbull, also went afloat, compiling a full report of the damage done and steps being taken to make it good as far as possible. Landing at the dockyard I inspected the hospital ship *Old Colony,* where I found all going satisfactorily and the American doctors doing splendid work."[57]

Ashore, Chambers struggled northward from the dockyard through the deep drifts of snow towards the ruined dry dock. He found the Norwegian steamer *Hovland* with her decks crushed in and her funnel over the side, yet undamaged from the fire that had burned out the remains of surrounding machine shops and other structures. As Chambers observed, "The dry dock was in the heart of the worst area, and the large sugar refinery close to was merely a pile of bricks, amongst which fragments of bodies could be discerned, the dock labourers having used the building as a vantage ground to view the unusual spectacle of a ship on fire."[58]

Despite the devastation, when he looked more closely Chambers found something he probably had not dared to hope for. The vital dry dock gate appeared to be intact, and therefore might be usable. He started back towards his office and was fortunate to catch a lift for part of the way in a sleigh, the only viable means of transport at the time. With this piece of promising news in hand, Chambers "spent the afternoon interviewing callers, making out reports, answering telegrams innumerable, as inquiries were now coming in from all sides, and preparing agenda for the evening's conference."[59]

In the naval dockyard, Captain Fred Pasco was still off duty. His condition was not regarded as serious, but he would not be ready to resume his responsibilities until Christmas Eve.[60] Walter Hose was still in command, and he wired Ottawa offering to continue in that capacity. He reported on the overnight difficulties in the harbour, noted that much confusion continued as to the status and whereabouts of people, and pointed to the challenges of identification. He also acknowledged the value of the help provided by the United States Navy, although no record can be found that recognition and appreciation for this service was ever subsequently registered at the national or interservice level. Although he did not note any assistance on the part of Rear-Admiral Chambers and the Royal Navy, this help was probably taken as a given. Hose reported that the dockyard was able to continue to issue supplies but that the engineering department was wholly crippled. With telegraph service restored and priority given to military traffic, the message was received and deciphered before the Ottawa staff got to work that morning. A note to file indicated that no action was taken: the concerns would be dealt with when Admiral Kingsmill arrived in Halifax.[61]

Later in the day, with the improved weather conditions, Hose was able to report further. Ships adrift or without crews had been shifted and secured, although *Saranac* was still ashore on Macnab Island. Early estimates of the disaster were that one thousand citizens had been killed and five times that number had been wounded. Ships known to have been badly damaged included *Curaca, Calonne, Middleham Castle, J.A. McKie,* and *Picton.* Only *Mont Blanc* was listed as sunk. No mention was made of *Imo.* Strain, fatigue, and confusion are sufficient to account for this obvious error.

Hose reported serious loss of life among the civilian crews and great destruction in the dockyard. As well, No. 13 House in the yard had been gutted by fire that afternoon, although no explanation was offered as to the reasons. Having evidently either accompanied or conferred with Admiral Chambers, the acting dockyard superintendent passed on the information that the dry dock buildings had been destroyed but the dock itself was believed viable. The report also anticipated the arrival of Admiral Kingsmill that evening. As well, it noted that Commodore Gaunt, the British naval attaché from Washington, had come to the city to look into conditions.[62]

There were other welcome arrivals. Doctors and nurses who had set out to help from various points in Nova Scotia and New Brunswick were desperately needed and quickly put to work. This influx continued to grow with arrivals from farther afield, including various relief trains carrying medical staff and supplies. By Saturday morning Frank McKelvey Bell, the district's senior medical officer, noted that "the medical work was assuming a semblance of order." Indeed, he reported with some pride that "within forty-eight hours of the disaster practically every patient in the City, in hospital or in houses, had received at least some medical care."[63]

The prompt and generous response of the State of Massachusetts is a particularly notable feature in any account of the aftermath of the Halifax explosion. First to arrive on the scene, on Saturday morning, was the Massachusetts Medical Unit of the state National Guard, which consisted of twelve surgeons, ten nurses, and two quartermasters. Frank Bell later remarked, "Too much cannot be said in praise of the American doctors, nurses and social helpers. Their work was excellent, their spirit willing, and their assistance generous and invaluable. Some of the best surgeons in Massachusetts, Rhode Island, and Maine were represented."[64]

Hidden beneath Bell's words, though, was a certain resentment towards the Americans, whose high-profile contribution was lauded in the local press as a shining example of "American efficiency." By contrast, the contributions of the Canadians, although just as important, received little praise in the media. Yet as Bell pointed out, the American personnel and supplies were not sufficient to form a complete hospital facility. The medical professionals had brought some basic emergency dressings and bandages and surgical instruments but "no hospital or other equipment." More seriously, medical orderlies – that most important element in dealing with a significant medical emergency – were not represented among the American teams. Fortunately, the Canadian Army Medical Corps (CAMC) had a ready supply at their training depot in the city. Bell promptly had a staff of orderlies assembled, and he detailed an officer "to draw all necessary medical or ordnance equipment as well as food supplies." In his report, Bell stressed the role of the CAMC in setting up facilities to accommodate the Americans:

> The "Bellevue" [Building on Spring Garden Road being used as an] Officers mess was the only available building. At eleven a.m. the officers were ordered out, and the engineers started work repairing the building, the windows and doors of which were shattered. The AMC orderlies and about 20 Jackies from the American Ship *Old Colony* worked with the nurses and doctors to clean and equip the building. All stores were drawn and in place and at 9 p.m. the same evening, i.e. in ten hours from the commencement of the work of repair, the hospital *completely* equipped from kitchen to operating room, stocked with food and medicines, was handed over to the Massachusetts Unit as a hospital ready for patients …
>
> It is only fair to the Engineers, A.M.C. and Ordnance Corps to state emphatically that this work, except for assistance in cleaning the building and handling cases of goods, beds, etc, was entirely done by the local units. Capt. H. Barrat, P.A.M.C. and Sergeant Major Anstey of the AMC Training Depot deserve the greatest credit for the rapid and well organized work.[65]

Similar efforts expedited the subsequent installation of a State of Maine Unit in the Halifax Ladies' College, the American Red Cross in Saint Mary's College, and a Rhode Island group in Bellevue and the Halifax Infirmary. Such impressive accomplishments underscore the extent to which the military medical organization had taken hold of the crisis. While Bell and his staff had controlled the military and emergency hospitals from the outset, the de facto regulation that he had assumed of all medical services would be formally sanctioned by a belated request from the Halifax Relief Committee only on 10 December. As far as Bell was concerned, this formal recognition of the military's role only reinforced the obvious. "It was ... apparent that had such a disaster occurred in any port not well organized for relief work and without great military assistance, the number of deaths and the amount of suffering would have been tremendously increased."[66]

While some of the sailors from the USS *Old Colony* were busy helping to set up local emergency hospitals on 8 December, other US Navy personnel were active elsewhere. Powers Symington of *Tacoma* had again landed a large party – this time equipped with pioneer tools in response to a request to assist in the continuing search of the ruins. With the arrival of the relief trains and additional manpower, he was beginning to feel that his ship would not be required much longer. However, the Americans' presence was not yet unnecessary: another two hundred men from *Von Steuben* would be landed on the 9th for more searches.[67]

At four o'clock on the afternoon of the 8th, almost forty-eight hours after John Wilson, the RCN's director of stores, had left Ottawa, his train finally arrived at the Halifax Ocean Terminal Station. He immediately set out on foot towards the naval dockyard. No streetcars were running, and Wilson noted that such conveyances as were out and about were all engaged in relief work. Arriving at the dockyard, he "was relieved to find that the reports which had reached us en route as to the loss of life in our Service were greatly exaggerated. Considering the damage caused to the buildings it is nothing short of marvellous that so many escaped unhurt and that in most cases the injuries received were not of a serious nature."[68]

Night fell before Wilson was able to undertake any detailed examination of the dockyard buildings, but he spent the early part of the evening conferring with a number of the officers *in situ*. He then composed a telegram for his deputy minister, which would be the first reasonably comprehensive assessment of the situation received at naval service headquarters. Finally, Ottawa would receive some indication of the health and condition of principal officers and staff and the state of critical dockyard buildings. All the buildings would require reconstruction to various degrees. Although the dockyard foundry was not usable, there was some prospect that the machine shop could be put back in shape in a week. *Niobe* would require replacement and repair of her roofing and upper works; otherwise, she was in good shape. Most importantly, all of the patrol boats and minesweeping tugs were all right.[69] Thus the operational capability of the RCN afloat would be largely unaffected.

That evening John Wilson was among those who attended the meeting organized by Rear-Admiral Chambers at the Hollis Street rooms of the Halifax Board of Trade. The group of worthies in attendance was concerned with the continued operation of the port of Halifax. The meeting and its outcomes, which do not seem to have been remarked in the explosion literature, should not be confused with gatherings held elsewhere to marshal civic resources and organize systematic relief or with the subcommittee on reconstruction that functioned under the Halifax Relief Committee. The civilians at Chambers's meeting represented the maritime business elite. The Halifax Board of Trade's president, Dugald MacGillivray, and board council member George W. Hensley of Pickford and Black (steamship agents and owners) were both present, as well as Captain (merchant) James W. Harrison, the marine superintendent of Furness Withy & Company (the Furness line), and James DeWolf of Tas DeWolf & Son (steamship agents and commission merchants). Walter Hose was among the naval officers attending, along with Commanders Holloway and Wyatt, representing the naval transport and examination services.[70] Commodore Gaunt, the RN attaché in Washington, had just arrived. The assemblage also included marine, rail, and shipping interests as well as officials of the Department of Marine and Fisheries and the Department of Railways and Canals. General Benson was represented by one of his senior administrative staff officers, Lieutenant-Colonel B.R. Armstrong, CGA. Colonel Lindsay, the militia officer who coordinated the CEF's transportation requirements, attended as well.

The most illustrious personage attending the meeting was Sir Robert Borden.[71] Upon hearing of the disaster, the prime minister had abandoned the election campaign and made his way to Halifax through the bad weather to visit the temporary hospitals and confer with city officials. He promptly hoisted the standard for a strong federal response to the disaster, beginning with a directive for $500,000 in immediate aid. He would also enjoin postponement of the federal election as well as delay in the implementation of conscription in the Halifax ridings.[72]

The prime minister opened the meeting and set the general tone by stating that "he had attended the meeting to indicate the desire on the part of the Canadian Govt. in co-operating in every way to reconstruct the Port of Halifax: this was of the utmost importance to the Empire. The meeting had been called with a view to asking the co-operation of all. As far as the Govt. was concerned the Premier repeated that they were most anxious to give every assistance and afford any aid within their power."[73] Rear-Admiral Chambers then moved to specifics, indicating that, while more time for preparation would have been useful, it was "imperative that a start should be made immediately. The port of Halifax was an absolute necessity to a successful prosecution of the War. He suggested that after hearing a few remarks from those present a Committee should be formed and a statement made out and forwarded to the Government stating what was actually required to be done and what the actual state of things was."[74]

Chambers summed up the general situation involving the numerous damaged ships and the mass of wreckage along the Richmond and Dartmouth shores. Piers 6, 7, and 8 were all totally demolished, but most of the frontage of Pier 9 was still intact. Future use of the essential dry dock was "very questionable." On the Dartmouth side, private facilities such as French cable wharf and the rope works wharf were intact or in a fair state. Several large ships were en route to Halifax carrying women and children and military medical casualties from the front. Could the port properly handle these arrivals, as well as deal with approaching trains carrying Chinese "coolies" for transport overseas?[75]

John W. Brookfield, who managed the dry dock, which had been built in 1889 by his father, Samuel, had been twice down to inspect the property and thought the dock itself was probably all right. Eighty to ninety men were available to start work on repairs at the dock and temporary shops could be erected. Workers would need seventeen or eighteen days to put the *Hovland* into shape and float her out, providing the pumps at the dry dock were still intact. The company's shop in Dartmouth, which had a large air compressor, could be put back into operation within two weeks; plates could then be punched and repairs done. Getting the facilities up and running was only one challenge. Finding skilled workers to staff the shops was another. Over half of the 238 dockyard labourers, many of them highly skilled, were killed or missing in the disaster. Every effort would be made to find replacements, but this would prove to be very difficult.

After some further technical discussion, the talk turned to the vital question of military transport. Neither Commander Holloway nor the two soldiers present saw insurmountable problems from the standpoint of actual embarkation or debarkation. Small vessels (tenders) could always be used if suitable dock space were unavailable, but the new Ocean Terminals in the South End seemed to offer a satisfactory alternative. The greater concern was that the troops usually appeared ahead of sailing time, and the city had no holding accommodation to spare. Colonel Armstrong thought the next two sailings should be deflected to Saint John until the situation improved. George Hensley opined that the situation depended on the railway company. If the railway could guarantee that the troops could be brought to the company's Deepwater Pier No. 2, which was south of the dockyard, "we can do the rest."[76]

At this, all eyes turned to Charles A. Hayes, the general manager of the Canadian Government Railway (still referred to locally as the Intercolonial or ICR). He responded:

> I think I am in a position to report to-night whether we will be able to land everything at the piers to-morrow. We will be in the North St. Station to-morrow afternoon. We have the terminals at the South End, that we can fall back upon to take the freight to the South terminals, and we have yards available for any train with heating plant to keep them warm if the steamers are not here. Our only difficulty is returning them [the trains]. We have had 87 cars put out of business. I can't say any more than that. Tomorrow afternoon we will be able to handle things better as far as the cargo business is concerned.[77]

Prime Minister Borden and Admiral Chambers both questioned Hayes closely over the details of clearing the track and providing terminal services for arriving ships. The railwayman emphasized that, with track already clear to the Deepwater Terminals, he saw no critical need to devote time and resources to replacing the wrecked wharves. Better, he said, to add facilities at the new Ocean Terminals. Following that, new sheds could be built to replace those damaged in the wrecked area.

In the midst of these promising discussions for reconstruction, the subject was abruptly changed by a sudden intervention from Captain Harrison: "I think that some rule should be laid down and enforced whereby steamers coming in and out at the present time should be compelled to come at a certain speed, and that no two ships should be passing through ... at the same time."[78] Harrison's statement was one of the first indications that thoughts were turning towards how the unthinkable calamity had been allowed to happen. Chambers smoothly allowed how he could speak to Harrison's question with some authority, "but I will ask Capt. Hose who is here [and] can put your minds to rest." Hose responded that "the regulations are just the same here as in any other defended port throughout the Empire, and I can't see that there should be any new regulations introduced; the proper signals are shown, and no vessel can come in with the signal against her."[79]

Harrison was not dissuaded. His rejoinder was an early indication of what would be a central theme of public outrage and discussion in days to come. Participants would implicate the RCN and question its credibility: "I might say that the regulations may be very proper and good but I don't think they are carried out by the pilots."[80] Thus, the die for much of the controversy to follow was cast at an early date.

Rear-Admiral Chambers cut off further debate on the point. "I don't think we have got to consider the pilotage yet, we are dealing with the reconstruction of the port." After this exchange, discussion turned to the formation of a strong committee of seven – representing shipping, naval, and military interests, and those of the dry dock – to deal with matters in detail and to draw up recommendations on the course to be followed. Commander Graham Holloway, as naval transport officer, was nominated to represent the RCN. George Hensley was elected as overall chair. Specialist subcommittees would follow, selected by the steering group. After some further discussion of options and technicalities, the meeting broke up, leaving Chambers satisfied that things had gone well and that port reconstruction matters were in capable hands.[81]

SOME HOURS AFTER THE MEETING AT THE Halifax Board of Trade, *Lady Evelyn*'s logkeeper noted that the wind was beginning to rise from the southeast. By 1:00 a.m. snow and hail were falling. Within hours, the wind increased to gale strength, forcing the ship to drop her port anchor and a thirty-fathom chain. When the hands were called at 6:00 Sunday morning, they immediately set about securing boat covers and movables on deck. For three hours, the wind in the harbour was logged at Force 8. The harbour filled with wreckage from the broken wharves and elsewhere.[82] Heavy rain set in, and the temperature rose through the morning as the wind swung into a sou'wester. At noon the log of HMCS *Grilse* recorded a temperature of 52°F. Even in Halifax, where rapid changes of temperature are not uncommon, such weather was rare at this time of year. Rear-Admiral Chambers bemoaned the results: "The streets were waist deep with semi-liquid snow, whilst small rivers rushed down many of the streets. If anything was required to add to the discomfiture of the unhappy town this was the last straw."[83]

John Wilson did not have time to wait for the storm to diminish. The director of stores was out in the dockyard going over the buildings and trying to assess the immediate requirements of the situation. One of the civil engineers, Mr Gainings, started putting together detailed reports on the structures, but, as Wilson subsequently reported, "It was evident from the first that many of the structures were damaged beyond repair and in other cases the question of whether it was advisable to spend further sums on the repair of ancient and dilapidated buildings, totally unsuited to present day requirements had to be faced."[84]

Speed was of the essence: the valuable dockyard stock required immediate shelter. Wilson decided new construction was warranted. As he later wired George Desbarats in Ottawa, temporary storehouses would be the fastest and most economical approach, and the dockyard parade ground would suit the purpose admirably. At the same time, Wilson tackled the perennial question of unsatisfactory office space for the dockyard in general. The old dwellings, which had always been inadequate, were now entirely unusable. Thus, any new construction would have to include a temporary office building.[85]

By Sunday afternoon Wilson was back at the Board of Trade rooms, where the reconstruction interests had reconvened their ad hoc committee. As he later summed up the meeting to Desbarats,

> After statements had been received from the Railway Department and the Graving dock as to the damage caused to their property we had a discussion as to the best method of proceeding to repair the damage in the shortest possible time. I placed before the Committee a brief statement of our requirements and stated that in view of the inevitable shortage of labour and difficulty of obtaining material, which would be enhanced if all the separate interests set to work independently and in competition with one another, it was considered advisable for all the Government interests to co-operate in the matter of handling the available labour and arrange for the purchase and forwarding of the material necessary to carry out the emergency work, and further that the permanent work should be left for more mature consideration and only absolutely necessary work should be undertaken in the meantime until a general survey had been made and the whole problem of the future of the Port considered.[86]

Wilson's proposal was readily accepted by the others and after the meeting they sat down to draw up a framework for joint action between the Departments of the Naval Service, Public Works, and Railways and Canals, bringing in joint management as well as consulting architects and engineers. From their work, tentative proposals would emerge, dividing the repair work of reconstruction of the various railway shops and facilities, the dry dock, and the dockyard. The final details would be hammered out five days later when the two ministers of the civilian departments, F.B. Carvell (public works) and Dr J.D. Reid (railways and canals), left the election campaign and met with prospective contractors to finalize the arrangements. In the event, outside contractors were not brought in because of concerns (by no means unfounded) of "probable disturbance to the labour market," which would be the case if large forces were brought from cities where wages were much higher than in Halifax. Sensitive to that issue, the two ministers decided that the work would be done by the contractors of the almost completed Ocean Terminals, aided by the forces of the relevant government departments. The naval minister, C.C. Ballantyne, had not travelled to Halifax with his colleagues for the consultations, but he agreed with their telegraphed proposals, despite mutterings from Desbarats in Ottawa that time and money would be saved by making repairs and additions to old buildings rather than constructing new ones. Wilson's new buildings for the dockyard were expected to be ready within four weeks.[87]

Sunday the 9th was also the date on which the Halifax Relief Committee (not to be confused with the later organized Halifax Relief Commission) was formally constituted. With the formation of this committee, the direction of the relief effort unmistakably passed into civilian hands, although, at least initially, the military continued to play a major role. Major-General Thomas Benson immediately waited upon the chairman, Mr R.T. McIlraith, KC, "and conferred with him as to the best lines of co-operation." With the chairman's agreement, Benson nominated expert military representatives to subcommittees coordinating resources and other assistance. Benson's officers were closely tied to subcommittees on executive (overall control), food, clothing, transportation, emergency shelter, registration, information, mortuary, and reconstruction.[88] In addition, what became the medical subcommittee fell under the direction of Lieutenant-Colonel Frank Bell. There was no need for RCN representation on any of the subcommittees, although sailors assisted search parties, coordinated by the militia, that daily took on the grim task of combing the ruins for survivors and bodies.[89]

With a measure of control and organization in place, and relief trains arriving with supplies and personnel, Powers Symington, the captain of

Tacoma, judged that his services were no longer required in Halifax. As he subsequently wrote in his report for Commander Squadron Two, Cruiser Force: "I beg to invite your attention to the fact that the officers and men of the *Tacoma, Von Steuben, Morrill* and *Old Colony* all worked hard in this emergency with a cheerfulness and a sense of discipline which was admirable. I believe that our efforts were appreciated by the people on shore, and needless to say we were very glad to do what we could."[90] By mid-afternoon, *Tacoma* hoisted her anchor and proceeded out to sea to return to convoy duty. Less than an hour earlier, *Lady Evelyn*'s logkeeper noted the arrival of HMS *Donegal,* a cruiser of the *Kent* class, which anchored off Jetty 1. The additional manpower and medical resources she carried would be welcome after the departure of the Americans.[91]

As *Tacoma* left Halifax her captain was less than optimistic about the port's immediate future: "No estimate could be made up to the time I left of the property damage or the loss of life. I am of the opinion that the dock yard will be of no further use before next summer, if then, and that the port of Halifax has suffered such a serious blow that it will very seriously interfere with the operation of the convoy fleet from now on."[92] Of course, Symington had not been privy to the work of John Wilson and others of the port reconstruction committee. Rather, his impressions were based largely on his own observations and experiences and reflected his considerable professional judgment. Indeed, the grim picture presented by the horrendous damage and ruination in the city and the harbour gave every appearance of supporting Symington's grave conclusions.

Despite the deep wounds, Halifax was still in business as a naval base and as a port. Not long after *Tacoma* disappeared from view, Chambers sent the good news to all stations: "Meeting of Representative heads of Shipping Transport Railways etc. held Saturday night 8th December. Committees appointed to collect information and arrange for reconstruction work. Delegates from United States arrived empowered to offer every assistance engineering and financial. In view of information elicited I consider that convoy work can be carried on immediately. JUSTICA and incoming Hospital Ships should be deflected to New York for present. Embarkation of troops can be arranged. Strong southerly gale blowing today – Sunday will hinder arrangements for departure of convoy to-morrow Monday 10th December."[93]

Orders were passed to all ports to send ships to Halifax for convoy as usual.[94] Graham Holloway already had the word out that the movement of

Chinese coolies could be continued through the port,[95] although some had to be diverted by rail through New York because the designated liners *Orduna* and *Saxonia* had been held there as a result of the explosion. Some troops had embarked at Saint John aboard the liner *Tunisian*, but the ship was now ready to proceed to Halifax. Over the next few days the situation would begin to return to normal.[96]

The arrival in Halifax of the director of the naval service is not documented, but he probably appeared some time on Sunday. Since Kingsmill was back in Ottawa on the 15th, he would have spent only four days in Halifax.[97] There is little to show how he spent his time: his name is not present on the minutes of the reconstruction committees or much else. Whether this demonstrates lack of effective leadership or the ability to rely upon subordinates who had already come to grips with their responsibilities can only be conjecture. With Wilson already on the ground to deal with dockyard problems and Holloway a prominent component of the reconstruction effort, one might lean towards a more generous interpretation of the circumstances.

Kingsmill himself later suggested to the chief press censor that there had been a good reason for him to keep a low profile locally: "The fact of the matter is that in and about Halifax, which is a hotbed of patronage, the Navy is not very popular as, from the first organization we have had to fight this very undesirable form of making appointments, that is patronage, and consequently gentlemen like the Mayor and the proprietor of the Halifax Herald do not love us."[98] Future events were to prove Kingsmill's wariness well founded. At this juncture, however, he was in the dockyard and among the patrol ships to see and be seen. Moreover, it would appear that he found at least one area sorely in need of his intervention – the Royal Naval College of Canada.

Conditions improved enough by Monday the 10th that the cadets assembled aboard *Niobe* could finally be sent off by train on what would be a two-month Christmas leave.[99] With Commander Nixon and others of his staff out of action for a time, Admiral Kingsmill seized much of the initiative in deciding the future of the Naval College. When he returned to Ottawa, Kingsmill brought with him a plan to relocate the college to either Kingston or Esquimalt.[100] Until the matter could be decided, he ordered Commander Arthur Atwood, RN (Ret.), the RCN's torpedo and gunnery training officer, to "take charge of the Naval College and its furnishings which are not under the immediate charge of any officer." The admiral set forth how instructional models and such should be "carefully collected and stored" and how the laboratory and physical instructional appliances should be treated. He called for care in the collecting and proper storage of all college property – including pictures, presentation shields, and cups – and detailed staff to look after the cadets belongings from their lockers and to see that these "are carefully packed in their chests of portmanteaux. The chests will be stored in one dormitory ready for shipment as ordered. Such articles of clothing as are required by the Cadets should be forwarded by express to them as requested, but it is pointed out that the Railways are much congested, and a favourable opportunity should be awaited."[101] Atwood was personally charged to see that the bedsteads and all desks, chairs, and other furniture were collected and stored and to "look upon the Yacht fittings as his particular care." A full report was to be rendered of all that had been done.[102]

Kingsmill's focus on the minutiae of packing up the Naval College presents a curious, if not bizarre, contrast to the matters that had occupied the attention of Rear-Admiral Chambers over the preceding few days. Nevertheless, such details were of some importance to the future of the RCN and had to be dealt with. Restoring the college to full operation would require labour and material resources that were in short supply and badly needed elsewhere. Indeed, given the extent of wartime activity and the consequent overcrowding of the Halifax waterfront, relocating the college might well have been a desirable option had the explosion not occurred. Now it became essential.

Another facility that could no longer be maintained in the dockyard was the Fleet Wireless School. Lieutenant Robert Ridges, RNCVR, the fleet wireless officer, had already had the foresight to halt the sending of wireless students to Halifax after the explosion.[103] With the building wrecked and the labour to restore it more urgently needed elsewhere, naval service headquarters decided to move the school to Ottawa. All untrained operators "not usefully employed" in Halifax were ordered on leave until a new facility was ready.[104]

The port reconstruction interests continued to meet several times through the week to hammer out details and priorities in dealing with damaged ships in the harbour and to confirm that steamers arriving for convoy purposes and fuelling "can be supplied by the Halifax tradespeople the same as usual."[105] Generally, arriving ships were adequately provisioned, although it would be a few days before the Harris Abattoir Company could supply meat as required. The supply of longshoremen was another potential problem: of the four to five hundred men who had been working on the waterfront before the disaster, about a hundred had been killed and the same number wounded. The president of the Longshoremen's Union thought that more men could be recruited from elsewhere, as long as accommodation could be provided. The limited number of available wharves also required careful coordination, and the committee reorganized their administration: Commander Holloway was given authority over the docking of overseas transport ships, Colonel Lindsay the troopships, and Captain Harrison the merchant ships.[106]

John Wilson had encouraging news for his deputy minister by 11 December, when he reported ongoing reconstruction developments as they affected the dockyard: "Situation clearing up, Issue, Victualling and Clothing Stores and coaling nearly normal. Naval Store Work will take more time. Weather conditions have been very bad ... Everyone doing utmost to get things running in good shape."[107] Although the Naval College building was no longer usable as an institution of learning, the roof was found to be sound and the windows had been boarded up. It would be utilized for offices and stores before the end of the week.

Yard electric lighting was back on the 11th. The lower machine shop, a small section of the boiler shop, and the coppersmiths' shop would be back in operation this same week. Meanwhile, preliminary work was in hand for the erection of stores and additional office space on the parade ground.[108]

December 11th was also the date that Rear-Admiral Chambers and his staff were able get the first post-explosion convoy away. It was a "slow" formation of thirty-three ships, with HMS *Highflyer* restored to active duty as escort. "There was a good deal of difficulty in getting away a few of the vessels, whose masters' nerves had possibly been a little upset by recent happenings, but on the whole the result was creditable to all concerned."[109]

Just minutes before *Highflyer* sailed out of the port, *Niobe* and the patrol ships began to land funeral parties.[110] Writers have remarked on the large public funerals that were held following the explosion, but generally the military fatalities were honoured only by their own. Bodies of soldiers and sailors that had been recovered from the wreckage and the water had been brought to the evacuated naval hospital. Most had lain there for several days awaiting coffins and the attention of clergy still ministering to the living. On the 11th, several hundred of the survivors, mostly military, gathered closely about a group of army chaplains who would conduct the funerals. Few of the dead had families that could come to Halifax to claim their bodies; thus, only their friends and companions in arms in the small naval family were present to mourn their passing. Colours on the ships and ashore were lowered to half mast. Curiously, the event was unrecorded in the Halifax newspapers. A staff reporter for the *Ottawa Citizen* wrote, "There was no funeral dirge, no muffled drums, no gun carriage and no solemn military pomp, though in a few cases friends had covered up the rough coffins with Union Jacks."[111]

The journalist's report implies the release of a vast amount of pent-up emotion. It describes the trembling voice of the Reverend Captain Veach of Truro rising softly above the low whisperings of the sobbing group of mourners. "Capless sailors and soldiers, here and there a sprinkling of women and civilians listened attentively to the grey-haired Nova Scotia chaplain consigning the bodies to the earth and their souls to God, after which there followed a slow shuffling of feet and companions of the unfortunate victims lifted the coffins and carried them through tear-eyed throngs to the waiting trucks outside."[112] The unclaimed sailors were carried to St John's churchyard and lowered into shared graves. Not far away were scores of conspicuous white crosses and a large monument that marked the last resting place of victims of another infamous disaster that had occurred five years earlier, the sinking of the RMS *Titanic*.[113]

At 4:30 *Lady Evelyn* ran up her colours, and shortly thereafter her crew were back aboard. That night her logkeeper noted that the "usual liberty" was again permissible. It was time to carry on.[114]

BY THE TIME THE MINISTER OF PUBLIC WORKS and his counterpart for railways and canals had authorized the contracts that included those for the construction of temporary buildings for the dockyard, John Wilson could report to Desbarats that materials had begun to arrive and that men would be at work the week of 17 December. "Work would be rushed to completion," he enthused to the undoubted chagrin of his normally cautious superior. Temporary repairs to the hospital roof would also be a priority to save the whole building. "Dockyard work will be in fair shape next week," he concluded. "Our offices will be opened on Monday in No. 5 house."[115]

On 18 December, the day following the general election, which had confirmed Borden's Union government in power, Wilson had even more favourable news: "Store office now open, routine business can be handled. Do not rush too much down all at once but let it come gradually staff still short Stepney and Story still in hospital but will be out next week. New store will be ready Friday, Main machine shop now running other work progressing satisfactorily."[116]

The same day, Captain Fred Pasco, who was just emerging from convalescence, provided news that the dockyard superintendent's place of work was being moved from the senior officers' smoking room on *Niobe* into the Naval College, following minor repairs to a dormitory in that building. Noted Pasco, "This room is not very badly damaged and I expect to be able to occupy it in two or three days, until such time as new offices are built."[117] Pasco hoped that the move would signal the resumption of the regular routine, although he observed that the loss of records in the fire at dockyard headquarters in November, and then again in the explosion, would likely mean delays in returning to normal.[118]

Although some semblance of normality had found its way back into the navy's operations and the function of the port, the picture was less sanguine in human terms. As Able Seaman Griffith wrote to his wife on 16 December,

> I got special leave to go up town on Thurs the 14 at 2:30 & have only been up once since. What a sight it is. Not a window anywhere. All the theatres closed & used for hospitals. Y.M.C.A. and Union Jack Club the same. There is no place now to write letters, so we are better off on board. I wrote to father & told him that I was safe. We have been on the Niobe now for two weeks. Tomorrow Mon we are going back on the boom & will quite likely be left there for two weeks. I shall be glad to get out of all the work & be able to do some washing & c. We have hardly had time to wash ourselves, let alone clothes ...
>
> Thank God a hundred times that you & the dear little girls were not here ...
>
> We'll be working pretty near night & day for a long time yet.[119]

Although it would not be a happy Christmas for members of the RCN in Halifax, they, like all who made it through the disaster, would give thanks for simple survival. For others who passed through the partly restored port on their way to the war, the scene they encountered must have seemed almost nightmarish. Kenneth Porter Kirkwood was a member of the Royal Naval Air Service travelling on the SS *Orduna*, which had left New York on the night of 15 December. In an unpublished reminiscence written some years later, he described the ship's arrival in Halifax to await convoy:

For the last few hours ... we have been slowly steaming up the harbour, and allowing a ghastly panorama of destruction to slide past our gaze. Far out on the rocks near the sea we saw the first wreck, a beached ship half-submerged. Then we passed one after another until the Belgian relief ship presented itself, and further up a remnant of a large boat we took to be the munition ship. Ships were sunk in the docks and only masts appeared through the debris. Railway cars lay upturned and wrecked along the shore. One freight car had either floated or been hurled to the opposite shore. On land buildings lay in ruins. Whole hillsides are devastated and denuded, and the straight intersecting roads alone indicate the blocks of houses that used to be. The spectacle is pitiful. There is very little snow here now but a damp mist hangs over the hills. The relief parties are still at work in the ruins looking for victims or helping refugees.

We lay in Halifax, without being permitted to go ashore, for a couple of days, and then steamed silently out into the Atlantic.[120]

6

Of Sailors, Lawyers, Goats, and Newspapers

The sequence of seemingly impossible events that had resulted in the monstrous explosion of 6 December was almost beyond comprehension. The reality of the battered port and its heavy toll of death and suffering brought to mind the ongoing but heretofore distant war. Such thoughts certainly seemed to preoccupy my grandfather, Able Seaman Bert Griffith. As he wrote his wife in Esquimalt two days after the explosion, "I have never seen death in this form before. I am sure that for ten minutes we have all been thru worse than in the trenches. The whole town is a wreck even the roof off the station. A German fleet could not have done so much damage."[1]

Not surprisingly, the initial perception that the tragedy was the result of enemy action or conspiracy won wide credence. There were many Canadians of German origin and many more from the multi-ethnic patchwork of Austria-Hungary. Some viewed these populations with suspicion. Rumours of various enemy designs against Canadian home defences had persisted since the war's outbreak, although there were few such actions. Public concern had actually diminished once the entry of the United States removed the perception of enemy plots south of the border.[2] Now the alarm was vigorously renewed. The local press, particularly the *Halifax Herald,* fed the hysteria. On the night of 9 December the paper reported the arrest of sixteen "enemy" civilians as the first phase of an operation intended to take "practically all the Germans in Halifax" into custody.[3] Concern was further fed by initial newspaper accounts of the cause of the catastrophe being that *Imo* "had for some inscrutable reason violated the rules of navigation."[4] Another published rumour was that *Imo*'s captain had been found with bullets in his head.[5] The vaguely teutonic accents of surviving Norwegian crew members heightened suspicion against the foreigners and, in one bizarre instance, *Imo*'s helmsman, Johan Johansen, was arrested by the militia authorities. Injured in the eye and leg and suffering from shock, he had – as in the case of other survivors from the two ships' crews – first been brought aboard *Highflyer* to be safeguarded as a material witness. Indeed, as the sole survivor from *Imo* who had both been on deck and involved in her navigation, his evidence would be very important. In the belief that he needed better treatment than was available aboard the warship, he was transferred to the new Bellevue facility – close to the courthouse. In this new venue, and out of touch with the naval authorities, otherwise innocent requests and behaviour aroused the suspicions of the hospital staff. He spoke strangely, asked for a newspaper to learn more about the disaster, wanted to leave the hospital because no one seemed to feel he required treatment, and offered money to a nurse to let him leave. When the officer that Frank McKelvey Bell had appointed to run the hospital searched the hapless patient's personal effects, he found a letter that he believed was written in German (it was Norwegian). The foreign "spy" – might he even be responsible for the accident? – was taken away under armed guard. When the lawyer retained by *Imo*'s shipping company subsequently caught up with his witness, he was in the county jail. His wounds were now serious: infection had set in and treatment was urgently required. The lawyer was able to secure the innocent Norwegian's release only after an urgent appeal to Major-General Benson.[6]

Mont Blanc was, of course, also of foreign origin. Although her crew were from an allied country, their pragmatic *sauve qui peut* response when their ship took fire was not the sort of gesture that bespoke gallantry or self-sacrifice in time of war. And the population had been led, by constant Allied propaganda, to expect both. The less than admirable behaviour of this crew occurred at a time, moreover, when Canadians outside of Quebec perceived the "French" in Canada to be unwilling to share the burdens of war. The bitter and vicious exchanges in the political battle over conscription were at their height in the weeks leading up to the federal election. The conscription issue was too emotional for most English Canadians to conceive its opponents in Quebec as anything other than a mob of cowardly traitors and slackers. And that conception was happily fanned by the press. Indeed, the night before the explosion, accounts in the Halifax papers told of terror, mob violence, suppression of free speech, and even the supposed attempted lynching of a Unionist candidate in Quebec.[7] The perception of British gallantry undermined by Gallic cowardice, however unfair, was both dangerous and powerful, and the unhappy crew of the *Mont Blanc* were tarred with the same brush. Indeed, in humiliating contrast to the ignoble behaviour of *Mont Blanc*'s crew, much would later be made by the *Halifax Herald* of the heroism of the "British bluejackets" who had "met death like heroes on *Mont Blanc*'s deck."[8] (It mattered not that the heroic sailors had come from the less illustrious RCN and HMCS *Niobe*.) Captain Aimé Le Médec required police protection as long as he remained in Halifax, where a powerful body of opinion was ready to believe him responsible for the disaster.[9]

More-dispassionate observers could reach some practical conclusions through common sense alone. As Captain Powers Symington wrote his superiors from his cabin aboard the USS *Tacoma*, "There would seem to be three very obvious lessons to be learned from this accident. First – heavy shipments of high explosives should not be permitted in any populous district. Two – benzol and picrates [sic] should not be loaded on the same ship with high explosives. Three – when shipments of high explosives are underway, all traffic should be rigidly controlled so as to avoid the danger of collision."[10]

What were the implications of these lessons? Had somebody bungled? Was traffic in the port poorly managed? Rumour, controversy, and fears that accident, incompetence, or design might produce yet another explosion undermined public confidence. Even minor incidents could provoke panic. One such episode involved the steamer *Picton,* which had been seriously damaged in the explosion and was towed away from the sugar refinery wharf before the surrounding fires could threaten the cargo of shells she carried. Since dragging her anchor in the storm of 7 December, she had been beached at Crowe Point in the Eastern Passage, which separated Macnab Island from the Dartmouth shore. Canadian sailors from the Patrol Service had boarded her several times, encountering a strange chemical substance on her decks, which they believed to be some sort of residue from the explosion. When stepped on, the particles would ignite. On the evening of 10 December, the ship was boarded by crew of the minesweeper *PV-IV*. The mysterious phenomenon occurred again, only this time a larger chunk flared and the men panicked. "Steamship *Picton* on fire am leaving east passage," the sweeper signalled the dockyard as she fled the scene. Before Canadian authorities could react, the captain of the armed merchant cruiser *Calgarian* had intercepted the warning and had gone afloat to investigate.[11] More immediate help was at hand in a four-man guard detail of militia that had been placed ashore to deter "any civilians boarding the vessel [*Picton*]." Once again, but on a much smaller scale, Canadian soldiers proved steadier than their naval counterparts. The men from the 63rd Regiment (Halifax Rifles) under Sergeant John Zwicker were aware of the risk posed by *Picton*'s dangerous cargo but they nevertheless immediately boarded her to extinguish the fire. As the regiment's commanding officer later reported with evident pride, "They even went down the hold of the vessel and put out a fire which had started in the straw in which the munitions were packed."[12] By the time Captain Newton of *Calgarian* arrived on the scene, the fire was out. As he investigated the cause, his professional eye immediately recognized what the problem had been. As he informed Rear-Admiral Chambers, who arrived upon the scene shortly afterward, the strange substance was phosphorus, not produced by clandestine saboteurs or provocateurs but rather by *Picton*'s own destroyed smoke-producing apparatus. The explosion had scattered the chemical all about the ship.[13]

In other circumstances, the belief that sabotage lay behind the incident would have been laughed off. In the atmosphere following the explosion, however, and given the press's penchant for "scare paragraphs," the panic of the sailors was understandable and the heroism of the soldiers genuine. The quick response of the dockyard's command was also in keeping with the frayed nerves in Halifax. Chambers was still aboard *Picton* when orders came from the dockyard that the boat should be sunk to avert the perceived danger. The newspapers made much of the incident – the *Herald* featured it as its lead story – representing the events as a second disaster narrowly averted only by the heroism of the soldiers. The *Herald* also prematurely reported that the "munitions steamer" had been towed out and sunk and that the danger was "overpast." Such action would probably have been taken but for the presence of the rear-admiral. Chambers, never eager to pander to public clamour for its own sake, knew that the boxed ammunition stored in *Picton*'s hold was in no way comparable to the deadly cocktail that had been carried aboard *Mont Blanc*. This ship was repairable, and every ship – not to mention the ammunition – was needed. Chambers therefore countermanded the orders, and the ship was anchored and secured. This pragmatic and rational response served only to intensify public outrage and indignation in the short term.[14] The following day, 11 December, Chambers was handed a formal resolution from the Board of Control of the City of Halifax:

> In view of the terrible catastrophe from the explosion of a munition ship in this port I beg on behalf of Citizens of Halifax that the Admiralty authorities will take every possible precaution to prevent the recurrence of any such disaster and in particular as representations have been made that the disaster was in some way due to improper loading of cargo upon ship which exploded, I ask that particular attention be paid in whatever manner is most suitable, to secure munition ships entering this port be loaded in such a manner as to prevent as far as possible any danger of explosion.[15]

Chambers passed the resolution along to the Admiralty with a note that a reassuring reply "would greatly assist in re-establishing public confidence." Although the Admiralty's response did emphasize additional instructions and safeguards, it had little effect.[16]

Shortly after the port convoy officer received the city's resolution, Major-General Thomas Benson telegraphed the chief of the general staff, General Willoughby Gwatkin, to ask that Ernest Chambers, the chief press censor, be sent down to help establish better control over the behaviour of the local and visiting media. Despite his best efforts to afford reasonable access, Benson was having problems with eager photographers trying to cash in on the disaster by ignoring the wartime fiats against militarily sensitive picture taking. He also wanted steps taken "to prevent the publication in the press of statements calculated to cause alarm and to interfere with the satisfactory prosecution of the inquiry into the recent accident in Halifax Harbour."[17]

In response, that same evening in Ottawa, Willoughby Gwatkin telephoned Ernest Chambers. As soon as he had finished his dinner, the chief press censor came down to the headquarters. Gwatkin had steadfastly exercised his responsibilities for militia operations in Halifax from a distance, leaving actual management of the crisis to his commander on the scene. He nevertheless made use of Chambers's good offices as a personal emissary to convey once again his willingness to render every assistance Benson might require "to cope with the present situation." Chambers and Gwatkin also agreed that Chambers's mission would be enhanced by his proceeding on duty and in uniform, reflecting his status not only as chief press censor but as a lieutenant-colonel in the militia and a representative of the chief of general staff.[18]

As we have seen, when news of the Halifax explosion reached Ottawa, one of the first responses of the Department of Marine was to order a full investigation into events. Although this action was played up by officials and politicians, it was a not uncommon response on the part of the department. The explosion had been caused by a collision between two ships and was therefore governable by Canadian marine law. Thus, the mere existence of an inquiry was not extraordinary; yet the profile resulting from the dimensions of the catastrophe, the widespread and continuing public distress, and the zealous press coverage inevitably made it so.

Under the Canada Shipping Act, the investigation of all significant incidents resulting in loss or damage to ships and marine facilities was administered by a section of the Department of Marine headed by the dominion wreck commissioner, Captain Louis Auguste Demers. He was a canny and experienced master mariner and public servant with long service in the merchant marine and as a professor in a Canadian marine school. He had also served as an official in the Fisheries Protective Service and was later chief examiner of the Marine Service before becoming responsible for marine accident investigations in 1909.[19]

Marine inquiries were entrenched within the judicial system and often the prelude to corrective action, resolution of insurance claims, and subsequent litigation. The Exchequer Court of Canada included an Admiralty Division made up of districts presided over by local judges. These judges might have other responsibilities in addition to those with the Exchequer Court. In the District of Nova Scotia, for example, the appointment was held by the Honourable Arthur Drysdale, a puisne judge of the Supreme Court of Nova Scotia. He was also reputed "a prominent figure at the bar, a very able politician, and one of the cleverest public speakers in the ... province."[20] In minor cases Demers himself might preside at the investigation or "preliminary inquiry," and subsequently pursue it through the court as necessary. Major cases required a more formal process, and the judge would preside personally with the assistance of one or more nautical assessors.

It was this latter system that had clicked into place on 6 December when Alexander Johnston, the deputy minister of marine, had advised the naval service of an inquiry over which Judge Drysdale would preside with the assistance of two nautical assessors. That same day, Johnston had instructed William Alexander Henry, KC, of Halifax to act as Crown counsel and to consult with the officer in charge at the dockyard with a view to detaining such witnesses as might be considered material.[21] He also telegraphed Nova Scotia's lieutenant governor, J. McCallum Grant, to advise him of the measures and to request he communicate to Henry "any information or suggestion that may be of value to him in assisting at inquiry."[22]

Nautical assessors would provide the technical and marine expertise the court would need. Johnston proposed that one be drawn from the merchant marine and one from the navy. Initially a local Halifax mariner was considered, but ultimately Johnston decided that Louis Demers himself would be the most suitable candidate. By virtue of his long experience in the Royal Navy, Captain Walter Hose, RCN, was nominated as the naval representative. There was nothing unusual in using naval officers as assessors in marine inquiries. Indeed, they could be very useful. As Demers was to point out some months later in a different context, they had the requisite qualifications in conformity with the act, "gave the Court a more imposing aspect," and were always on hand to discuss evidence and sign the findings when framed. With merchant ships coming and going as their commerce required, their masters were not always so readily available. More importantly, most masters were reluctant to sit in judgment over their confrères.[23]

Johnston took one other measure to protect as much as possible the integrity of the pending inquiry. This concerned the pilotage service. Even prior to the explosion, the Marine Department had been aware of problems in the pilotage service at Halifax and elsewhere. These services were organized and administered locally, saving the department money, but making control and regulation more challenging. With its board drawn from the local political and business community, the pilotage service was also an attractive source of patronage. The service in Halifax had been a particular concern. According to the observations of one official, in addition to "no proper standard of qualifications for the pilots, no proper discipline amongst the pilots was maintained, and no proper records were kept." Despite growing public concern over pilotage matters, under existing law the government had no authority to act in this area, and could only make recommendations, yet "the local Pilotage Authority refused to take any suggestions from the Department in regard to improvements in the service."[24]

Proposals made in late 1916 by the Masters and Seamen branch of the Marine Department to improve regulation of pilotage had not been acted upon.[25] The disaster in Halifax would certainly place the pilotage system under close scrutiny and might bring some of these concerns to the surface. Johnston therefore moved quickly to cut off any prospect of local officials conducting their own inquiry. Given conflicts of interest, such an attempt could not hope to get to the bottom of the matter, nor could it hope to effect needed change. Johnston's telegram to the secretary of pilotage commissioners in Halifax was blunt and to the point: there would be no action taken by pilotage authorities to investigate the "recent casualty in Halifax Harbour."[26]

The Crown counsel to the pending inquiry carried the name of his father, William Alexander Henry, a late judge on the Supreme Court of Canada. The son had acquired a fine education in Scotland, France (where he had become bilingual), Nova Scotia, and Massachusetts, culminating in a law degree from Harvard University. He was one of Nova Scotia's more distinguished practitioners with a thirty-year career behind him.[27]

As Crown counsel, Henry would carry the burden of both organizing the proceedings and advising the court. As such, he would be very visible in the unfolding of events and very active behind the scenes, conferring with judge, counsel, and witnesses and advising the government through the Marine Department. In the immediate aftermath of the disaster, as officials, the military, and Haligonians were struggling through the blizzard of 7 December, Henry was putting his brief together to organize the inquiry. Meetings with Rear-Admiral Chambers, Lieutenant Governor Grant, Judge Drysdale, and other officials contributed to the identification of witnesses and arrangements to detain them in Halifax. Others had to be found through advertisements in the media. Henry had to find a serviceable and available courtroom and negotiate arrangements and agreements as to other participating legal counsel.[28] No time could be wasted. Pressure came directly from the top, with instructions from Prime Minister Borden to Minister of Marine Ballantyne that the investigation be "instituted without delay."[29] Even Borden must have been pleased with Henry's industry: the details on the composition of the inquiry appeared in the press on 11 December,[30] and the proceedings were slated to begin the next morning in the courthouse on Spring Garden Road.

Expectations were intense, and in some quarters extreme. The Halifax *Morning Chronicle,* a newspaper with some repute for editorials of seriousness and substance,[31] greeted the announcement with the observation that

> in the list of famous cases arising out of tragedies at sea which have been tried in the Marine Court of Inquiry at Halifax, none has been of such stupendous importance as the one which will open on Wednesday Morning. The facts as there disclosed ought to determine the responsibility and fix the blame for the collision with its consequences so appalling and overwhelming for this community. It is imperative ... that the inquiry shall be searching and complete. To secure that end every facility which our public authorities can afford should be placed freely at the services of the Court. The people are vitally interested in the outcome of this inquiry and the people should be formally represented at it by the department of the Attorney General or the chief law officer of the Crown in Nova Scotia. The Deputy Attorney General is eminently well qualified to represent the interests of the people, and to be of valuable assistance to the court in investigating all the facts and bringing out the whole truth about the cause of a catastrophe which in its burden of tragedy and sorrow has probably never been parallelled in history.[32]

Throughout the coming days, the *Chronicle* would manage to maintain a relatively dispassionate view of the inquiry. Indeed, while offering its readers detailed reports of the daily proceedings, its editorials would continually stress the public interest. Its main competitor, the *Halifax Herald,* would not be so circumspect.

The *Herald* was owned by Conservative senator William Dennis, a venerable journalist and local political figure of immense reputation and wide influence. A lengthy listing in H.J. Morgan's *The Canadian Men and Women of the Time* (1912) gives testimony to his ability, enterprise, and dedication to public service.[33] Dennis was also a friend of the federal Conservatives who dominated the Union government and a former alderman with ten years' service. As such, he was a key figure in the system of local patronage, which made him no friend of federal or provincial officials, such as Admiral Kingsmill, who endeavoured to eschew political considerations in making appointments and spending tax dollars.[34]

The *Herald* had become particularly adept at the form of wartime reporting that, in the style of the *Globe* of Toronto, built upon intense national emotion.[35] Its editions were filled with patriotic rhetoric and hyperbole on behalf of allegiant causes and the war, and the paper metaphorically led the inflammatory charge against the enemies of the British Empire, whoever they might be. Throughout this period, its editions had been particularly fervent on the issues of conscription and the pending election. They had also included warm praise and grateful thanks to the officers and men of the army's Halifax Garrison: "The splendid service rendered by the military from the moment after the great disaster to this present hour ... all done so efficiently and well, has won the heartiest admiration of all our citizens and drawn forth words of praise from our American friends who have witnessed their splendid efforts. Our Halifax troops have done nobly; they have been splendidly officered, and a grateful city records its sincerest thanks."

Now the *Herald* turned its attention to the pending inquiry:

> The investigation into the cause of this horrible disaster should not begin or end with an examination of the crews of the steamers concerned. If men higher up or lower down, through incompetency or duplicity, are to blame let it be known. If this was the work of the arch enemy whose methods do not stop at killing women and children then the people want to know it. Halifax is deeply concerned in this. All Canada is deeply concerned and the people will not rest satisfied until the truth is known. We owe this much to the dead, the suffering wounded and to the friends who are left to sorrow.[36]

Those wondering what approach the paper might take were not in suspense for long. On the day the inquiry was to begin the *Herald* led with the headline "Some One Blundered – Who? Court May Decide." Practising journalism as yellow as that found in today's tabloids, the paper published lengthy speculations – based on hearsay and scattered unofficial interviews – as to the testimony to come.[37]

As the participants assembled that morning, they found that Captain Demers had not yet been able to get through from Ottawa. William Henry was thus reluctantly forced to announce a deferral to that afternoon and then again until the following morning when the dominion wreck commissioner finally arrived.[38]

As Donald A. Kerr, a notable Halifax lawyer who has studied the inquiry, observed in his astute summary of the litigation process, the setting at the courthouse on 13 September "was almost Dickensian. The Inquiry convened in a large room with twenty-five-foot ceilings ... The windows had been blown out by the explosion and were boarded up. Power was unavailable and the room was dimly lit with two oil lamps. Drysdale peered down through the gloom from an elevated Victorian pulpit, flanked on either side by master mariners who were to serve as his advisors."[39]

As Crown counsel, William Henry would conduct the initial examination of witnesses, but other interests with a stake in the outcome had also retained legal counsel among the senior members of the Halifax legal community. The natural antagonists in the proceedings were the representatives of the shipping companies owning *Mont Blanc* and *Imo*. Each had a brief to defend their respective owners, crew, and pilots and present them in a favourable light, particularly from the standpoint of liability. Their principal opportunities would come in cross-examination. *Mont Blanc* was represented by Humphrey Mellish, KC, as well as Joseph Nolan, a lawyer who served the shipping company in New York and who had requested and received the privileges of the Nova Scotia bar for his visit. Mellish, who had a distinguished legal career dating back to 1890, was about to be elevated to a judgeship.[40]

Imo was represented by the able and colourful Charles J. Burchell, KC, a distinguished specialist in marine and commercial law who was at the height of what would be some sixty years' service at the bar. According to Donald Kerr's seasoned professional perspective, Burchell was a superb all-round lawyer. In an adversarial confrontation, however, he was a street fighter. "To put it in the kindest possible way, he gave a virtuoso performance at the Inquiry. Repeatedly, he browbeat and misled witnesses, disregarded all the rules of courtroom etiquette and, on a number of occasions, violated the standards of legal ethics to which lawyers must subscribe. The trouble was, it worked. He pandered shamelessly to the press and they ate it up. He had only to insinuate some misbehaviour on the part of a witness and the next day the newspapers would publish it as fact, totally disregarding the witness' [sic] rejection of any such inference."[41]

Beyond Crown counsel and the representatives for *Mont Blanc* and *Imo*, several other lawyers were present as well. The attorney general of Nova Scotia, whose office would be responsible for the initiation of any criminal charges that might arise out of the inquiry, was represented by the Crown prosecutor, Andrew Cluney, KC. Both the Halifax Pilotage Commission and the City of Halifax were also represented by King's counsel, Thomas R. Robertson and F.C. Bell, respectively.

The inquiry opened with the ordeal of a full day's testimony from an apprehensive Aimé Le Médec. Francis Mackey, the pilot responsible for guiding *Mont Blanc* into the harbour, subsequently spent two days on the stand. Others appeared for shorter periods. Despite frequent interventions and the tactics employed by Burchell, the general lines of questioning were consistent with what one might expect from a routine marine investigation. Every imaginable aspect of the sequence of events was probed in detail: rules of navigation, traffic in the harbour, weather, tidal forces, courses, speeds, whistles, propeller motion and direction, sightings, commands, language and comprehension, visibility and positions vis-à-vis other vessels, and navigation points. Witnesses were asked to manipulate model boats over a chart of the harbour. Inevitably much of this detail was conflicting. As William Henry observed in a report to Alex Johnston just after the first round of hearings,

> The survivors from the "Mont Blanc" including the pilot have given on the whole a very consistent story, and were their evidence the only evidence there would be little difficulty in fixing the blame for the collision, but occurring as the collision did in the sight and hearing of many persons on other ships and on the shores the evidence of this latter class of witnesses has been most conflicting, no two persons telling the same story as to the speed and positions of the ships, the signals exchanged, etc., and this condition of affairs will be more accentuated when the rest of the testimony has been put in.[42]

The careers, qualifications, and, particularly, alleged drinking habits of the pilots were closely questioned, and testimony that all were men of sober habit was entered upon the record. The source, loading, and handling of *Mont Blanc*'s explosive cargo received particular scrutiny, and the question of why she had not displayed the red flag many associated with the presence of ammunition aboard a ship was posed at an early stage.

The court sat from 13 to 21 December, when it adjourned for the Christmas season and to permit Justice Drysdale to preside over national service appeals against conscription in his home county of Hants. The inquiry would reconvene on 21 January 1918 and continue to the end of the month. Over its 19 days, 61 witnesses would be examined and 1,770 pages of testimony taken. Addresses of counsel on completion of the testimony would occupy two full days at the end.[43]

In addition to Le Médec, Mackey, and several of the officers from *Mont Blanc*, witnesses called during the December portion of the inquiry included several survivors from *Imo*. None except Johan Johansen, her helmsman, had any clear impression of events, and his wounds permitted his appearance only later in the inquiry. The absence of material witnesses from *Imo* actually worked to Burchell's advantage – they offered Mellish little opportunity for cross-examination. The French-speaking witnesses from *Mont Blanc*, however, along with Mackey, were shamelessly grilled and discredited at every opportunity by Burchell's constant probing and hectoring. He fully played up every aspect of their abandonment of their burning ship and their apparent failure to provide any warning to mariners on other ships, including *Imo*. He thus characterized his clients as victims, along with the unwarned innocents of Halifax.

Other witnesses called before Christmas were survivors of ships damaged in the explosion, among them crew from *Picton, Calonne, Middleham Castle,* and a passing motor boat that had been moving up towards Bedford Basin. During this initial period, no naval members or officials of other departments or agencies were called, although the civilian steward from the chartered minesweeper/tug *Musquash* testified, along with William Nickerson, the senior of the few survivors from *Stella Maris*.

Ernest Chambers, the chief press censor, arrived in the city on the second day of the inquiry for his promised discussions with General Benson over the security and censorship problems posed by the explosion. As he subsequently reported back to Willoughby Gwatkin, the general officer commanding "was anxious that there should be impressed upon local and visiting journalists the importance of abstaining from publishing statements which might interfere with the successful prosecution of the official inquiry at present going on there and which might produce anxiety and mis-giving among the community at large. He explained that the explosion was of such a peculiarly startling and sensational character that the poise of the community had been completely upset and there was still much unnecessary apprehension as to a repetition of the explosion."[44]

It was a touchy situation. The wartime censorship requirements in the defended port had to be applied, but sensibly, and the freedom of the press had to be respected. All in all, Chambers's visit went better than he had probably hoped. After convening a meeting of representative journalists, Chambers presented the censorship requirements that he believed were appropriate under the circumstances. He was relieved to find "a disposition on the part of the newspaper men to cooperate readily to any reasonable extent."[45]

So far so good. Thomas Benson was very pleased with the results of Ernest Chambers's appeal to the journalistic community. Rear-Admiral Chambers, however, was "unable" to meet with the chief press censor during his visit. Perhaps the admiral preferred to stay out of the Canadian picture as much as possible. In any case, the press censor had a generally satisfactory meeting with Captain Eldridge, the naval intelligence officer at the dockyard. There was one sticking point between the two, however. Journalists knew that some forty British seamen from *Highflyer* had died in the explosion, but they wrongly believed that all had died in the heroic effort to save *Mont Blanc*. The newspapers wanted to print the story, but Eldridge was adamant that he could not disclose any information about Royal Navy casualties "unless authorized by the Admiralty in London." So a false impression persisted that it was heroic British sailors and not a party of Canadians who had died on the deck of *Mont Blanc*. Eldridge had acted correctly, but the cloak of rigid censorship, however necessary to the war effort, did little to inform the community or build its confidence in the RCN.[46]

The onslaught from the *Herald* subsided slightly after Chambers's departure from Halifax on 15 December, although it continued to give the proceedings front-page coverage and posed questions in its headlines such as "Did Another Hand Than Pilot's Direct Imo's Course?"[47] Something of a respite followed Borden's election victory. The coalition was now in place that would carry the country through to the end of the war with a policy of universal military service. For a few days, this outcome carried the front pages, but by the time the inquiry shut down for its lengthy Christmas sojourn, the *Herald* was once again fanning public discontent to new heights.

In its edition of 21 December, the *Herald* printed a letter to the editor and a personal account from one of its reporters, both of which proved incendiary. On the preceding day, two wounded and apparently "still suffering" crewmen from the *Calonne* had been brought from hospital to testify at the inquiry. Their appearance caused something of a sensation. There was some question, due to their obvious physical impairments, as to whether they should be required to give evidence, but Judge Drysdale permitted it with the proviso that counsel should limit their cross-examinations. As they awaited transportation back to hospital, one of the witnesses, Alfred Kayford, the ship's third engineer, spoke to the *Herald*'s reporter covering the inquiry. According to the subsequent article, Kayford reportedly asked the newspaperman,

"Say, mate, when is the big enquiry going to be held?" The reporter, who has been present already at fourteen sessions of the present enquiry and who has listened to the accumulation of evidence which will fill a many hundred page book [sic], was somewhat astonished at the enquiry and said to Cayford [sic]; "What do you mean by the big enquiry? This is the only enquiry I know of and it looks as if it had only got a good start."

"But," persisted Cayford, "all this enquiry seems to be after is to fix the blame on some pilot or somebody for bringing on the collision. I should think they would have an enquiry to fix the blame for the explosion. I've been ship-mates with explosives to Alexandria and a lot of other ports and this is the only port in the world where I ever saw cargoes like that brought right into the heart of a city, you might say, in a harbour full of ships and up thru narrow water. They always have some outlandish place where very few people live for such cargoes as that. Why is it different in Halifax? Who is to blame? That's what I'd like to know and so would all my shipmates who are left alive. I don't suppose it matters to those who are dead but I know some of them have folks at home to whom it matters."[48]

On a similar theme was a letter to the editor from J.R. Middleton, featured under the heading "Behind the Personal Responsibility of the Pilots Is the Personal Responsibility of the Naval Authorities."

After one of the most frightful disasters the modern world has known, the citizens of this city are being treated, under the title of "Enquiry as to the Disaster," to the spectacle of several seamen and a pilot, being "examined," and "cross-examined," by eminent counsel, in an effort to prove that one of the vessels in the collisions [sic] went to "port" when she should have gone to "starboard," or that the other "blew her whistle once" or "twice," as the leaning of counsel may be. Doubtless this is interesting to navigators, and remunerative to said counsel. Of what interest is it, however, to the citizen of this city who, in the fortunate case of being alive, finds himself, or herself STRIPPED OF EVERYTHING which previously had made his, or her life?

What the people of this city want to know, and what they have got to know is:

WHY was the "Mont Blanc" coming into Halifax?

WHO was the naval officer who issued permission for her to come, and

FROM WHOM did HE get the authority?

WHERE lays the ultimate responsibility for permitting such ships to come into our midst ...

So far the naval department have preserved a judicious silence ... We now want their answers.[49]

While the voice of the *Herald* was the most strident, the *Morning Chronicle*'s editorial on the subject expressed a rightful concern: "It is important of course, to determine whether one captain or the other, this pilot or that pilot, was at fault, or whether there was contributory negligence or blame on both sides. But the inquiry, we respectfully submit, should not rest there, and no mere technicalities or red tape should prevent this whole affair being probed to the very bottom."[50]

The *Chronicle* understood that the naval authorities controlled the movements of all ships in and out of the harbour:

It is imperative that the public should know by whose authority the Imo was ordered to leave her anchorage in Bedford Basin at a time when it must have been plain to the competent naval authority that the two ships would meet in or near the narrow channel which leads from the inner harbour to the Basin. It is also imperative, not only for the purposes of this investigation, but for the City's security in future, to ascertain why a proper patrol was not maintained by naval craft to keep the course clear for the munition boat. The naval authorities have a large number of boats of various sorts at their command in this harbour, but so far as we have learned, none of them were employed in escorting the Mont Blanc on her way to Bedford Basin. Why? The public has a right to know, why these and other precautions which we might mention were not taken and, above all, why the risk of allowing these two steamers to meet ... was taken.[51]

Even though the jurisdiction of the court might not cover all desirable lines of inquiry, the *Chronicle* called for it to be given authority so that "every source of information bearing upon this tragic calamity shall be exhausted."[52] Only days later, the Halifax Board of Control sent a resolution to the prime minister, urging him to take steps to ensure that the inquiry fully ascertain all the causes and what measures should be taken to prevent a recurrence.[53]

These concerns were legitimate, and the Marine Department was in favour of expanding the investigation to cover some of these matters. Alex Johnston had telegraphed Drysdale as early as 18 December stating that the question of pilotage in Halifax Harbour should be considered by the inquiry.[54] The same day, Johnston sent an amplifying letter to the judge. Johnston explained that both he and C.C. Ballantyne were very concerned that remedial measures be proposed "should it appear that they are required. I do not want to unduly urge it – that while the war continues at any rate, the Minister should become the pilotage authority at Halifax in much the same way as obtains at Quebec and Montreal."[55]

Changes in the basis of the inquiry might have created a need for some additional time for counsel and the judge to reconsider their mandate and discuss it with government officials. Even so, the month's recess to accommodate Judge Drysdale's schedule was excessive. There is evidence that the government had hoped to get Drysdale back to work earlier, but he had resisted on the grounds that his calendar was filled with military tribunal appointments.[56] Although it would have been impolitic for the Marine Department to press Drysdale too hard or appear to interfere, the lengthy halt in the proceedings not only delayed resolution but contributed exponentially to public indignation. The two were interconnected. Without the reassurance of clear findings from the inquiry, the public was not convinced the danger was over. The *Herald* contributed to those fears, asking during the inquiry's recess "Does the Menace Still Exist and Is Halifax Still Exposed to the Risk of Munition Ships Exploding in Harbour?"[57]

In the face of growing indignation about why *Mont Blanc* had been allowed unsupervised in the harbour in the first place, Rear-Admiral Chambers sought to reassure the population. On 20 December he telegraphed the Canadian government and imperial authorities, as well as the British embassy in Washington, that, where possible, vessels with large cargoes of high explosives from the United States should not pass in proximity to Halifax. Instead they should travel to Europe in convoys direct from Norfolk, Virginia.[58]

Obviously, authorities saw a pressing need to alleviate public suspicions that the inquiry would be less than full and searching, particularly in the face of the *Herald*'s almost daily flogging of disaster-related issues as well as the more trenchant analysis of the *Morning Chronicle*. The latter, the Crown counsel informed his retainers in Ottawa, "fairly well crystallized" the public attitude in Halifax. Nevertheless, from a legal standpoint, the question of munitions ships in the harbour was a large one that had to be approached with considerable caution:

In the first place the whole subject matter of such an investigation is so closely allied with the carrying on of the war that it would be considered improper that anything in the nature of a public inquiry should be instituted. The whole matter of the convoying of ships across the Atlantic from Canadian ports is in the hands, I understand, of the British Admiralty. It seems to me that no Court of Inquiry authorized by the Canadian Government would have jurisdiction to investigate proceedings of the Admiralty. In the case of the "Mont Blanc" in particular, another important consideration is involved. This ship was loaded in the United States with a cargo destined for France and no doubt owned by the French Government. The war interests therefore of two of our greatest allies are involved, which would make, I think, the holding of such an investigation a very delicate matter. The "Mont Blanc" was sent here by the representatives in New York of the British Admiralty for the purpose of being convoyed across the Atlantic, with the possibility however of being found deficient in speed for the slowest class of convoys and it was apparently not considered unlikely that she would be left to cross the Atlantic alone. The instructions which were given to her Captain at New York were received from the British Admiralty's representative there. His orders were to report to the naval authorities here.[59]

Like Rear-Admiral Chambers, Henry saw a need to reassure the citizenry that proper measures were in effect, and he suggested to Alex Johnston that a public statement should come from the government.[60]

Meanwhile, local naval officials responded to the debate by tightening their control over ships carrying explosives, a reaction that may well have made them seem even more culpable. Although the Narrows was sufficiently wide for even the largest ships to pass safely, instructions were issued to prevent any opposing movement if a ship loaded with explosives was under way.[61] On 26 December complaints were received that officers had begun refusing permission to vessels carrying explosives to stop at the Imperial Oil refinery dock on the Dartmouth shore between the two submarine barriers. This zeal effectively prevented even transports or ocean liners carrying shells for their own guns from topping up their fuel tanks.[62] Rear-Admiral Chambers was still trying to sort out the muddle almost three weeks later, advising nervous officials in Ottawa that the danger with any ship was "very slight when proper precautions taken."[63]

On 27 and 28 December, despite the announcement that a permanent federal commission would be formed to administer Halifax relief, the *Herald* also expanded its attacks to include the system of harbour regulations and pilotage in effect at Halifax. The paper alleged that regulations were unsatisfactory, and reported on conflict of authority between the civilian harbourmaster, the pilots, and the navy. Other articles criticized the presence of Captain Hose on the inquiry panel: while he might be competent to comment on the actions of ships' masters or pilots, "into the conditions REALLY responsible for the disaster he is not legally competent to enquire or to adjudicate."[64]

Senator Dennis followed his paper's line by sending a lengthy telegram of political advice to the prime minister, prefacing it with the observation there was "but little doubt" that the disaster was due to "dense stupidity or criminal carelessness" of port officials, both dominion and imperial. He also claimed that relief efforts were being mismanaged and that much dissatisfaction existed among the victims, who had suffered from the severe weather and who were "naturally discontented, discouraged and disheartened." He urged Borden to send an inspiring New Year's message with appropriate assurances of restoration and relief and to promise "exhaustive investigation" into the disaster and "rigorous punishment" of any parties guilty of "stupidity or carelessness." The prime minister, he insisted, had to inspire the discouraged with determination, to "lift them above [their] desolate environment and fill their souls with high hope for [the] future."[65]

Sir Robert had far more substantive plans. The federal cabinet ministers who had been the most involved in the disaster's aftermath arrived in Halifax on the 29th as a cabinet subcommittee to size up conditions and advise the prime minister and the government. The visiting ministers included C.C. Ballantyne (marine/naval), F.B. Carvell (public works), J.D. Reid (railways and canals), Major-General S.C. Mewburn (militia and defence), and A.K. Maclean (without portfolio). Maclean, like Borden, was the incumbent in a Halifax riding, where voting in the federal election had been delayed in the aftermath of the explosion. The cabinet ministers were accompanied by Alex Johnston from the Marine Department and George Desbarats from the naval service.[66]

Ballantyne evidently spent some time with Senator Dennis that day: the *Herald*'s evening headline broadcast the minister's pledge for a "Complete, Comprehensive, Searching Inquiry." Ballantyne had apparently authorized the paper to state "that the people can feel FULLY ASSURED that the matter had been dealt with promptly and that rumours of existing and recurring dangers should be promptly suppressed." Not surprisingly, these assurances were published alongside the now habitual diatribe about fixing blame and meting out drastic punishment.[67]

While Johnston and Desbarats were in Halifax pursuing their departmental agendas, the visiting ministers strived to achieve the necessary political objectives of demonstrating visible sympathy and concern, restoring public confidence, and consulting on how relief and reparation work could best be organized and funded under the umbrella of the pending relief commission. After touring the damaged areas, the federal ministers adjourned to the Legislative Council Chamber and later to the Board of Trade rooms, where they were addressed and questioned by local and provincial politicians and representatives of the business community. Inevitably, the marine and naval service minister was the target for some of the more difficult questions. He was presented with another resolution, this time from the most recent weekly meeting of the Commercial Club of Halifax, calling for investigation and punishment, sufficient safeguards and rigid regulations, and full reparation for property losses and injuries. The full text had already been published in the press.[68]

Arriving late at the Board of Trade session, C.C. Ballantyne was presented with a question from the mayor of Halifax. P.F. Martin "wanted to know who was in charge of the Port of Halifax. The City had been trying for two weeks to find that out but could not get the information. He also wanted to confer with the minister regarding regulations for munition ships coming to the port."[69] Undoubtedly, Ballantyne wanted to be convincing and eloquent and to restore public confidence and defend his department and the naval service. Yet his statement, as summarized in the *Chronicle*, seemed more defensive than reassuring:

> The minister said the port was in charge of the Canadian naval authorities of which Capt. Martin was at the head. During Capt. Martin's absence at present, Capt. Hose was acting for him. The Minister said he felt a section of the Canadian press appeared to have been unfair to the Canadian naval authorities and he regretted so many people had been given erroneous ideas. The Admiralty authorities had not been remiss and extra precautions had been taken. The Minister trusted the people of Halifax would not be misled by alarming false reports in a section of the press as to the port authorities. They would be glad to give any information and their offices were open to the Mayor or to any other citizen.

The administration of the port and control had not been lax careless [sic] and he had been well satisfied with the work of ship control here. The situation was realized fully but no fault could be found with the work of port administration. Halifax was the best regulated port in any part of Canada.[70]

During his visit, Ballantyne also released a statement that action had been taken towards making impossible a repetition of the disaster as had befallen the City of Halifax. Events soon made it clear that he had failed to convince the populace. The next evening, Rear-Admiral Chambers received a report that a ship was on fire in Bedford Basin. As he subsequently reported to the Admiralty, "The people in the neighbourhood were leaving their houses and going into the woods, though the night was a bitter one, below zero and a blizzard blowing. A vessel sent to the basin was unable to get through the narrows in the blinding snow and went ashore. I have since been quite unable to discover that any fire actually existed whatever."[71]

Ballantyne's visit to the city had not been a great success. His efforts to reassure the citizens of Halifax and bolster the reputation of the navy had rung hollow. Nor had he persuaded the government's erstwhile friend, Senator Dennis, to cut the navy much slack. Although the *Herald* was willing to give Ballantyne himself the benefit of the doubt, it nonetheless suggested that the minister's vote of confidence for the inquiry might be a "preliminary coat of whitewash."[72]

Criticism of the inquiry and of government officials was not limited to the local press. The *Ottawa Journal* scolded Ballantyne for what it perceived as interference:

Lecturing the press seems to be a favourite pastime for amateurish statesmen, the extravagance of the lecturer being usually in proportion to the lecturer's lack of knowledge of the press ... The port of Halifax is in charge of the naval authorities. What the public want to know is this – how does it come that a ship carrying 3,000 tons of high explosives was permitted to wander about in the immediate vicinity of a great residential district? Why was the Mont Blanc without a patrol boat preceding her? Why did she not carry something to denote the deadly character of her cargo? These are things that should engage the immediate attention of the minister of marine. Lecturing the press for lack of public responsibility can be wisely suspended for the present.[73]

Despite the controversy surrounding Ballantyne, the cabinet subcommittee managed to achieve some tangible progress. Much of the confusion surrounding Halifax relief had been cleared up. At the same time, Alex Johnston had met with Judge Drysdale to discuss the jurisdiction of the marine inquiry. Could it properly discuss movements of ships carrying explosives in general and appraise the pilotage system in effect at the port? Interestingly, both men seem to have decided to seek the Crown counsel's recommendations, which were recorded in a letter to Johnston on 2 January. Henry's estimate became the basis upon which the inquiry would ultimately proceed.[74]

As Henry observed, certainly no Canadian court could have jurisdiction to pronounce upon the loading of a French ship in an American port, with a cargo owned by the French government, ordered to Halifax by British Admiralty authorities in New York. Specifically, then, the inquiry could not concern itself with the doings of *Mont Blanc* until she arrived at the examination ground, when she came under the jurisdiction of the Canadian naval authorities. Henry saw no reason, however, why the court could not inquire "into all the circumstances relating to the 'Mont Blanc' from that time on, including the system governing the movement of ships in and out of the harbour, with a view to ascertaining whether that system adequately protected life and property in the areas surrounding the harbour."[75]

Henry also opined that the inquiry had no legal basis to examine the pilotage system except as it pertained to the particular incident. A separate investigation under another section of the Canada Shipping Act would be necessary, which could commence as soon as the current task was completed. Significantly, having outlined his view of the inquiry's scope, Henry proceeded to tell Johnston that, "as the Court has power only to report and make recommendations, no harm would be done even if it exceeded its jurisdiction." Indeed, Henry had already assumed that

> the real object of the investigation is to establish that the system, as administered by the Pilot commissioners, is faulty and not up-to-date, and to provide a justification for transferring the control of the pilotage to the Minister. I have had for a number of years a very strong opinion that the system should be changed. It will afford me very great satisfaction to do what I can to bring about improved conditions. If there are, therefore, any particular matters which your Department would like brought out, I would be glad if you would advise me of them.[76]

It was fortunate for the RCN that the pilotage system had been targeted for as much scrutiny as Henry could reasonably introduce. Otherwise the navy's position would have been even more distressing. Its role in controlling traffic in Halifax Harbour was to be examined and in as much detail as needed. William Henry asked for "all available information, which, in view of war conditions, can properly be made public." In a strategy to streamline the process, he suggested that the navy prepare a statement to be read by officials on the witness stand. Although he acknowledged that members of the inquiry could cross-examine the officials, using the prepared statement might obviate the need for a large number of navy witnesses.[77]

William Henry's schedule did not slacken much during the lengthy period when the inquiry was adjourned. On the last day of December, for example, he met with a special committee of the Halifax Commercial Club to discuss the resolution they had handed to C.C. Ballantyne and to brief them on the further conduct of the investigation.[78] His efforts to satisfy their concerns were evidently futile. At the club's next weekly meeting, the proceedings of which were emblazoned in the *Herald,* members continued to pressure for determination of cause and assignment of blame and to condemn the delay as highly improper.[79] The club mailed additional resolutions to Ballantyne's Ottawa office, and the minister promised that when the court reconvened it would sit until the investigation was complete. If required, a further investigation or commission would be held, but not before the end of the current inquiry, so as to avoid any conflict.[80]

It would be wrong to think that the public was entirely consumed with establishing cause and blame. For many, issues of relief and compensation were also at the forefront. Here, too, intense dissatisfaction hounded official efforts. As one of the prime minister's political correspondents observed, the "Relief Committee" had "no friends" and was "attacked from all quarters." Victims of the explosion expressed outrage that the committee continued to lack a scheme to pay for damage to the town. "The answer from the Committee to perpetual enquiries are [sic] very vague and indefinite, and tend to alarm the sufferers."[81]

The massive relief effort to assist the population and restore the damaged areas is beyond the scope of this study. However, it must be mentioned here for its undoubted influence on the emotional state of the community as the inquiry proceeded. More importantly, citizens awaiting compensation for losses had an enormous stake in the identification of the guilty parties, whom they undoubtedly would expect to pay restitution. Should the inquiry determine that the accident was the result of the incompetence or negligence of officials of the Canadian government and/or its naval service, some of this burden might rest on the Crown in Canada. Certainly this possibility appears to have been considered at the time by the Prime Minister's Office, and there was some inclination within cabinet to "accede to the demand." Indeed, the governor general inquired on the government's behalf with the Ministry of Munitions in London to determine the practice with respect to granting indemnity for damage as a result of the transport of munitions.[82]

From the standpoint of the *Morning Chronicle,* the question of responsibility and reparations was simple:

> The problem with regard to the responsibility ... has been complicated by much ill-advised discussion; but it is, in reality, a very simple one ... we do not, of course, mean responsibility for the immoderate act or acts which led to the collision of the "Mont Blanc" and the "Imo," ... but for the state of affairs which made that collision possible. That responsibility no longer needs to be determined by formal legal inquiry. It has been established beyond question by the open confession of the Federal Minister whose Department appoints and controls the official managers of Halifax Harbour.
>
> In that confession it was publicly admitted that the Dominion Government has been and is in full charge of the navigable waters of this harbour ... When a crime has been confessed by its perpetrators, further court proceedings are merely formal for the purpose of establishing the probable truthfulness of the confession ... equally indisputable is the fact that the explosion could not and would not have occurred had there been proper harbour management ... The Dominion Government in effect admits that it is bound both at law and in equity to make good the private and civic losses so occasioned. It is bound, therefore, in so far as it is able, to make full reparation to every person damnified by the misdeeds or negligence of its chosen agents.[83]

While accusations of its ineptitude were flying about the press, the RCN was busy continuing the clean-up of Halifax Harbour. Personnel and tugs had been hard at work for a month, although this effort would not be acknowledged in Ottawa. Instead, after his return from Halifax, Alex Johnston had sent an abrupt note to his counterpart in the naval service that "some effort should be made to clear the harbour." Such careless and misleading words added insult to injury. By the time of Johnston's message, the clean-up was "practically complete." As well, RCN minesweepers had swept the vicinity of the explosion to a depth of forty feet to ensure that there was no menace to shipping. Small naval vessels still had to carry out daily patrols to pick up drifting wood because tangled masses remained along the shore, mostly what was left of the ruined piers. Every time strong winds and waves came up, additional wreckage would break away from the shore and the damaged wharves. Captain Pasco asked that the harbour-master, a civilian, be authorized to arrange with a contractor to clear away this wreckage. This request, while not particularly important in itself, was symptomatic of the lack of clarity about who was responsible for what in Halifax Harbour, both during the clean-up and even before the explosion. This absence of clarity would come out when the inquiry resumed. In the meantime, C.C. Ballantyne showed no inclination to have responsibility for such a contract assigned to the harbour-master. He ordered the naval authorities to get on with the necessary arrangements without delay.[84]

It did not help matters that Captain Edward Martin had not yet returned from England as the dockyard's permanent superintendent. Fred Pasco was still temporarily in command, having recovered from the wounds that had forced him to turn his responsibilities over to Walter Hose on 6 December. He was less able than Martin to provide the background material William Henry would need to make best use of the naval and other witnesses he would bring before the inquiry.

The subtleties of chain of command and changes in command responsibility within the RCN were beyond the ken of the public and were additionally complicated by the separate responsibilities in the port of the Royal Navy and Rear-Admiral Chambers. The citizenry were further baffled when both Chambers and Walter Hose – now restored as captain of patrols following the return of Pasco – disclaimed "being invested with any authority over harbour matters from Headquarters." Although, strictly speaking, this was correct, it must have smacked of evasion to the frustrated and suspicious citizens of Halifax. More disturbingly, similar disclaimers were attributed by one of the prime minister's political correspondents to the chief examining officer, Commander Frederick Wyatt.[85]

Within this atmosphere, the *Herald* continued its assaults on Canadian naval officials and posed "questions" they should be required to answer when the inquiry resumed.[86] One edition alleged that "Captain Hose Should Be Under Investigation and Not an 'Investigator' in the Halifax Disaster."[87] The sailors in Halifax responsible for Canadian naval interests were beginning to wilt under the barrage and were becoming increasingly anxious and defensive. As Pasco telegraphed Kingsmill, "Herald continues to abuse Captain Hose daily." Pasco then asked for permission to inform the paper that Hose had been uninvolved in the management of the harbour before 6 December.[88] Kingsmill was not inclined to placate the outcry; he saw any attempt to open a dialogue with the paper as self-defeating. He asked for copies of the offending material but assured Pasco that "no harm [would] result from Herald abuse. Better treat it with contempt. Let Herald continue to bark up the wrong tree."[89]

The barrage against Hose continued. Even Mayor Martin sent a telegram to the prime minister requesting that Hose be removed from the inquiry. Martin minced no words: "He should be examined not examiner. Have Ballantyne remove him."[90] When the mayor's demand was referred from the Prime Minister's Office, Desbarats, the deputy minister, had just departed for two weeks of meetings in Washington.[91] Thus for once, Admiral Kingsmill was free to speak to the minister directly. Their conversations are not recorded, but Ballantyne vigorously defended Hose's position on the inquiry in a lengthy response to the prime minister. The captain of patrols was highly qualified and respected and, at the time of the tragedy, had not been in any way responsible for anything to do with the movement of vessels in Halifax Harbour. Ballantyne also explained his continuing efforts to provide reassurances that the investigation would be full and complete and added his hope that Haligonians would withhold their criticisms of the port authorities and the court until the findings had been rendered. "I might further add that all this sentiment has been created by the alarming and unjustifiable articles that have constantly appeared in the Halifax 'Herald' since this great catastrophe. Anything you could do with Senator Dennis to have his paper cease publishing its attacks on the Naval Authorities, Court of Inquiry and the Administration of the Port of Halifax, would greatly tend to allay the nervous tension of the Halifax citizens caused by the recent terrible catastrophe."[92]

Borden accepted Ballantyne's argument to keep Hose on the inquiry and informed Mayor Martin accordingly.[93] No efforts to tame the excesses of Senator Dennis's publication are recorded; in any case, they probably would have been to no avail. Although careful to respect wartime censorship requirements with respect to the movement of ships, the canny publisher was speaking to and for a substantial body of public opinion when it came to the operation of the port, and he knew how to sell his newspapers. Kingsmill realized there could be no respite for the RCN from the "unjust attacks," but did his best to hearten Pasco, finishing with the observation that "the 'Herald' would be only too glad to enter into a controversy, and no correspondence with that paper is to take place."[94]

As a member of Parliament for Halifax, Borden was particularly sensitive to the longer term political effects of the continuing controversy. He set out to gather his own brief on harbour control matters, asking Ballantyne for a written explanation of the role played by naval officials vis-à-vis the King's harbour-master in the regulation and movement of ships in Halifax Harbour. He particularly wanted to know about provisions for munition ships.[95] Thus, before the issue was even scrutinized by the inquiry, officials in the Marine and Naval Service Departments were set to work to outline their views of the distinctions in detail and to predict some of what might be revealed to the court. Interestingly, while acknowledging a continuing role for the civilian harbour-master, officials were clear in their agreement that the RCN was the ultimate authority for movement in wartime. With respect to the movement of ships carrying munitions, the regulations had been fixed in 1911. They dealt with the landing and shipping of explosives, but none envisioned the passage through the harbour of ships carrying such cargoes while they awaited convoy. According to Admiral Kingsmill, naval authorities had not altered these latter regulations "in any way" before the tragedy of 6 December.[96]

Now, to protect Ballantyne, who had stated while in Halifax that the navy had effected changes that rendered another explosion impossible, Kingsmill was obliged to ensure that regulations had, in fact, been changed. Thus, in the last days before the inquiry resumed, the director of the naval service sought confirmation from Fred Pasco that the necessary measures had been put in place. Indeed they had. An arriving ship loaded with explosives would remain in the Examination Anchorage until the "favourable moment" when all ship traffic would be halted and the arrival would be escorted to her berth by the CXO's tug. She would be anchored in an isolated part of Bedford Basin until her designated convoy departed, at which time similar procedures would apply. Berths would not be shifted without the personal approval of the captain superintendent. Traffic control would also be improved by the operation of signal stations on *Niobe* and at the Narrows.[97]

One of the visiting ships that had been governed by the enhanced rules was the SS *Galileo*, which had arrived on 14 January with a cargo of munitions and had been berthed in the designated area in the northeast part of Bedford Basin. On the afternoon of Saturday the 19th, two days before the inquiry was to resume, Captain Fred Pasco received a report of a fire in her coal bunker. The indispensable *W.H. Lee* was despatched from the dockyard with an officer and working party for yet another rescue mission. Fortunately, the fire was not serious: empty space separated the bunker from the hold containing the ammunition. Nevertheless, the sailors worked throughout the next day discharging the contents of the bunker into a barge alongside. That evening the danger was reported over. Pasco summed up his terse report on the matter to Kingsmill on 22 January. *Galileo* would refuel the same day and sail with a convoy the next.[98] The admonition he received back from headquarters was gently phrased but said much for the contrast between the practicalities of seamanship in Halifax Harbour and the political state of mind in Ottawa: "Thank you for your 463. If you would report these things & what you are doing it would put the Department in a position to relieve the Minister of a great deal of worry & anxiety. Times are not normal with regard to Halifax. You must keep us informed of any untoward happenings."[99]

In the event, *Galileo* had a further part to play in causing worry and anxiety to the minister, contributing to public nervousness, and undermining the credibility of the Royal Canadian Navy. So did *Picton*. In consultation with Ministry of Munitions staff, *Picton* had been moved alongside Pier 24 in the new Ocean Terminals so that the 1,500 tons of ammunition still carried in her hold could be unloaded and inspected. The intent was to prepare the uninjured material for reshipment and to dispose of any that had been damaged.[100] As Rear-Admiral Chambers later reported to the Admiralty, "As considerable nervousness was displayed by the towns people over the ship being brought alongside, every precaution was taken and though the matter did not come within my jurisdiction, I had myself visited the ship and sheds to satisfy myself that the work was being properly conducted."[101]

Great care had to be exercised in handling the ammunition cases. Nevertheless, a few particles of almost invisible phosphorus from *Picton*'s destroyed smoke producer were still scattered among them.[102] Thus, as the court of inquiry prepared to reconvene on 21 January, two different ships were poised to play their part in a further series of ill-timed events.

Goats to the Slaughter

The Drysdale inquiry finally reconvened at 10 a.m. on Monday, 21 January. Predictably, now that the inquiry was to cover more than a mere examination of the minutiae of a marine collision, public anticipation was that expressed concerns would be satisfied and that those to blame would be identified and punished. Government officials believed that an agenda was in place to further the aim of reforming pilotage in Halifax through the exercise of federal control, to promote general confidence in the government, and to permit naval officials to credibly acquit themselves of harm in the general management of the port. In the end, few of these wide expectations would be met, and the credibility of the Royal Canadian Navy in particular would be stretched to the point of a crisis of confidence. And where there is a failure of expectations, scapegoats are generally not only sought but found.

Upon resumption of the inquiry, Judge Drysdale's first act was to pronounce that an injustice had been done to Captain Walter Hose with the clamour to have him removed from the inquiry. The judge emphasized that the naval officer had not been in any way responsible for the movement of ships at the time of the explosion and that he would therefore continue to be a member of the inquiry. Yet the next day, the effectiveness of Drysdale's announcement was undermined by publication in the *Herald* of the full text of a letter from C.C. Ballantyne to the judge requesting that he make such a statement and accusing the newspaper and Mayor Martin of having "done their utmost to create a false impression" about Hose.[1] One can only speculate as to how and why the letter got into the hands of Senator Dennis.

The proceedings largely took up where they had left off in December, and it was not immediately clear that the scope of the inquiry had indeed been broadened. Among the first witnesses called were the chief engineer and the helmsman from *Imo,* as well as the Canadian Government Railway's terminal agent. A gloomy but unapologetic Captain Aimé Le Médec made another appearance. The lines of questioning were so similar to the December sessions that they roused a complaint from the next morning's *Herald* that "no attempt was made ... to get at facts other than those connected with the navigation of the ships and the responsibilities of the pilots."[2] Yet a development of somewhat broader interest took place when Pilot Edward Renner took the stand that afternoon. He had been the pilot assigned to what became known as the "unknown" American "tramp steamer" that had preceded *Mont Blanc* up the harbour. Renner could not remember the ship's name, and records kept at the Pilotage Commission were insufficient to provide the necessary reminder. Renner's faulty memory served *Imo's* lawyer, Charles Burchell, in very good stead. Burchell exploited with great drama the (possibly sinister?) presence of a "mystery ship" that had earlier passed *Imo* on the wrong (Halifax) side, thereby forcing her to proceed down the entire harbour on the Dartmouth side.[3] (Interestingly, the name of the ship responsible for this dubious contention has never been published. RCN intelligence files indicate that she was no "tramp" but almost certainly the New York-registered SS *Clara,* a former Austro-Hungarian merchant ship owned by the United States Shipping Board Emergency Fleet. These records show she arrived in Halifax at approximately the same time as *Mont Blanc.*[4])

The appearance of witnesses was influenced by when they were available and when they could be fitted in and by the subjects on which they would be examined. Thus various technical experts testified on explosives effects, or methods of steamship inspection, in no apparent order.[5] A representative from New York of the Compagnie Générale Transatlantique was brought in to testify about whether special flooding arrangements had been considered for the numerous French vessels carrying explosives. That there were not was the end of a futile line of inquiry exploring the possibility that *Mont Blanc*'s crew might have reduced the risk by sinking her themselves.[6]

New witnesses included those who had been waiting to appear since December and those added to supplement testimony. Others had been too seriously injured to testify in December. Among them were two members of the RCN: George Abbott, the seaman whose despatch boat had passed the stricken *Mont Blanc* on her way down from Bedford Basin to *Niobe*,[7] and Mate Herbert Whitehead, RNCVR, the skipper of the drifter *CD-73*. Whitehead had been on sick leave at home in Sudbury but was now well enough to testify. The court kept him most of a morning as Burchell and Captain Demers in particular and counsel in general probed his version of the sequence of events for inconsistencies.[8] Despite the pressure, he proved a star witness. As William Henry later reported in a note to Alex Johnston: "Everybody who heard him give evidence, including the Court, was very much impressed by his keen powers of observation, his retentive memory, and his clear exposition of the matters which came under his observation."[9] Would the more senior members of the RCN fare as well?

Before that could be seen, several non-naval officials were called upon to testify, including the port warden of Halifax and the superintendent of lights and buoys for the Nova Scotia coast. On 22 January, Francis Rudolf, the harbour-master, was questioned in detail about existing harbour regulations and the nature of his subordination to the authority of the RCN through the chief examining officer. Although officials with the Marine and Naval Service Departments in Ottawa saw a continuing role for the harbour-master in management of the harbour, the perception in Halifax was rather different. After Rudolf testified that no boat had been made available for his use, the *Herald* reported that responsibility for the harbour had clearly been taken out of his hands.[10]

Rudolf's testimony also highlighted the confusion surrounding rules for ships carrying explosives or combustibles in the harbour. Humphrey Mellish, the lawyer who represented *Mont Blanc*, cleverly pointed out that, by provincial statute, the city had an authority to take protective measures against careless use of explosives. Stating that this statute did not apply to the harbour, Rudolf was forced to acknowledge that the harbour had no special provisions for the control of explosive-laden ships. Yet Rudolf had established some informal arrangements on his own. For example, he drew up regulations that ships carrying kerosene to the Imperial Oil works in Bedford Basin would fly red flags. Those carrying crude oil to the refinery at Dartmouth would not, however.[11] The next day's testimony by Captain Fred Pasco would show that display of red flags was required practice when explosives were being physically handled, but it did not necessarily follow that such a display was required for ships under way. Indeed, it could prove suicidal, "giving information to enemy agents."[12]

William Henry had notified three naval officers that their testimony would be required at 10 a.m. on 23 January. In addition to Fred Pasco, he intended to call Commander Frederick Wyatt and Terrence Freeman, the reservist mate who had first encountered *Mont Blanc* outside the port. Pasco and Freeman were available at the appointed time, but Wyatt would have to be rescheduled. The ships gathering in Bedford Basin, the munitions ship *Galileo* among them, were due to sail in a large convoy that morning. Wyatt would have to see them safely out of Halifax before coming to court.[13]

On the morning of the 23rd, while Wyatt busied himself with his convoy, the acting captain superintendent gave his version of events in the dockyard on the day of the explosion up to the time when he turned command over to Walter Hose. He was neither defensive nor apologetic in acknowledging that no special regulations had existed at the time of the explosion with regard to ships carrying explosives. Nor did he know of any place in the world, aside from the Suez Canal, where regulations existed requiring one ship to stop when two were passing "in narrow waters."[14]

Because Pasco had played a part in drafting regulations for the port of Sydney in Cape Breton, Henry asked whether he might have considered any special measures in that port to guard against the possibility of violations of the rules of the road.

A. I didn't. It certainly did not occur to me that a ship would be coming up a harbour like a piece of fireworks ready to be exploded.

Q. Or it didn't occur to you in broad daylight in the harbour that two ships, one entering and the other leaving, would come into violent collision?

A. That does happen; I don't expect a ship to blow up because she has had a collision.

Q. That didn't suggest itself to you as reasonable or likely?

A. No.[15]

Pasco expressed surprise that shipping authorities would even allow a vessel like *Mont Blanc* to carry such a combination of deadly cargo and that any crew would consent to stay with such a ship. He was also astonished that such a cargo would be brought into the harbour without his being informed of its "special dangerous nature." Henry then made certain that the court received full details from Pasco of the special measures he had taken since the explosion to prevent the possibility of another accident.[16] Andrew Cluney, representing the provincial attorney general, asked about the berthing of *Picton* at the new terminals while the ammunition aboard was being off-loaded and inspected. Pasco described the activity as perfectly safe and no danger to the community in the event of mishap.[17]

Before Pasco completed his testimony he was asked if any person on duty in the dockyard on 6 December could have prevented the *Imo* leaving her anchorage that morning. His response – "Commander Wyatt could have stopped her; that had better come in his evidence"[18] – was innocent enough. Wyatt was the proper official to answer such a question, but he was not available for immediate response. At the time of Pasco's testimony, the man who conceivably could have stopped *Imo* – had he seen any reason to do so – was on the deck of *Niobe* supervising the departure of that morning's convoy. Shortly before Pasco had finished giving his evidence, all the ships but one had passed down the harbour. *Galileo,* with her load of shrapnel shells, had been delayed in coaling and was not ready to take her place in the convoy. Captain Turnbull, the assistant port convoy officer, was adamant that she needed to sail as soon as possible in order to catch up, but he was not able to estimate when she would be ready. Of course, under the new procedures applying to ships carrying ammunition, other traffic had to be halted, and incoming traffic was accumulating. Accordingly, as soon as the last outbound ship, excepting *Galileo,* had cleared the outer gate, Wyatt ordered the signal changed to allow waiting ships into the harbour. He then hurried off to the courthouse, leaving one of his assistants, Mate Roland Iceton, to supervise matters. Wyatt omitted, however, to hoist the signal necessary to prevent *Galileo* from sailing.[19]

On the stand, the testimony of the chief examining officer seemed forthright and innocuous enough. Indeed, the press reports gave Wyatt's words far less play than Pasco's.[20] In describing his responsibilities, Wyatt distanced himself from overall accountability for traffic control by indicating that he was "not the harbour master" but "on certain occasions" did "some of his work," because the latter had no boat. He acknowledged that there were no special procedures in effect on 6 December for ammunition ships reporting for convoy. He also admitted that he knew the *Mont Blanc* would enter Halifax Harbour the morning of 6 December and that she would be carrying "high explosives." At the same time, any ship departing the port would require his permission before moving.[21]

Q. Did you know of any other ship leaving that morning?
A. No, there was a ship coming up.
Q. Had you given permission to any other ship to leave that morning?
A. Nothing.
Q. So that from your stand point the Mont Blanc had a clear passage up?
A. Perfectly clear passage; no obstruction whatever.

When asked whether the master of the ship or the local pilot was responsible for allowing *Imo* to go out that morning, Wyatt clearly replied that such matters were up to the pilot. Wyatt referred to measures he had introduced in May 1917 requiring pilots to inform the chief examining officer before allowing the movement of any ship in the harbour. Asked again, "So the responsibility for the Imo coming out that morning would be upon the pilot in your opinion?" Wyatt responded, "Absolutely."[22]

Under cross-examination by F.C. Bell, the lawyer representing the city of Halifax, Wyatt allowed that, while he had known that *Mont Blanc* was carrying high explosives, he had not realized the particular combination of inflammables it carried. He insisted, however, that this information would not have affected his decision to give *Mont Blanc* free passage up the harbour; he firmly believed that, with no outbound movements authorized, there was no risk of collision. Then, when Bell posed a hypothetical question as to what Wyatt would have done had he seen *Imo* coming out, the CXO responded that he would have tried to stop her at the outside gate by firing at her, or by signalling the coastal fortifications to do the same. Indeed, such a situation had occurred only two days before the explosion, although he had been unable to stop the ship involved.

A. The pilots have not been in the habit of carrying out my instructions as they should latterly: there were one or two instances and I reported to my superior officer; the ships have been shot at and stopped; and let go anchor and I went to see what was the matter.

Q. Previous to the collision ships that violated the regulations were actually stopped?

A. Yes.

Q. Were the pilots punished?

A. There has never seemed to be any way of punishing pilots for violations.

Q. Do you know whether your report was forwarded to the pilot commission?

A. I could not tell you anything about that; I reported the matter as far as I was concerned. I heard nothing more.[23]

Although Wyatt generally declined to give the names of the pilots who had disregarded his orders, he did mention that one of them had been Pilot Mackey, who had later apologized to him. But his earlier charge that Pilot Hayes of *Imo* had acted improperly in taking the ship out of the harbour without authority would not stand unchallenged. Engaged in conversation by the counsel for *Imo* as the court broke for lunch, Wyatt evidently expressed regret to Burchell about having spoken ill of the dead. He would rue this gentlemanly but ill-advised act. The lawyer had no brief to protect the interests of the Pilotage Commission or Pilot Hayes, but when the court reconvened for the afternoon he asked for and received permission to defer his cross-examination to the following day. Wyatt was excused to hurry off to his duties and attention shifted to Mate Freeman and then James Hall, sheriff of Halifax County and chairman of the Pilotage Commission.

Freeman's testimony served merely to confirm the sequence of events and the procedures in effect at the time of the explosion. Nevertheless, Henry made use of it as another means to emphasize that corrective measures had been taken by the navy to prevent any recurrence. Burchell, by contrast, took the opportunity to make insinuations about the young sailor's low level of knowledge. Although Freeman knew that *Mont Blanc* was carrying dangerous explosives, he had no idea what benzol was. In short, he had not realized how dangerous the cargo was.[24]

James Hall defended the records and sobriety of pilots Hayes and Mackey and answered questions about the structure of the Pilotage Commission. He acknowledged a shortage of pilots but was unclear as to the reasons for it. When Judge Drysdale suggested that the Pilotage Commission might depend on "recommendations" as to who got appointments – thus insinuating that patronage was common – the response was to the contrary but nevertheless telling: "We have tried to avoid that as much as possible." Although Hall acknowledged that complaints had been levelled against the commission, he was not clear on the details. Interestingly, he also acknowledged that Pilot Mackey was still employed guiding ships into and out of the harbour, including one that carried munitions, prompting an incredulous Captain Demers to ask if the witness thought it right that Pilot Mackey should be continued in office pending the outcome of the inquiry. Yet Hall would only lamely reply that there was quite a bit of "haphazard work" in the "tracing" of pilots and no direct supervision.[25] Demers did not pursue the matter further.

As the Marine Department had hoped, a clear case was building to demonstrate that the pilotage system was unacceptably lax and informal and required improvement. Yet circumstances had also conspired, at least in public eyes, to draw the navy firmly into the same circle of evident incompetence and negligence.

While Wyatt was on the stand, *Galileo* and her cargo of ammunition had begun moving down the harbour. At the same time, other ships were moving inward through the gate, as permitted by the signal displayed by *Niobe*, which Wyatt had changed before his departure. Mate Roland Iceton had been down at the gate in the examination tug monitoring the convoy's departure. Just before departing for the courthouse, Wyatt had phoned him to return to *Niobe*. Iceton knew that *Galileo* had not yet sailed but when he got back to the depot ship he found the signal permitting movement up the harbour and was advised by Rear-Admiral Chambers's assistant, Captain Turnbull, that *Galileo* could pass downward at any time. He called John Makiny's armed tug, *Nereid*, alongside to be prepared for escort duties, but the first inkling he had of the ammunition ship's departure was about 11:30, when she slipped through the Narrows down past *Niobe* and then by an upward-bound oiler, the SS *Appalache*. *Nereid* went racing off to her task of intercepting *Galileo*, and Iceton frantically telephoned out to the entrance in an effort to stop the passage of any more incoming ships.[26]

Galileo and *Appalache* passed without incident. In any case, neither carried a cargo that posed a degree of risk comparable to that of *Mont Blanc*. Still, the violation did not pass unnoticed, and news of it spread quickly. So much for the safety measures guaranteed by the navy, to say nothing of the credibility of the service or the assurances of its minister.

Frederick Wyatt had long feared being "made the goat" for an accident in Halifax Harbour. His worst nightmares were about to come true.[27] The next morning, 24 January, he was back on the stand for what would be an ordeal of almost three hours. Charles Burchell was waiting for him and was at his street-fighting best. Unlike Pasco's generally unruffled and straightforward testimony the preceding day, Wyatt's evidence had offered a number of opportunities for exploitation. Burchell was ruthless in probing for inconsistencies and implicating the navy. Wyatt's language on the stand reads as rather strident and defensive, but he fought gamely through the rivetting confrontation. The opening sallies, as Burchell clearly sought to discredit and intimidate him, were telling:

Q. Is your title Captain or Commander?
A. Commander.
Q. You spoke to me after you left the witness stand yesterday morning and expressed regret that you had to make these charges against the late Pilot Hayes, as you didn't think it right to lay a charge against a dead man or words to that effect?
A. Yes.
Q. Even if a charge of this kind is true you don't think it British fair play to make the charge against him?
A. I have to clear myself.
Q. And to clear yourself by throwing the responsibility upon him?
A. I clear myself by declaring the absolute fact.
Q. I suppose if it is unfair and unwarranted it would be still more against British fair play?
A. I am stating the fact.
Q. You are an Englishman?
A. Yes.
Q. You know what British fair play is?
A. Yes.
Q. For a man to make a charge against a dead man which is unfair and unwarranted would be very much against British fair play?
A. Neither unfair or unwarranted, seeing it is an absolute fact.
Q. Assuming it is unfair and unwarranted it would be against British fair play?
Mr. Mellish objects.[28]

As he dragged Wyatt through every imaginable detail of the workings of the Examination Service and its relation to other services in the port, Charles Burchell probed, bluffed, insinuated, and tried to draw out criticisms of others. Throughout, he made the most of the willingness of the press to seize upon every utterance as fact. In doing so, he managed to create an impression that the generally well-understood and straightforward practices by which wartime shipping was controlled and coordinated in the harbour were, instead, webs of confusing roles and jurisdictions, where incompetence prevailed. Wyatt held to the contention that his function was uncomplicated by dealings with or its relation to ships' agents or captains, customs and revenue, coaling, the Patrol Service, the port convoy officer, clearance of neutral shipping, warships, small boats, the guard ship in Bedford Basin, intelligence, and routing of convoys and individual ships. Despite continued abuse and inappropriate language from Burchell, which at one point drew an indignant protest from the Crown counsel, Wyatt also held firmly to the contention that he relied on the pilots of the port to keep him in touch with the movement of ships. As Wyatt had stated in earlier testimony, this had been promulgated as a local regulation on 4 May 1917; it provided that "no ship will be allowed to leave the port or move anywhere in the harbour without the pilot acquainting the Chief Examining Officer as to what ship he is moving and to what anchorage or wharf or if going to sea."[29]

Wyatt forcefully defended the measure as the easiest, quickest, and most accurate way of getting the job done, because only the pilot was in a position of knowing the vital question of when the move would actually take place. The guard ship in Bedford Basin could not provide this service because those aboard were in a position only to observe the passage when it occurred. The pilots in general had not been keeping Wyatt informed, however; the *Imo* incident was just one case in point.

Under Burchell's poking and prodding, Wyatt had difficulty identifying more than one or two specific instances in which the pilots had not observed proper procedure. Then, as Burchell hounded Wyatt over his seemingly imperfect memory, Wyatt indicated that he could produce a letter he had written to Captain Martin, the captain superintendent – "I have it in my pocket now, complaining the pilots had not carried out my orders in regard to that regulation."[30] Three letters were subsequently entered into evidence. On 21 June and 1 August 1917, Wyatt had written to the captain superintendent to complain that pilots were not carrying out his orders regarding the movement of vessels and that their reports were coming in spasmodically.[31] In the third letter, written on 15 September, Wyatt asked Martin to punish offending pilots under Defence of the Realm regulations. Wyatt wrote:

> Under existing circumstances it is impossible to berth vessels properly in the stream, and vessels are continually sailing without any reference to myself, such as contained in my orders to the pilots and regardless of whether the net defences are open or not, on many occasions having to drop anchor on arriving at these defences until they have been opened at the proper hour. Under these conditions it is not possible to regulate the traffic in the harbour, and it is submitted that I cannot in this regard accept the responsibility of any accident occurring.[32]

Burchell pursued the last point brilliantly, and Wyatt leapt for safety.

Q. No complaints prior to the 6th December were made by the captain of the Dockyard to the Secretary of the Pilotage Commission with regard to the failure of the pilots to report?

A. I don't know if the captain superintendent has complained; I personally have complained and written to the captain superintendent about it; what he does afterwards is none of my business.

Q. The Secretary of the Pilotage Commission will tell us whether or not any complaint was made to the commission about the matter?

A. That does not interest me; I write to the Captain Superintendent and I am finished.

Q. You don't think it is any part of your duty to see the regulations are carried out?

A. I can't go over the head of my superior officer.

Q. You throw the responsibility upon Captain Pasco?

A. He was not here at the time.

Q. On whom do you throw the responsibility?

A. The superintendent at the time, Captain Martin.

Q. He was over you?

A. Yes.[33]

By implicating his superior, Wyatt had put himself beyond the pale. Burchell pursued him relentlessly to underscore the contradictions and drive the point home:

Q. I take it on the morning of the collision that you are the one man who was responsible for the traffic regulations in Halifax Harbour?

A. Yes.

Q. And I take it that since the 6th December and to the present time you also are the man responsible for the traffic regulations in Halifax harbour? Is that right?

A. No, I won't accept that responsibility; I am acting under orders to do such and such things and I am not the harbour master of this harbour.[34]

It was a tense moment. While it appeared to offer a route to personal salvation for Commander Wyatt, it also served to underscore the apparent disarray of the RCN in its management of Halifax Harbour. Burchell returned briefly to that governance, drawing Wyatt through the new measures brought into force since the disaster. He then sprang upon the preceding day's incident involving *Galileo,* using it to cast the navy in as unfavourable a light as possible. The hectoring continued for some time. Wyatt scored some minor points late in his testimony when Burchell tried unsuccessfully to bluff him about the presence of witnesses from the dockyard who could attest to his personal cowardice in the disaster's immediate aftermath. Burchell was for once forced to beat an embarrassed retreat in the face of Wyatt's indignant demands that counsel name these witnesses.[35] All in all, however, Burchell's cross-examination and tactics served to discredit the chief examining officer, cast him in a guilty light, and even make him appear haughty and ridiculous.

Burchell's allusions to the testimony of as yet unheard witnesses were not always bluffs. He told Wyatt he thought it fair to tell him he would introduce evidence from the secretary of the Pilot Commission and its clerk to show that they had attempted to conform to the regulations Wyatt had set out in May over reporting ships: "The pilots themselves tried to keep in touch with you and give you the information that you asked for and found it impossible to do so because they could not get in touch with you; then an arrangement was made in an attempt to carry out the order, that the clerk in the pilot office should be informed by the pilots when they were going to take a ship out and that the clerk in the office kept informing your office for some weeks giving the information."[36] Wyatt professed having no memory of these calls and claimed hearing only on occasion from individual pilots dealing with specific cases. Under Burchell's continued grilling about office hours and access to telephones, Wyatt recalled no specific instances of receiving calls from the clerk with sometimes lengthy lists of vessels.[37]

    Q. The clerk further tells me that after keeping up this practice of calling up your office and giving the names of these ships for six or seven weeks he found you were not taking the names down and, as he puts it, you were laughing at him at the other end of the telephone and then he discontinued the practice at the end of the six or seven weeks?

    A. He had a peculiar idea in his head.[38]

That afternoon, as a shaken Wyatt was finally allowed to stand down, he was replaced by James Creighton, the secretary of the Pilotage Commission. While the latter's testimony was vague and inconclusive from the standpoint of demonstrating that the commission was efficient and well controlled, it did reveal that Wyatt's orders had been posted for the information of the pilots and that the clerk had indeed reported movements to the Examination Office for some weeks. He had discontinued the practice when he sensed that the Examination Office was indifferent to the information. Since that unspecified time, no pilot had been cited or punished for disobedience of naval orders. The greatest sensation during Creighton's testimony stemmed from the revelation that the clerk was a mere lad of fifteen. In later testimony, young Edward Beazley confirmed that he had indeed been making the daily reports but had felt the information was not being taken down and that he was being laughed at by the examination staff. He had not informed Creighton or the pilots that he was no longer making the calls to the office, and that was where matters had stood from that time.[39] Thus, Burchell could confidently conclude that, despite his angry denials to the contrary, Wyatt's orders to the pilots were something of a "dead letter."[40]

The issue of traffic control had become a serious concern for the inquiry. Clearly the relationship between naval officials and the Pilotage Commission was dysfunctional, and every appearance suggested that traffic was not being managed responsibly or efficiently. As the session of 24 January continued, that impression heightened exponentially when George R. Smith, an official of the local shipping firm Pickford and Black, who had acted as agent for *Imo* while she was in port, took the stand. His information was most disquieting. According to Smith, on the evening of 5 December he had received a telephone call purporting to be from the Examination Office. The caller, after asking about the destination of a Danish ship in the port, then inquired whether *Imo* had yet sailed. Smith informed him that she would be leaving in the morning. The implications were stunning: had Wyatt perjured himself?[41]

The day did not close without another event reinforcing public distrust of the navy. While the court had been in session that morning, Mayor Martin of Halifax and the president of the Board of Trade, Dugald MacGillivray, had paid a visit to the Ocean Terminals, where *Picton* was berthed. The two were upset with the apparent lack of fire precautions they found where the ammunition was being unloaded. Their letters of protest to Major-General Thomas Benson and Captain Fred Pasco cited fire hoses locked up 200 feet from the hydrants, no firemen in attendance, insufficient sentries at the pier, and a "blazing" tar pot in the immediate vicinity. "Under these circumstances," Martin wrote to Pasco, "we cannot feel assured that sufficient safeguards will always surround the handling of munitions and therefore must object to the loading or unloading of explosives altogether at any pier in the City."[42]

The fallout from the day's events was considerable. Not surprisingly, William Henry's billing records show that he had two meetings with Commander Wyatt over his evidence and the evidence of George Smith, with a view to recalling the chief examining officer and his assistants as witnesses. Henry also had a lengthy conference with Captain Pasco that evening as to the advisability of his being re-examined. The Crown counsel had learned that Captain Edward Martin had returned from his mission to England and would be arriving in Halifax the following day. He and Pasco discussed whether Martin should also be called to the stand. Henry then went to Judge Drysdale's residence to discuss "the matters referred to by Capt. Pasco and taking the Judge's instructions thereon." Drysdale ultimately decided that there was no need to bring Pasco back to the stand, nor would it be necessary for Martin to be examined. Although his reasons for this decision were not recorded, Drysdale may have been trying to turn the focus of the inquiry away from the less material issue of traffic control and back onto the facts of the collision. This would prove impossible.[43]

Despite news of a terrible mining catastrophe at Stellarton, Nova Scotia, in which more than eighty-five miners perished, the banner "Startling Evidence Before Judge Drysdale's Commission" shared the front page of the *Halifax Herald* on 25 January. Much was made of the revelation that a fifteen-year-old boy had been responsible for the pilot reports and that Frederick Wyatt had taken no special precautions with respect to the *Mont Blanc*, even though he had known the dangerous nature of her cargo. The passing of *Galileo* and the oil tanker in the harbour "Within a Stone's Throw of the Mont Blanc–Imo Tragedy" was played up and sarcasm heaped on the navy's abilities to enforce the new traffic rules. The paper called for the immediate appointment of a royal commission to investigate the "Astounding Pilotage Conditions at Halifax" and renewed demands to retire Walter Hose from the inquiry. But most of the malice was aimed at Wyatt. The inferences of "incompetence," "inefficiency," "bungling," "impotency," and "pigheadedness" arising from the cross-examinations of Burchell and others, and from the testimony of other new witnesses, were granted the status of fact in the next two days' issues. Indeed, the issue for 26 January referred to "Further Agonizing Revelations of Naval, Harbour, and Pilot Mismanagement." The rhetoric had become so strong that even Justice Drysdale was moved to record his objections when court reconvened on the morning of 26 January.[44] "I desire to say to those who are reporting for the press that very improper statements are being made; the evidence is not being reported fairly and properly; misleading statements are given to the public as evidence … I will have to take some steps to prevent the public being excited over a thing like that when it was not in fact stated."[45]

The most emphatic demand from the *Herald*'s banners of 25 January had been "That Commander Wyatt Shall Not Continue Another Hour in Charge of Halifax Harbour."[46] Before it had appeared in print, Senator William Dennis had already telegraphed the prime minister: "In order allay public feeling, strongly urge that Commander Wyatt be immediately suspended from command of Harbour: evidence fully justifies suspension pending findings of Court."[47] Few disagreed. City officials in Dartmouth also lodged a protest with Borden, demanding the "instant appointment" of a "competent official" to control the traffic in Halifax Harbour.[48]

CAPTAIN FRED PASCO HAD A LOT ON HIS PLATE the morning after the unhappy events of 24 January. Admiral Kingsmill and C.C. Ballantyne in Ottawa were demanding to know what had gone wrong with *Galileo*.[49] Pasco also had to investigate and deal with the latest expression of continuing public obsession over *Picton*. Last, but not least, was the performance in and out of court of Frederick Wyatt. On 23 January, Pasco had written to the chief examining officer for an explanation of the latest incident involving *Galileo*.[50] When Burchell grilled him on the stand the following day, Wyatt had claimed only vague knowledge of the episode, acknowledging simply that he had received a letter on the subject, probably the note from Pasco.[51] In reply to Pasco's missive, Wyatt had submitted a bland and misleading statement that the last ship in the convoy had sailed on the morning of the 23rd, before the *Appalache* and other incoming ships had been allowed to proceed. He omitted any mention of *Galileo,* instead asking Pasco that "in justice to myself, I be given the name of the person who gave you this misinformation."[52] As far as Pasco was concerned, this final display of arrogance and prevarication sealed Wyatt's fate.

Pasco must have felt he was dwelling in a house of cards in a strong breeze. Putting first things first, however, he ordered Commanders Holloway and Holme to the Ocean Terminals to inspect the safety measures in effect around *Picton* and the surrounding docks. They found the mayor's claims much exaggerated. Indeed, as Pasco immediately telegraphed Admiral Kingsmill, what Holloway and Holme observed on the scene "entirely" contradicted the mayor's statement.[53] Pasco acknowledged that a lengthy and comprehensive report had to be prepared as the basis for an equally long open letter that same day to the City of Halifax, explaining the measures to ensure the safety of *Picton* in minute detail. In his letter, Pasco informed the mayor that his concerns would be put before the authorities in Ottawa. He nonetheless asked him to accept his personal assurances that *Picton* was safe and to convey these to the citizens of the city.[54]

Hoping that the investigation and letter would end the controversy over *Picton,* Pasco then tried to address the concerns in Ottawa over *Galileo.* The incident was too complicated to explain in a telegram, so Pasco briefly informed Kingsmill that the problem had stemmed from the ship not sailing as scheduled with the convoy, saving the details for a longer letter.[55] Then, turning his attention to Commander Frederick Wyatt, Pasco asked Kingsmill for authority to suspend him from duty "in view of unsatisfactory control of Traffic generally ... culminating in most unsatisfactory report on crossing of two vessels in Narrows Jan. 23rd."[56]

Sharp words were undoubtedly exchanged the next day between the captain superintendent and his disgraced chief examining officer. Although there is no record of the conversation, Wyatt produced a laboriously hand-written defence. In it, he indicated that Captain Turnbull had informed him that *Galileo* had been delayed and must depart quickly to catch up with her convoy. Wyatt claimed Turnbull had said "something about taking a chance," which Wyatt was unprepared to do. Nonetheless, he left it to Turnbull to make arrangements with Mate Roland Iceton. Beyond this, Wyatt claimed to know "nothing of the matter of these two ships crossing."[57]

Ultimately, after receiving a secret telegram from Admiral Kingsmill on 26 January, of which no copies were made, Pasco took the decision to suspend Wyatt as his own. He specified that the action had been taken only because Wyatt had not informed the captain superintendent of the circumstances of the *Galileo* incident and, despite any perception to the contrary, that it was "irrespective of matters pertaining to present enquiry."[58]

As Pasco took his decision, *Galileo* was again in the press, this time as a result of the previous day's testimony of Mate Iceton at the inquiry. Most of the questions posed had dealt not with the Halifax explosion but with the *Galileo* incident. Iceton's generally lucid account both set out the conflicting needs that had led to the botched signal and the circumstances of the subsequent safe passage of the two ships in the stream. He also corroborated Wyatt's claims that, at the time of the explosion, requirements for pilots to report ship movements were being routinely ignored. The latter was the basis of the *Halifax Herald*'s next banner headline. The *Herald* also reported a conflict with the evidence of George Smith. Iceton had been alone in the Examination Office on the evening of 5 December at the time Smith said he had been telephoned about the *Imo*. Iceton testified that he had made no such call to the offices of Pickford and Black that evening. Burchell did his best to impeach the young man's knowledge, experience, and integrity, comparing him unfavourably with the respectable Mr Smith.[59]

On 26 January, Captain Edward Martin unexpectedly took the stand to answer questions on harbour control and naval administration. This appearance gave the public its first inkling that Martin was no longer serving in Halifax. It became clear from Crown counsel's initial series of questions that Martin had returned only the previous day, had not yet taken over as captain superintendent, and would be "going away from Halifax" in two days for "an indefinite period."[60] There was no explanation of the reason for his departure or of the reversal in the court's decision that he would not be called. But without doubt the latter was at the insistence of representative counsel and the nautical assessors. Indeed, after Henry turned Martin over to their "tender mercies," they grilled him for a considerable time.[61]

Most of the questioning of the former captain superintendent was along familiar lines and offered general assurances and nautical truths that do not bear further repeating. Still it need be noted that, before Crown counsel completed his opening series of regulatory, procedural, and other questions, he also carefully broached a consideration of fundamental concern.

Q. Was it considered necessary, Captain Martin, that in the harbour regulations provision should be made for the possible infringement of the rules of navigation – make provision based upon the happening of a collision in Halifax Harbour occurring in defiance of the rules of navigation?

A. You mean that if we had to alter the rule of the road – the ordinary rule of the road?

Q. No; but as I understand it there are certain indefinite International rules of navigation laid down?

A. Yes sir.

Q. In preparing the regulations for the Port of Halifax, did you contemplate that those rules would be observed, or that those rules would likely be broken?

A. Oh no, observed.

Q. It has been suggested that precautions should have been taken in traffic regulations in Halifax Harbour, in view of the fact that there was almost another collision occurring in the narrows – do you think that was a thing the harbour regulations should have provided against?

A. I don't see when there are set rules which every seaman knows, why I should make rules for one little corner which would only mix him up.[62]

The remarks received little attention in the press reports. Even the generally reliable *Morning Chronicle* was selective in the way it presented the testimony. While the *Chronicle*'s account was accurate enough from the standpoint of detail, the editor yielded to the journalistic instinct to play up the more controversial aspects of public concern at the expense of mundane evidence more related to the original purpose of the inquiry. If mentioned at all, such detail was buried deep in the small print. According to the paper, Martin acknowledged that, had he still been in command at Halifax on 6 December, he would have regarded *Mont Blanc*'s arrival as "an exceptional circumstance." As the headline proclaimed, he would have given the ship "a clear passage or else anchored her." Nothing was made of Martin's amplifying remarks that no special measures were needed for most ships carrying ammunition.[63]

The *Chronicle* account noted that Martin had informed the court that he had not been aware of any difficulty in getting pilots to report to the chief examining officer. When William Henry showed him the three letters Wyatt claimed to have submitted, Martin could not confirm having received them "without going over my files." The *Chronicle* printed the text of all three letters. "I am almost certain that I should have taken action on a letter like this," Martin testified, holding in his hand what was presumably the third letter, in which Wyatt had abjured responsibility for any future accident. The former captain superintendent agreed to Henry's request that his secretary would search the files for the letters.[64]

Nova Scotia's Crown prosecutor, Andrew Cluney, followed up Commander Wyatt's stated disclaimer that he had no knowledge of whether pilots were punished. Captain Martin was also rather unhelpful on the matter. As Cluney probed rather insistently for specifics on naval regulations for Halifax as they applied to the pilots, the captain outlined how these had been drafted before the war and then "filled in as circumstances have occurred since the war." The directive of May 1917 concerning pilotage was an example. What would Martin – who conceded he had been aware of "trouble about the pilots" – do if there were continuing difficulties with them not obeying the instructions? Martin vaguely acknowledged that if "all things failed" he would consider it his duty to "go to Ottawa" to resolve any problem. Pressed further for specific instances of pilots disregarding naval instructions, Martin could not remember when he might have first been aware of any problem. Exasperated by several failed efforts to coax specifics out of him, Cluney finally bluntly asked:

Q. Did you or did you not, as a matter of fact, make any complaint to Ottawa about the way the pilots were ignoring the regulations?

A. I have.

Q. That complaint is in writing?

A. Yes.

Q. Could you produce it?

A. Yes, there is a case there notably of a ship being brought in here. We took precautions by letter and also by phone to give notice to bring the ship to another place.[65]

Martin continued to ramble vaguely as Cluney repeatedly tried to spark his memory. Finally, Martin spoke of the need for cooperation, as some authority(ies) he did not name had seemingly decided early on that the objective was not as much to have the pilots "seek us out and report to us like in an ordinary military sense" as it was "to communicate generally, to get into communication." By implication, the May 1917 directive, "was not an order – it was more to cooperate."

Q. And they [the pilots] were in no way subject to the Naval Discipline – they were not as an auxiliary force in any way?

A. No sir, we got a ruling on that from Ottawa.[66]

This last statement was extremely germane in that it implied direction from above not to stir up any controversy over the pilotage, but Cluney did not pursue it directly. Rather, he alluded to the recent *Galileo* incident, which Captain Martin had not heard of since his return. The response was telling, but, like the remark about Ottawa, Cluney let it pass.

Q. Have you any suggestion to make to the Court, Captain, by which the omission or the negligence, or carelessness of the pilots in obeying the orders from the Chief Examining officer, or yourself, or from any other officer of the Naval Service Department at Halifax, could be carried out or enforced under the existing conditions?

A. That is to say that if I had a complaint so serious that I should consider it necessary for this pilot never to be used for the period of the war, could I have it done – have I the power -

Q. I am not asking if you had the power – can you suggest any means by which those orders can be enforced?

A. No.

Q. Under existing conditions?

A. No.

Q. Then you will agree with what Commander Wyatt says, that the carrying out of these orders about taking ships from their anchorage, on the part of the pilots, is a matter over which you cannot exercise any control any more than giving an order, and if it is not obeyed you have no remedy?

A. No, we look to the Commission.

Q. And you depend on the pilot to carry that out – carry out that order?

A. Yes sir.

Q. And if they don't carry it out you are helpless?

A. Except by the patrol boat, fire the gun and ... take charge of the ship.[67]

Unfortunately, Cluney did not pursue these statements to ask Captain Martin why "Ottawa" had apparently ruled against any sanction of individual pilots by the RCN. When Cluney had finished, Captain Louis Demers returned to the subject of the three letters attributed to Wyatt, particularly the most recent, which had been "very strongly worded to my mind." Captain Demers read the letter out, then asked:

Q. This letter should awake your attention, or the attention of a superior officer – in connection with this letter can you remember whether you have taken any steps to meet it?

A. No. I cannot.

Q. Your letters which you are going to produce by searching your file will show that?

A. Yes, otherwise I cannot understand if the matter was so serious which this officer, should not have reminded me sooner, in case I had forgotten it, and not wait until August, and from then leave it until September 15th. I cannot think that these letters were not answered.

Q. Is it permissible for a subordinate to make any suggestions to a superior officer?

A. Yes.

Q. Has Commander Wyatt at any time made any suggestion to you about the traffic regulations?

A. Yes sir.

Q. Were those letters filed?

A. Yes.[68]

The *Chronicle*'s report did not seize upon this ambiguous implication of serious communication problems in the naval chain of command, but it accurately quoted Demers's questions as to character and reputation.

Q. Commander Wyatt comes under your direct control and supervision?

A. Yes.

Q. Have you had any cause to complain of his attention to duty in the past?

A. I have I think once – whatever it was.

Q. Serious?

A. No.

Q. Trivial?

A. Something.

Q. Was there a warning issued to him?

A. Yes sir, a warning issued to him by the Director of the Naval Service.

Q. Will you have a copy of that on your files?

A. No, it was personally I think.

Q. It was on the strength of a letter written by you to Ottawa?

A. No, verbal report on his visit. It was not a thing that was necessary to be taken up at once. I really forget what it was.

Q. Nothing about the Service?

A. Yes it was to a certain extent.[69]

This exchange may have been in reference to Wyatt's marital situation. Prior to the catastrophe in Halifax, a letter to the Naval Department from a law firm in London revealed that Wyatt had a divorced wife and a child in England. While Wyatt's remarriage to a woman in Halifax was legal, the letter alleged that he had not met the financial obligations imposed by the divorce decree and that his family in England was destitute. In 1917, of course, divorce was rare and ungentlemanly comportment, especially for people in Wyatt's position. Admiral Kingsmill made it clear to the CXO in a personal letter that he viewed this behaviour on the part of an officer of the Canadian naval service "with grave displeasure." Wyatt naturally had promised to set things right and offered a rational explanation of the misunderstanding, mentioning a letter, "unfortunately not kept," from his ex-wife stating "she had not need of funds."[70] This scandal would be of little consequence today, but in 1917 it would have raised doubts about an individual's character and reliability. It might also leave that individual feeling bitter and defensive. Moveover, in the light of Wyatt's actions during the aftermath of the explosion, the situation could be interpreted as a characteristic evasion of responsibility followed by a self-serving defence.

In any case, Demers did not probe further into the question, and no other counsel took up the chase, leaving the matter as it stood, faithfully reported by the *Chronicle*. Martin's vague remarks were nevertheless something less than a ringing endorsement of his subordinate, and indisputably suggested some undisclosed but unsavoury aspect to the character of the chief examining officer. Wyatt's credibility took some further blows towards the end of Captain Martin's cross-examination. Burchell had the witness confirm that naval authorities had wanted information from the pilots only for purposes of record and to regulate traffic through the "gate." The intention of the order had not been to govern traffic in the Narrows.

> Q. The evidence we have now is that for some weeks prior to the 6th of December, probably some months prior, the pilots had not been reporting when they were taking ships out – that being so, and the chief examining officer knowing that he was not getting any reports from pilots, if he wanted to stop the traffic on the morning of the collision the down coming traffic, the proper thing for him to do would be to telephone the Guard Ship not to let any ships come out of the Basin while the Mont Blanc was on her way up?
>
> A. Yes.[71]

Cross-examination by William Henry secured Martin's opinion that, given the events that had delayed *Imo*'s departure from Halifax, it would have been "only fair" for the pilot to have notified the Examination Office that she was not going to sail on the evening of 5 December.[72] The weight of that opinion was soon undermined, however. Captain Demers, who posed the final questions to Martin, followed up Burchell's line of questioning. Ultimately, Captain Martin agreed that, despite any difficulties that the CXO might have had in getting information from the pilots, other adequate means were available to determine the sailing status of ships. Had Frederick Wyatt wanted to know if *Imo* had sailed, he could have had the information from the secretary of the pilots' office.[73]

The completion of Martin's testimony left the idea that *Imo* had been cleared to sail on 5 December but had not done so. Despite the delay, Wyatt had not seen fit to exercise any initiative over the ship's future movements. It was clear that the naval authorities had long since discarded the notion that intense monitoring was necessary or even desirable in a port where it was considered reasonable to expect that the normal rules of the road would be obeyed by all.

In its customary sensationalist report of the day's happenings, the *Halifax Herald* played up remarks by Judge Drysdale that the inconsistencies between Martin's and Wyatt's recollections of the controversial letters required resolution and that Wyatt should be re-examined the following week. The *Herald* confidently predicted that the settlement of this conflict of evidence would "be one of the features" of ensuing proceedings.[74]

The public focus of the inquiry was now squarely upon the Royal Canadian Navy. The court did not sit on Sunday, 27 January, but William Henry's billing records suggest that the Crown counsel had a very busy day of rest. He had to prepare for the next day's testimony from Lieutenant Arthur Adams, RNVR, of the naval control staff aboard *Acadia*, on the procedures for clearing neutral shipping and from Captain George Eldridge, the naval staff officer aboard *Niobe*, who would describe the details of the routing of ships and his office's working relationship with the Examination Office. Despite the matters left hanging from Captain Martin's testimony, the former dockyard superintendent was still inexplicably required in Ottawa "immediately"; he would depart the next day. Henry had one last opportunity to confer with him at length over the search for the originals or copies of Commander Wyatt's letters, after which the lawyer went on to another lengthy meeting on the same subject with Richard Price, the captain superintendent's secretary. The search would have been impeded by the death in the explosion of *Niobe*'s head writer, Chief Petty Officer William Morgan, and the wrecking of the ship's office. Finally, Henry had a long session with a despondent Commander Wyatt, "arranging for him to attend for further examination and discussing matters upon which he is to be further interrogated." Henry also spent several hours perusing the evidence so far taken, as Judge Drysdale had asked him to prepare a "summing up" for the assistance of the court, to supplement the presentations that would be made by other attending counsel after all testimony had been completed.[75]

Quite a few witnesses were on the docket for the last full day of testimony on 28 January. Lieutenant Adams and Captain Eldridge both provided satisfactory particulars of their responsibilities, which are of some interest from the standpoint of the workings of the port but passed uneventfully with respect to the determinations of the inquiry. Pilot Mackey and the chairman of the Pilotage Commission made brief encore appearances, and a customs officer took the stand to explain customs clearance procedures for neutral shipping.

When Richard Price appeared that morning, he revealed the results of his "thorough search" of the captain superintendent's office files and card indexes for evidence of Wyatt's letters. Nothing had been found beyond a few reports concerning specific incidents of pilots anchoring vessels in the wrong berths or damaging gates or wharves. The captain superintendent's secretary did acknowledge that a few loose papers in the dockyard office had been lost during the fire four weeks before the explosion and that more loose documents had been lost during the explosion, although the actual files had survived intact. Price had seen the contents of the alleged letters published in the *Chronicle*, but he could not recall having seen the documents themselves.[76] This was also the testimony of Charles McGannon, who had served for some time as writer in the Examination Office. After stating that he had not been ordered to type such correspondence, he acknowledged that Commander Wyatt frequently did typing himself, particularly if the matter were confidential.[77]

Wyatt returned to the stand with his character and credibility much in question. Few, it appeared, were willing to give him the benefit of the doubt. Henry quickly moved into the contentious issues. First, there was an accounting of the chief examining officer's whereabouts on the evening of 5 December, when George Smith of Pickford and Black had received the call about the status of *Imo*. Wyatt testified that he did not know Smith and that there had been no such call. Indeed, he could prove he had been at a colleague's wedding reception at the time in question. Further, he stated that he had received no information from naval control or intelligence officials about *Imo* and that he generally did not expect to receive any such information from these sources.[78]

Attention now turned to the letters. Wyatt was somewhat vague as to how they had been prepared. He

> ... would not swear as to who typed them, – probably this last one, which I consider a very important one, I probably would do that myself. It is not a thing I would wish my Writer to know about. I don't say I did but probably.
> Q. You have no recollection about it?
> A. It is a long time ago and many things have happened since then.[79]

Asked where he had retrieved the copies he had presented to the court, Wyatt stated they had been laying among a large collection of loose documents in his office on a shelf reserved for "Letters to Captain Superintendent ... Anybody could go in and take them away if they wanted to," he added.

> Q. Can you tell us Commander Wyatt, whether you had any personal interviews with the Captain Superintendent on the subject matter of these letters?

A. With regard to the last one sir, two or three days after, very shortly after, he ordered me to his office, about 10 or 10:30, and he handed me a sheet he had there – the Defence of the Realm – and he pointed out to me that in this regulation he showed me that he could not punish the pilots – this sheet was in reference to the Defence of the Realm.

Q. He showed you the sheet?

A. Yes sir, and we discussed on what we could do and he said he could not punish the pilots, – under that.

When Henry inquired whether he agreed with Martin's conclusion in this regard, Wyatt replied "That is beyond me to say."

Henry's questions continued:

Q. Is there anything else Commander Wyatt that you would like to speak about?

A. I would like to say that the last paragraph I put in there, in which I said I would not be responsible for any accident, was because for months and months I saw an accident, or collision was coming, and I could see there was somebody going to be made the goat for this and I did not wish to be made the goat – you can call it intuition or what you like; but that was my idea.[80]

It was the old salt Captain Demers, an official of the Canadian government, who pressed Wyatt most closely in the cross-examination. (For once, the combative Burchell had only brief questions on minor matters. Perhaps he felt that Wyatt's credibility had already been demolished.) The dominion wreck commissioner rightly focused on matters that seemed to imply a serious problem in the capacity of either Martin or Wyatt, if not both. When discussing Wyatt's letters and the powers under the Defence of the Realm regulations, Demers asked if any effort had been made, or specifically whether Wyatt had made any effort, to notify the Pilotage Commission "that if such and such a thing were not done something would happen?" "That was not up to me," Wyatt replied. Thus, presumably, he neither knew nor cared whether the commission followed up to make things safer. The revealing exchange that followed clearly established that Wyatt had long since lost either the power or the will to exercise initiative and that he was not receiving the necessary level of support and supervision from his superior officer. It is worth considering at length.

Q. You are the Examining Officer?

A. Yes sir.

Q. Does that admit that you are responsible for the traffic of the harbour?

A. No sir, I admit I have had to go down and shift ships which has not been done by the harbour master.

Q. For the knowledge of ships leaving, and keeping tab on the departure and arrival of ships?

A. Keeping tab on paper.

Q. Since the pilots could not be relied upon for that information what other steps did you adopt in order to protect you to see that you knew of ships arriving and leaving?

A. I had the gate vessel and also the examining ship.

Q. For vessels leaving Bedford Basin what information did you have other than from the pilots?

A. I had no means of telling when vessels were leaving the Basin.

Q. You assumed right away, without making any inquiries whatever from the Guard ship in Bedford Basin there was no ship sailing.

A. Yes sir, I saw there was nothing coming.

Q. Is it proper to take anything for granted? Personally you are a responsible man, and all these arrivals of vessels devolve upon you? Was it necessary for you to take extra precautions in view of the fact that pilots could not be depended on as being your only source of information?

A. I suppose it would have been necessary.

Q. You failed to do it?

A. I did not do it.

Q. Did you discuss these points with Captain Martin that in view of the attitude of the pilots, that they did not give you the information – did you devise or make any suggestion to him at all about other methods to him to be adopted?

A. No, I did not suggest to the Captain Superintendent. – I don't suggest to the Captain Superintendent.

Q. Are you permitted to suggest to your superior officers?

A. I would be permitted to suggest.

Q. Have you made any suggestions to Captain Martin at all since you have been in charge of the examination office?

A. Not by letter.

Q. Verbally?

A. I have often spoken to Captain Martin about things.

Q. Were your suggestions accepted in a good way, kind way?

A. That is why I don't suggest now, because I don't think my suggestions have ever been looked upon as worth anything.[81]

Poor Wyatt. He faced not only more tough questions from Captains Hose and Demers but also complaints of the seriousness of his charges against the pilots from Thomas Robertson, counsel for the Pilotage Commission. As the ordeal ended, he stood down humiliated, discredited, and seemingly ridiculous. In his fortnightly report to the Admiralty that day, Rear-Admiral Chambers observed that "the responsibility seems to have been very largely brought home to the Examination Officer, who is relieved of his post."[82]

One Haligonian who had not joined the condemnation against the RCN in Halifax was Crown counsel William Henry. Indeed, on 28 January, the day of Wyatt's last appearance on the stand, he had written Alex Johnston at the Ministry of Marine that he did "not consider that any negligence on the part of the Naval Service Department or any of its officers has been established. On the other hand the Pilotage System has been shown up rather badly, and much important evidence has been obtained."[83] This information would be valuable. On 25 January, C.C. Ballantyne had announced that a royal commission would be formed to investigate the Halifax pilotage system.[84]

On completion of Wyatt's testimony, Henry had another long evening. He wanted to recall the departed Captain Martin from Ottawa in one last attempt to resolve the impasse between his evidence and that given by Wyatt. After a long meeting with Pasco on the subject and an equally long visit to Judge Drysdale's home, Henry sought the assistance of Captain Eldridge in wiring Martin in code.[85]

> Secret for Captain Martin.
>
> Chief Examining Officer testified today Monday was sent for by you shortly after his letter to you of 15th September and discussed with you your powers over pilots under defence of realm regulations when you pointed out that you had no such power as claimed by him. He was sure you would remember this interview if called to your attention. Please wire if you have any recollections of it. Court anxious to give you opportunity to testify further if you so desire will you return for that purpose, if so when can you be here.[86]

Henry would not receive his reply until 31 January, too late to recall Martin as a witness. In any case, the response contained no hint that further testimony from Martin would have been to any effect: "Please tell W.A. Henry that I do not remember the conference which Commander Wyatt claimed to have had with me ... also that I have no further evidence to give, but could go to Halifax if deemed necessary. This information should be given to Mr. Henry without delay."[87]

On 29 January the court heard its last testimony, the brief questioning of the customs officer, and adjourned after Judge Drysdale set out the order in which counsel would present their summations and rebuttals. With a royal commission to investigate pilotage now announced, the judge confirmed during his remarks to the inquiry that he did not want to go into the pilotage system in Halifax other than as it had reference to the case at hand.[88]

The matter of Wyatt's letters remained unresolved, a fact seized upon by the *Herald*. The paper also had a field day with Wyatt's testimony to the effect that the disaster had been "no surprise to him."[89] Beyond press speculations and innuendo, many valid questions remain on these points. Was former Captain Superintendent Martin covering up his failure to heed the warnings from his subordinate? Had he exercised due and diligent command of the dockyard? Had Wyatt faked the letters in order to avoid being held responsible for his apparent incompetence in maintaining effective control over movement in the harbour, an impression seemingly confirmed by his relief from duty? In naval circles, there was also the question of Wyatt's evident disloyalty to his superior officer. This was highlighted by the clumsy way he seemed to have gone about making his concerns known and his apparent negligence in leaving the matter lie, in the face of the obvious difficulties involved in confronting an aloof and apparently unapproachable superior officer. Added to this was the matter of his personal life and the obvious stigma that had attached to his reputation with his seniors over his failure to provide for his divorced wife and his child in England. Perhaps the spectre of letters claimed "unfortunately not kept" concerning his honourable intentions in that quarter threw a shadow over alleged correspondence on the harbour control. It is almost without doubt that, in his somewhat vague testimony against Wyatt, Martin had been referring to the admonition from Admiral Kingsmill on the subject of Wyatt's divorce. Had these details become known, they would unquestionably have caused additional sensation and further influenced the court and the public against Wyatt.

Facing both public and professional opprobrium, on 29 January an embittered Commander Wyatt requested "release from any further service in the Naval Department of Canada." Alert, however, to the possibility that he could be the subject of criminal charges that would require his continued presence in Halifax, neither Pasco nor Kingsmill would countenance Wyatt's request until completion of the inquiry. The navy would risk no blame in the event he fled the scene.[90]

The adjournment of the court on 29 January coincided with another unfortunate event that again focused unwelcome attention on the Royal Canadian Navy. Despite all precautions and Fred Pasco's resolute assurances, a fire broke out that morning where *Picton*'s ammunition was still being offloaded and inspected in the new terminals. It was not much of a blaze. As Rear-Admiral Chambers found when he hurried to the scene, an undetected nodule of phosphorus had stuck to an ammunition case as it was removed from the ship. As the case was slid along to the examination table, the friction caused the substance to "burst into flame igniting a bundle of cordite sticks from a broken cartridge."[91] Two of the workers maintained their composure and dashed for a nearby fire extinguisher. They were able to subdue the blaze in a matter of moments, before the arrival of the Halifax Fire Department. However, others on the scene had panicked and fled. The alarm quickly spread. Schools in the South End were evacuated and others again fled their homes. Halifax officials and the media were furious, and the wave of indignation crested in the offices of Sir Robert Borden and Ministers Ballantyne and Reid that same day. Pasco's repeated assurances that there had been no danger fell on deaf ears, and he was ordered to have *Picton* removed from the area forthwith.[92]

The *Morning Chronicle* was scathing in its lead editorial on the incident. The navy did not understand the situation they were dealing with.

> There must be no more "hap-hazard" methods in the all-important matter of the protection of life and property, and those in authority must be made to understand that the people are in no mood to tolerate incompetence or delay in establishing the most complete and effective system of safeguards. The military authorities, we notice, are much exercised over the fact that the schools were ordered to dismiss their pupils when the alarm of fire spread yesterday morning and are eager to "run down" the person who sent out this warning. Let them not waste their precious efforts over this. However desirable it may be to check

the spread of alarmist reports, they have other and more important work to do. They cannot plead a shortage of manpower – at least not in officers.[93]

Influenced by press reports and editorials on the inquiry itself as well as on events such as the latest incident on the *Picton,* the public had largely reached its own conclusions on the matter of responsibility for the Halifax explosion. As the court prepared for two days of summation by counsel – 30 and 31 January – before the members retired to consider their decision, it remained to be seen if the judgment would confirm these conclusions or risk the arousal of further public indignation.

With much at stake, the *Herald*'s attacks on the naval service intensified. The 30 January edition led with a headline, "Naval Service Housecleaning Is Expected Here." The story was datelined from Ottawa.

> Sensational disclosures in connection with the administration of the port of Halifax before the Drysdale commission has [sic] aroused considerable uneasiness in government circles here. There is a strong feeling that such extraordinary laxity and apathy as the evidence seems to disclose could not possibly have existed under any reasonably efficient system of port administration *and whereas a few weeks ago there seemed to be a disposition to whitewash naval officials, there is now strong determination that the cause of the disaster be probed to the bottom and responsibility squarely fixed regardless of who is hit in the process.*[94]

The story continued with a personal attack on Senator Dennis's old nemesis, Admiral Kingsmill. "The truth is that Ottawa does not take Admiral Kingsmill any too seriously. He is jokingly referred to as the man who was created an admiral for losing a ship, is more famous in the capital for his social than for his naval exploits, and the knighthood recently conferred upon him is mostly regarded as one of those insoluble mysteries which every now and again baffle the ingenuity of the public mind."[95]

Dennis apparently had some inside information at hand. The next day, as counsel continued their summations, his paper claimed that there had been a "remarkable change" in attitudes in Ottawa, that certain cabinet ministers had been "staggered" by the revelations in testimony, and that the prime minister himself, who had been following matters closely, had "personally intervened."[96]

> There are rumours that there may be a complete reorganization of the naval department at Ottawa, but it is hardly likely that anything will be done until the

findings of the Drysdale commission are received. The feeling here is that there is "too much Pomposity and too little Efficiency" among certain naval officers in Ottawa. Deputy Minister of Naval Affairs Desbarats is admitted to be a competent official, tho, of course, he is a civilian and consequently lacking in naval experience. Commander Stevens, naval chief of staff, is spoken highly of as an efficient officer. Admiral Kingsmill, however, is not generally accepted as possessing the qualifications essential to the important post which he holds.[97]

These claims contained a kernel of truth – namely, that dominion officials had recognized the necessity for further appeasement of public opinion. Efforts from Ottawa to limit the political damage had been proceeding apace since just before the inquiry had reconvened on 21 January. Indeed, C.C. Ballantyne had become increasingly worried that a policy of simply defending his naval officials and waiting for the crisis to play itself out might not be enough. The criticism of Walter Hose's presence on the inquiry panel had been weathered thanks to both Kingsmill's strong support of his professionalism and the captain of patrols' own solid performance in the court. Judge Drysdale later referred to Hose's presence as "invaluable" and "his industry a source of pleasure to me."[98]

The minister of marine and the naval service evidently made full use of Desbarats's continued absence in Washington in mid-January to solicit complete candour from Admiral Kingsmill with respect to potential chinks in the armour of the naval service. Kingsmill responded that

the importance of the Port of Halifax has increased so very much of late that I consider it would be advisable to make a change there. My decision has been strengthened of late by various things that have transpired since the disastrous explosion of December 6th. The officer who at present holds the appointment is Captain E.H. Martin, R.N.

Captain Martin has held this appointment for some seven or eight years, which is I consider too long for efficiency.

I visited Halifax in October last and found that things were not running very smoothly.[99]

Kingsmill did not detail the nature of the problems with Martin. Many factors could have been involved: an uneasy personal relationship with the director of the naval service, the stress and fatigue of the fifty-eight-year-old captain, or simply a not altogether successful transformation of a prewar sinecure into a post of vital responsibility in a critical port. Certainly the loss of Captain Martin's wife during the early years of the war must have been a particularly serious burden to his spirit.[100] Be that as it may, after his visit, Kingsmill had quietly extracted the captain superintendent from the scene for a time, with a mission to take charge of important secret despatches to British Columbia. He had hoped Martin "would benefit by the change." In the same spirit, Martin had been chosen for the more important mission to England upon which he had been engaged when the tragedy occurred.[101]

For some time before the explosion, Kingsmill had been entertaining the possibility of Martin exchanging assignments with Vice-Admiral Oswald Story, RN (Ret.), the captain superintendent of the Esquimalt dockyard. Story, who had settled in Canada after leaving the Royal Navy, had taken over at Esquimalt in October 1914 and had been credited with solving problems of initial confusion and disorder in civil-military relations and in establishing a smooth administration. As Michael Hadley and Roger Sarty have established, the exchange would have nicely finessed the problem posed in the summer of 1917 by the appearance of Rear-Admiral Chambers on Canada's east coast – making Vice-Admiral Story the ranking naval officer. Unfortunately, Story was also senior – by virtue of time in rank – to the British vice-admiral (M.C. Browning) who from Bermuda directed RN operations in North American and West Indian waters. Such distinctions being the source of infinite difficulties among officers, nothing further had been done. As Kingsmill now observed in his recommendation to Ballantyne, the RN's regional command had recently changed to a vice-admiral of greater seniority (W.L. Grant). Thus a change between the two Canadian dockyard commands could again be contemplated, and "this would seem to be the proper moment."[102]

Yet Ottawa was sensitive to the fact that the public announcement of a change of command in Halifax would surely be taken as confirmation that the naval administration of the port had indeed been unsatisfactory. As well, despite the obvious merits of replacing Martin, any such move before the conclusion of the inquiry might be prejudicial to fair findings. Instead, to protect Martin and to quietly keep him away from the Halifax dockyard and out of the public eye, other useful employment would be found for him in Ottawa. Martin would return only to give his evidence at the inquiry. Then he would again be whisked away to help organize the temporary removal of the Naval College to the premises of the Royal Military College of Canada in Kingston. No one could reasonably question the need for someone to act in place of the still disabled Commander E.A.E. Nixon of the Naval College, except perhaps Nixon himself. Kingsmill therefore felt obliged to explain the stratagem in order to ease the commander's mind: "You will hear of the appointment of Captain Martin for special duty at Headquarters in connection with the Naval College. This appointment does not interfere with your position in any way. It has been made so that the man in the street at Halifax should not consider Captain Martin as being relieved for any reason in connection with the late disaster or from anything that has transpired at the Enquiry."[103]

Frederick Wyatt's problems with the *Galileo* and the resulting uproar from Halifax upset Kingsmill's plan. By now the straight-shooting Ballantyne had quite had his fill of being made to look the fool, to both the public and, presumably, his cabinet colleagues, by the continuing ineptitude still emanating from the dockyard. He insisted that changes be made as soon as possible. Nevertheless, Ballantyne and Kingsmill agreed that these would be made in such a way as to give Senator Dennis and his cohorts the least possible satisfaction. This decision explains Pasco's earlier move to suspend Wyatt as chief examining officer on a disciplinary technicality based on the *Galileo* incident.

Before the end of January, then, Martin had readily accepted the proposal to exchange with Admiral Story. Other changes were planned as well.[104] Fred Pasco would eventually move to Saint John. The "well-liked" senior naval officer from that city, Commander Charles Stuart, RNR, reported immediately to the Halifax dockyard to take interim control of the Examination Service in place of the disgraced Wyatt. Stuart, who was promoted to captain, would then serve as assistant to the new captain superintendent, once Story had arrived.[105]

Having insisted on these changes, Ballantyne took a further hand in damage control, writing two personal letters to Dugald MacGillivray, president of the Halifax Board of Trade, on 29 January. Evidently the minister had given up on swaying local politicians; he chose instead to appeal directly to his fellow businessmen in the local commercial community. The first letter was a standard appeal for assistance in "allaying the fears of the citizens that every precaution is not being taken," even though he acknowledged that the administration of the port by Canadian naval authorities had not been "absolutely perfect." Still, he countered somewhat lamely, he believed it to be the best compared with other ports in Canada.[106] The second was an unusually frank and detailed disclosure of the entire *Galileo* incident, explaining it largely as a result of Commander Wyatt's appearance in court and his mind being "no doubt much occupied by the evidence that he was going to give." Although there had been no danger, Wyatt had been suspended because of his failure to make suitable arrangements to ensure that, in his absence, the situation was handled in accordance with the new regulations. That explained, Ballantyne informed MacGillivray of the transfers of both Stuart and Story and reminded him that Martin had been in England at the time of the explosion. Ballantyne closed with the usual assurances, welcomed any suggestions, and gave MacGillivray "perfect liberty" to make his letter public.[107]

Admiral Story's transfer from Esquimalt, "With Full Authority to Effect Necessary Changes," was the *Herald*'s feature item two days later, on 31 January. The story went on to speak of rumours of a general "shake up" in Ottawa as well. C.C. Ballantyne was congratulated, however, "on the evidence he has given that it is not his intention to be shackled by the bureaucratic system that seems to have fastened its tentacles around the department."[108]

The *Herald*'s report had appeared at another awkward moment for the Marine Department and the naval service. On that morning, the court was preparing for the last day of summation by counsel before it retired to consider its findings. As the closing scenes played out with Edward Martin now conveniently absent from the scene, Frederick Wyatt was the most visible manifestation of the navy's errant ways.

The entire first day of summations had been taken up by a remarkable *tour de force* on the part of Charles Burchell. He had gone to quite extraordinary lengths to speak to his brief, seemingly belabouring every point and nuance of the evidence that had been presented. At one point an increasingly frustrated Judge Drysdale interrupted him to request that he move along more quickly and stop reading from the evidence of witnesses. "State your point and tell us which witness you rely on."[109]

Perhaps surprisingly, in view of the histrionics that had accompanied his cross-examinations of some of the naval witnesses, Burchell now confined himself almost entirely to the physical circumstances of the collision, with little reference to the wider considerations that had so occupied public attention. Indeed, Wyatt escaped his attacks entirely. Rather, Burchell was particularly hard on Frank Mackey, *Mont Blanc*'s pilot, and on the "confusing and contradictory" evidence that had been presented by witnesses from *Mont Blanc*: "I say Pilot Mackey, all through the case, has been that kind of witness.

He would say for a minute anything that he could see that would help him immediately, acquiesce in any suggestion."[110]

Burchell accomplished much in portraying in a favourable light *Imo*'s somewhat questionable progress down the left side of the harbour, but he did not rely on the specifics of ship navigation alone. He also scored telling points with respect to the "special and dangerous" cargo that *Mont Blanc* had carried into the unsuspecting port, arguing that in such situations "the rules of good seamanship required the most extra and special care in navigating her narrow waters."[111]

When Humphrey Mellish finally received his chance to speak for *Mont Blanc* on 31 January, he also refrained from gratuitous attacks on the naval and marine authorities. It was a practice he had maintained throughout. Donald Kerr has characterized Mellish's performance in the court as low profile, lacklustre, almost timid, "and certainly not the vigorous performance one would have expected from counsel of that calibre."[112] Certainly Mellish did not share Burchell's penchant for aggressive tactics and polemic. His sub-dued manner may also have stemmed from his belief that the case for *Mont Blanc* rested on relatively solid ground and that the prejudicial state of pub-lic opinion over the behaviour of her crew mandated a straightforward and quiet argument that kept to the essentials of the matter. Such restraint also fitted his imminent appointment to a judgeship.

Throughout the inquiry, Mellish had seemed to attend Burchell's behav-iour with a quiet disbelief. In his summation, however, he chose to attack it vigorously, particularly Burchell's treatment of Frank Mackey:

> He has been openly and with dramatic intensity, and premeditated insult, been accused of perjury ... The bones of the departed have been drawn before him, and the tolling of the funeral bells have been brought to his attention, and he has been charged in the most direct, emphatic and insulting fashion of abus-ing his conscience and his oath, and I think it is only fair to say that this labour-ing of the mountain has resulted in the birth of a mouse, and that nothing has come of all these threats that have been made to this pilot, to discredit him by witnesses who were going to be called to prove he was a deliberate perjurer ... It is for the court to decide whether he is in the main telling the truth; but my learned friend said he was not frank with him. I will say that my learned friend did not treat him with respect, and in a manner that would suggest he himself was frank.[113]

When Thomas Robertson rose one last time to the hopeless task of restoring any faith in the reliability of the Pilotage Commission, he did not neglect to share as much of the blame as possible with the Royal Canadian Navy and Commander Frederick Wyatt. He argued that if the Pilotage Commission had ignored the May 1917 rules mandating that pilots inform Wyatt before allowing the movement of any ship in the harbour, they did so "with the knowledge of the Chief Examining Officer." For Robertson noted, "outgoing ships were not being reported to the Chief Examining Officer," a fact known to Wyatt, and possibly to Martin.[114]

Nova Scotia's Crown prosecutor had also saved some unpleasant comments with respect to the navy. Indeed, Andrew Cluney did not in any way address his remarks to the circumstances of the collision. His claim was to represent the public interest, and of course the vital matters that concerned the public were the circumstances surrounding the explosion and its disastrous consequences. Echoing the oft-printed reports in the *Herald*, Cluney observed that

> it would seem to be rather a peculiar fatality attended this whole transaction with regard to this ship: the loading of the ship; the sending of her to the port of Halifax; allowing her to enter loaded as she was; and the circumstances attending the bringing of her up the harbour; and allowing this other boat to leave the anchorage at Bedford Basin – I think that presents to this court such a series of blunders and acts of stupidity ... that it might not be difficult for the court with the evidence before it and on its findings to make representations to the proper authorities, whoever they may be, to safeguard and prevent a repetition of this occurrence.[115]

Perhaps it was straight political pandering, but he was saying what the public wanted to hear.

Cluney then began to apportion blame for this series of "blunders." Unfortunately for the navy, on the face of it, his assessment left little to challenge. Retracing the arrival in port of *Mont Blanc*, he reminded the court that "Captain" Wyatt permitted the French ship to enter, not knowing whether *Imo* was still in port. Yet he acknowledged "a divided responsibility, not direct perhaps, at that particular moment, but there is divided responsibility shared in by the pilots of the port of Halifax, Captain Martin, the superintendent of the Dockyard, and who was not here; I am bearing that in mind; and Commander Wyatt ... it has turned out there has been a lack of cohesion and cooperation between the pilots and the naval authorities; one independent of the other."[116]

If anyone was responsible for the loose state of affairs in the port, and regulations being routinely ignored by the pilots week after week, Cluney argued that it had to be Captain Martin. In outlining the requirements for a new captain superintendent, Cluney effectively criticized the performance of Martin himself. "The man who holds the position of Superintendent of the dockyard of this port," Cluney intoned, should keep himself "fully informed on everything going on; informed as to every subordinate officer or official under him; seeing that regulations affecting the pilots or auxiliary services connected with the shipping of this port ... are carried out and not ignored and let go in the hazardous sort of way as before December 6th."

That said, Cluney returned to Wyatt. Claiming that, on this subject, "the evidence speaks for itself," Cluney said, "I have this observation to make; if there is one individual more than another who is responsible for the ship being in the harbour on the 6th December, it is, I think it cannot be said it was any other than Commander Wyatt."[117]

In legal argument there is evidently much difference between saying nothing and saying little, for Cluney carried on for some time yet concerning the responsibilities of Martin and Wyatt, the differences in their evidence, and systemic problems in the working of the port. Cluney claimed that, despite the assurances of the minister of marine, these problems continued still, thus bringing to mind the farces played out with *Galileo* and *Picton*. Finally, before taking his seat, he presented an eloquent argument on behalf of the safety of lives and property in Halifax in which he suggested removing, as much as possible, the handling and storage of ammunition and explosives from the vicinity of the city.[118]

The last attorney to speak before the inquiry adjourned was William Henry. Although Crown counsel did not usually provide summations in marine cases, it will be remembered that Judge Drysdale had asked him to provide the court with a final "summing up" from his own viewpoint, dealing with any and all aspects of the evidence. Somehow, despite the charged emotional atmosphere, he also realized that he would have to make use of this opportunity to endeavour to restore a much needed sense of perspective to the proceedings. As he explained in his opening remarks, the obligation of speaking his own mind now was a matter he approached with some diffidence, having been left free by both the government and Judge Drysdale to control the conduct and presentation of the investigation through the calling and questioning of the witnesses. He prefaced his remarks by observing that "after 30 years active advocacy in the courts I anticipate a certain amount of difficulty in keeping my remarks in the limits of strict neutrality, and if it should happen in the course of my remarks I may be seen to be departing from it, I wish to assure you I am actuated with only one motive, to present the facts as accurately as I can and assist the court as far as lies in my humble power in arriving at the correct conclusion I have no doubt they will arrive at."[119]

Before addressing the case before the court, Henry spent several minutes rebutting Cluney's emotional remarks over continuing conditions of public risk in the port by placing on record complete details of the *Picton*'s controversial career in the harbour. Henry argued that the work of offloading the ammunition at the new terminals had been essential, that the risk to life and limb had been minimal, and that the navy had ensured practical safeguards were in place. However accurate his assessment, Henry was no doubt wasting his time in proffering it: public opinion was beyond being soothed by practical assurances.

Henry then went over the matter of the collision with detailed analysis of witnesses and corroborating testimony and attempts to account for circumstances of movement. It is of interest to note that, of the two stories told by the ships' crews, Henry found the testimony from *Mont Blanc* more consistent and reasonable. It was, he argued, borne out with a greater degree of corroboration from external witnesses on matters of speeds and signals. Of the external witnesses who had appeared, Henry felt Mate Herbert Whitehead of *CD-73* to be the most credible by virtue of his placement at the time and his nautical expertise and character.

Considering the overall weight of evidence, Henry thought that, under the circumstances, *Imo*'s presence on the Dartmouth side of the harbour could not be justified. Moreover, given the "prolonged rending crash" Whitehead had described, Henry thought it probable *Imo* was moving at a speed of as much as six knots – above the speed limit for the harbour – when the collision occurred. He was particularly struck that, despite *Imo*'s being lightly laden, the force of her impact was enough to turn the heavily loaded *Mont Blanc* through four points of the compass.[120] The "pinch of the case," however, was before his Lordship and the assessors. Despite his own opinions, Henry did not think it proper for him to say "whether I think the facts at the moment preceding the collision did or did not justify the departure from the rule[s of the road]."[121] Henry also argued that whether or not *Mont Blanc's* cargo should have been directed to Halifax was a moot point beyond the province of the court but one that should perhaps be addressed by the Allied powers. Regardless, he insisted, it was not the fault of the Canadian naval service.[122]

The attacks on the RCN and its officers in both the court and the press had been particularly disturbing to Henry. What should have been something of a side issue had become the apparent centrepiece of the inquiry, highlighted by the continuing episodes of ostensible ineptitude in the harbour and the unresolved differences in the testimony of Captain Martin and Commander Wyatt. Martin had managed to slip away from the scene. Admiral Kingsmill had despatched a last-minute telegram on the day of the captain's testimony advising that he should remain until assured that the court had no further need of him, but it had not arrived in time to prevent his departure.[123] Delayed communications also prevented the former captain superintendent from responding in time to Henry's request for further testimony, although Martin's eventual reply suggested he had nothing new to offer, with no memory of the meeting Wyatt claimed they had had. Martin's convenient lapse of memory left the situation an unresolved embarrassment. How could Henry explain the continued disparity between the accounts of Wyatt and Martin? How to restore perspective to the inquiry?

As he moved forward from a discussion of technical aspects of the explosion, Henry focused on the much flogged question of what Commander Wyatt had known about the nature of *Mont Blanc's* cargo. Henry noted that "Commander Wyatt has been severely criticised not only by Counsel – Mr. Cluney who represents the government of Nova Scotia, but very severely criticised in the press, because he didn't take any special precautions in regard to this ship. The first observation that it occurs to me to make in that connection is that he was not required by the regulations to make it. He did not make the regulations. He had not power to alter them."[124]

Henry then took up the somewhat more challenging problem of Wyatt's admission that, had he known *Imo* had not yet sailed, he might have made arrangements so that the ships would not have passed in the harbour. This Henry dismissed as Wyatt speaking with hindsight after the tragedy. In reality, it would have been entirely reasonable if, at the time, he had said to himself, there is no reason to apprehend danger to this vessel, the harbour is wide, she is not going up until daylight in the morning, I will keep her there tonight and when we open the gates in the morning it will be broad daylight: there was no reason to anticipate any particular danger: let her go up. I say the concurrence of the naval opinion we have had before this court on that subject is if he had done that, even with the knowledge there were other ships likely to come down, he would not have to be censured, it was [a] perfectly proper thing for a naval officer to do nothing – the harbour was guarded by regulations – rules of the road which would make it absolutely impossible if they were observed as he had every right to suppose they would be.

Henry continued on this theme of "the rules of the road," referring to the domestic and international laws that covered the movement of all ships under specific conditions. These, if properly followed, he argued, would have prevented any collision and consequent explosion. Moreover, naval officials like Wyatt or Pasco would quite rightfully have had confidence that ships in the harbour would follow these rules, and it was unfair to have expected them to have anticipated otherwise:

> The regulations of the road were ample, that the rules of the road were suffi-
> cient to safeguard us against all dangers – that is to say a reasonable safeguard.
> And I also think that any provision in the regulations for stoppage of traffic in
> Halifax harbour under certain conditions would be a regulation made on the
> assumption that a law was going to be violated, such a regulation was not
> needed so long as the law was observed – I mean the rule of the road. I do not
> think it was incumbent on anybody either in making the rules and regulations
> for Halifax harbour or in carrying them out to go on the assumption the law
> of the land was going to be violated. I think that is exoneration of the Naval
> Service Department and its officers.[125]

Henry's argument was clear and logical. The vessels in question had collided due to a violation of the international laws regarding the navigation of ships. During the inquiry, witnesses had provided instances of the safe passage of the Narrows by the largest ships in the world. The difference was that these were navigated by men who obeyed the rules of the road. From these facts, Henry concluded, "While I have the utmost sympathy for the people of Halifax in the irreparable losses they have sustained, the incalculable suffering they have endured with the utmost fortitude, I have no sympathy with the attempt to find a scapegoat for the explosion which took place on the 6th of December and to find that scapegoat among the officers of the Canadian Naval Service. I do not think that is where the blame belongs."[126] Few men in Halifax besides William Henry would have been willing to state the matter thus. To do so was a remarkable act of professional integrity, even though, essentially, it was simply an effort to introduce a needed dose of reality to the proceedings.

Henry somewhat blamed himself for bringing out testimony that Wyatt had not known *Imo* would be coming down the harbour that unhappy morning. He was now convinced that a great deal of the subsequent hostility thrown Wyatt's way in court and in print developed from a misunderstanding of this incidental reference:

> I freely confess I thought it was an exceptional case and there was carelessness on the part of a particular pilot. I did not understand, [n]or did anybody, until the matter was gone into further, that the pilots had been systematically neglecting the duty for several months; it was not exceptional and he did not consider it was and he only mentioned it as a reason he didn't know the Imo was coming down. I think this incident has been magnified out of all proportion in its value to the investigation. Whether Wyatt had the means of knowing, could have ascertained or not, is not the issue ... It depends on the question whether this was such an exceptional occurrence he was bound as a matter of fact and duty to close the port. I think not. I think he was justified to think there would be no danger to allow it to go up even if another ship were coming down.[127]

Frederick Wyatt had not asked the pilots to report ship movements to him in order to control the movement of vessels in the harbour. Rather, the information was needed in order to report sailings "somewhere" (the Admiralty and other headquarters) and to regulate the opening and closing of the "gates." A pilot might propose to sail at a certain time and be advised that the gates would not be open until later. Indeed, on 6 December Wyatt knew that the gates would be closed at 9 a.m. that morning. Chances are that *Imo* would not have been able to depart the port until later had she passed *Mont Blanc* safely.

With respect to the collision, Henry now made the most important statement he would make during the inquiry and one of crucial importance to anyone who seeks to understand the circumstances of the Halifax explosion:

I should mention it is an extraordinary coincidence, almost unbelievably extra-ordinary that the first ship which came to this port since the beginning of the war or in the history of Halifax, loaded exclusively with explosives should be the only ship to be in serious collision in Halifax Harbour. We know there have been slight collisions from time to time of a minor character, I don't think there has been a ship sunk or badly damaged in the harbour to my knowledge at all events, and any collisions have been in time of fog or darkness, their lights not being carried. There is an extraordinary coincidence the only ship which came here which might be termed, as Mr. Cluney has said, a floating arsenal, that was the one ship for some inscrutable reason of Providence, that one ship should be the one picked out by hazard to be collided with and exploded. The Imo could have run into 999 out of 1000 and fire would not have been caused and even if it had been caused there would be no explosives on board to explode. I think in the way of appeasing the panic of the public that thing should be emphasized that this was the first ship that could have caused this disaster and it was not a usual thing, and not one likely to occur, probably never will occur again – and we have not been exposed to this danger during the three or four years the war has been going on.[128]

This, then, was the crux of the matter for Henry. It provided the basis for his sympathy for the navy and frustration with the overwrought excesses of the media.

The press, he felt, had distorted aspects of inquiry, forcing him to address matters he didn't consider vital to the issue at hand. Chief among these was the "unfortunate misunderstanding" in the testimony of Wyatt and Martin. Henry found incredible the suggestion that anyone in Wyatt's position would have forged the letters to Martin.[129] Yet it was equally unbelievable that a man of Captain Martin's stature, experience, and honourable reputation would testify that letters supposedly directed to him had not been delivered. Henry confessed that the former captain superintendent was a personal friend and made public their exchange of telegrams. Ultimately, Henry found it extraordinary and disappointing that with a matter of such apparent importance Martin could not "say positively after reading the letters, I never saw these letters before in my life." Henry understood that the tribunal would conclude either that Wyatt had committed forgery or that Martin had per-jured himself. By doing so, however, they could "besmirch the reputation of a man who turns out months afterwards to be entirely innocent of the verdict that was passed against him." There were plausible alternatives to account for the disappearance of the letters – a breakdown in the delivery system, perhaps, or a misplaced file. The fire in the dockyard office some weeks prior to the explosion was another potential explanation. Were these possibilities not at least as plausible as accusations of forgery or perjury? Said Henry, "If there is any reasonable possibility of there being an explanation that does not involve that dispute between these two gentlemen ... [the court] should adopt that possibility rather than say that one or the other of these gentlemen has been guilty of conduct that should almost certainly subject them to the tender mercies of the criminal courts."[130]

Although Henry's summation was winding down, he had a few final but telling aspects to highlight. Acknowledging that an exhaustive examination of the pilotage service would take place at another time, the Crown counsel nonetheless expressed concern with what had been revealed on that subject at the inquiry. Testimony had provided an "exhibition of hopeless, helpless inefficiency." Important correspondence from the naval service had been treated "in the most casual way," handled by a fifteen-year-old boy, and never brought to the attention of the Pilotage Commission. Telephoned reports of ship movements to the CXO had been discontinued on "some fancied grievances about the way the messengers were taking the messages," without consulting or informing the secretary or members of the Pilotage Commission.

Henry then directed some critical words towards Charles Burchell for both his lack of courtesy and his disparagement of outside witnesses who had come to assist the court and who had no personal axes to grind. A case in point was his vaguely slanderous attempts to impeach the testimony of Mate Roland Iceton.

The last issues addressed by Crown counsel concerned the detrimental impact of inaccuracies in fact and terminology that had been admitted before the court. A particular problem had been caused by use of the term "munitions ship" to describe any ship carrying explosives. Unnecessary public upset had been created, for it was now assumed that any ship carrying munitions was loaded "to the hatches" with high explosives. Perhaps, Henry remarked, "our good friends the newspapers" could set things straight. He further deprecated the manner in which witnesses had introduced idle street rumours without having to support them with any actual evidence. Such false and misleading impressions had then circulated through the community as if they were facts. In one case Pilot Mackey was wrongly said to have narrowly escaped another collision after 6 December. A more serious example was the *Galileo* incident, where the falsehood that a collision had been "narrowly averted between a munition ship and a petroleum carrying ship in the Narrows" had been taken as truth. Henry summed up the incident yet again, concluding that Iceton was blameless and had simply been following instructions, and that the entire incident reflected the popular determination to scapegoat the CXO and his subordinates.[131] With that, Henry returned to his place. Moments later, the court adjourned to consider its verdict.

The Crown counsel had spoken with wisdom and discretion but against the grain of public opinion. The *Halifax Herald*'s banner the next day attacked his defence of Commander Wyatt as "astonishing," berated Henry for not devoting himself "to a ruthless exposure of all the facts," and sneered at his efforts to find "'some' Explanation for the Direct Conflict of Naval Officers' Testimony." The next day, the *Herald* proclaimed, "If Federal Officers Fail, Nova Scotia's Attorney-General Should See to It That ANY Man Responsible for the Great Disaster Is QUICKLY Subjected to 'The Tender Mercies of a Criminal Court'!"[132]

In a surprise move, two days after the adjournment, Henry informed the court "of the existence of testimony corroborating the evidence of Commander Wyatt" with respect to the alleged letters. By that time, it was too late to introduce testimony: the court had already reached its judgment, although it would not be made public for a couple more days. In any case, as Henry stated in his report to the Ministry of Marine, the new evidence concerned "a subsidiary phase of the matter, which did not really affect the responsibility for the collision."[133] The report does not specify what the new evidence was or whether its nature was informally revealed.

The court rendered its judgment on Monday 4 February. It was only three double-spaced pages. The explosion was the result of the collision of the two ships and that collision had been caused by a violation of the rules of navigation. The pilot and master of the *Mont Blanc* were "wholly responsible for violating the rules of the road." They were also guilty of neglect of the public safety for not having taken proper steps to warn Haligonians of the probable explosion. Pilot Mackey should be dismissed by the pilotage authorities and his licence cancelled because of gross negligence. For that negligence and for violation of the rules of navigation, "the attention of the Law Officers of the Crown should be called to the evidence taken on this investigation with a view to a criminal prosecution of such pilot." The court also recommended the evidence to authorities in France with a view to cancellation of Captain Le Médec's licence and with the wish that he be "dealt with according to the law of his country."

The pilotage authorities were censured for not having immediately suspended Mackey from further service. The court did not consider that disobedience by the pilots of the chief examining officer's orders had been "the proximate cause of the collision." Still, the court observed that the Halifax pilots too often had attempted "to vary the well known rules of the Road." Pilot Renner, who had brought the "American tramp steamer" (the SS *Clara*) into the port, was also considered deserving of censure.

With respect to naval control of the port, the court noted that the traffic regulations in effect "did not specifically deal with the handling of ships laden with explosives." While it was recognized that explosives must move "whilst the war goes on," specific regulations on this subject were required forthwith by the "proper authorities."

Commander Frederick Wyatt was found to be guilty of neglect in performing his duty as CXO. He had not taken proper steps to make certain that regulations were being observed, and he had failed to keep himself "fully acquainted with the movements and intended movements of vessels in the harbour." There was more: "In dealing with the CXO's negligence in not ensuring the efficient carrying out of traffic regulations by the pilots we have to report that the evidence is far from satisfactory that he ever took any efficient steps to bring to the notice of the Captain Superintendent neglect on the part of the pilots."[134] Given such a statement, it would seem that Henry's new evidence might not have been entirely irrelevant. The information remains unknown, however, and one can only speculate that it might have changed this aspect of the findings and perhaps have reflected badly on Captain Martin.

The judgment, which went directly to C.C. Ballantyne, the federal minister of marine, included no explanations or analysis. None was evidently needed. The next day's *Herald* reported the arrest of Aimé Le Médec and Frank Mackey. The headline also recorded the paper's "Demands That Commander Wyatt Be Immediately Arrested and Also 'subjected to the Tender Mercies of a Criminal Court.'" They need not have feared; the former CXO had already been taken into custody. Provincial authorities laid charges of manslaughter against all three men.[135]

Covering the Tracks

Evening, thou that bringest all, whatever the light-giving dawn scattered;
thou bringest the sheep, thou bringest the goat, thou bringest the child
to its mother.

Sappho

In his role as Crown counsel, William Henry had gamely tried to present the considerations that the court might most rightfully and rationally have applied in rendering its decision. Yet, clearly, his forthright reasoning had little more success with the court than it had with the public or the press. There was no indication, however, why the court, in rendering its decision, had so vigorously repudiated the sage (although unpopular) advice of the Crown counsel. Regardless, the decision of the inquiry was unquestionably what the public had been looking for. Moreover, such an outcome and the prospect of a speedy end to the matter were certainly consistent with much of the federal agenda for the inquiry, particularly with respect to easing public "concern." But had the inquiry capitulated to public opinion and political pressure?

For the most part, the written proceedings suggest that Justice Drysdale in particular, as well as Louis Demers and Captain Walter Hose, RCN, showed much independence of opinion in their questioning and argument. It is less clear that this independence extended to the formulation of the conclusions reached in the terse and unexplained judgment. How can one account for the inquiry's rather astonishing findings and for its failure to consider the eleventh-hour evidence that may have been favourable to Commander Frederick Wyatt?

William Henry attempted to address such questions as he tried to explain the outcome to anxious officials and politicians who had been monitoring developments from Ottawa. Although he had been hoping for better, Henry was not completely surprised by the conclusions reached by Arthur Drysdale and his assessors, given the state of feeling in the city. Yet the finding against *Mont Blanc* had nevertheless come as "a great surprise to most people." The general expectation among informed mariners and legal practitioners had been that *Imo* would have been found primarily at fault for being on the wrong side of the channel. Henry predicted – rightly, as it turned out – that, on appeal, higher courts would not take the same view of the facts. Indeed, the matter would advance through a split vote in the Supreme Court of Canada to the highest court in the legal system, the Judicial Committee of the Privy Council in Britain. It would be resolved only in February 1920 when their Lordships ultimately declared *Imo* and *Mont Blanc* equally to blame. Interestingly, the lengthy judgment of the Judicial Committee made no mention of traffic control issues or the RCN.[1]

Henry's greatest concern in terms of the original inquiry was its conclusions concerning the part played by the Royal Canadian Navy in the affair. In the letter to Alex Johnston at the Ministry of Marine, he was restrained but clear on this point:

> Of the judgment delivered by the Court it would not be proper, perhaps, for me to say all I feel. I am and have been throughout satisfied that the Department of the Naval Service and its officers were entirely free from blame and should not be held responsible in any way for the disaster. The harbour regulations were sufficient, in my opinion, to safeguard the port, in view of the existence of Rules of the Road designed to prevent collisions, and I cannot see why regulations

should have been framed based upon the assumption that the Rules of the Road would be infringed.

The officials charged with the carrying out of the Regulations were not, I consider, to blame for not taking precautions not required by the Regulations. The evidence was all to the effect that Commander Wyatt would not have been to blame, even if he had known that the "Imo" was to sail on the morning of December 6th, in permitting the "Mount Blanc" to enter the harbour. The Court has disregarded that evidence, apparently, and placed some of the blame upon him.[2]

Although Henry saw Wyatt and the RCN as blameless, both the local and national press, feeding on the findings of the inquiry, found much to condemn in the service. From the vantage of the national capital, the influential Ottawa *Evening Journal* was scathing:

The controlling of traffic in Halifax harbour was a policeman's job. The sergeant of any city traffic squad, with the might of the law behind him, could organize the traffic ... in a couple of days and keep it running smoothly and safely. Any pilot or ship master who dared to break the rules of the road laid down by the policeman would be yanked off his vessel and sent to jail ... The sergeant of any city traffic squad would regard the thing as easy.

Yet upon this simple policeman's job the Canadian Naval Service, with all its frills and feathers, its admirals and commanders, captains and lieutenants, fine uniforms and gold lace fell down.

Having established the ineptitude of the navy and the need for an overhaul of its command, the paper commented on the cosy relationship between officials in Ottawa and those at least partially responsible for the navy's shortcomings:

We see that Captain Martin is the guest of Admiral Sir Charles Kingsmill at Rockliffe. Captain Martin was in charge of Halifax harbour. He was away in England when the disaster occurred, but, as we have pointed out, the conditions that permitted that disaster had prevailed long before he went away.

...

The Minister of this department, and the Dominion Government, must see that the confidence of the people of Canada in the whole administration of the Canadian Naval Service is shattered ... The Canadian Naval Service has received a black eye. If for no other reason than that of providing the British Admiralty with assurances for the future, drastic action by the Dominion Government is imperative.[3]

Admiral Sir Charles Kingsmill was sufficiently distressed by the public expressions of non-confidence in the navy that he raised the question with Ernest Chambers, the chief press censor. Was it in the public interest in time of war to allow such intense condemnation of naval officials? What of the effect on the morale of the sailors, to see their superiors so rebuked? Chambers, who was sympathetic to Kingsmill's position, had already discussed the situation with his superior, Thomas Mulvey, KC, the undersecretary of state. Mulvey's response may not have satisfied either Chambers or Kingsmill. Despite the government's general preference to keep the Halifax disaster as much as possible out of the headlines, and the necessity for wartime censorship of the press, there were nevertheless certain rights and rules that must be respected. As Chambers reported back to Kingsmill, "Mr. Mulvey explains that it was distinctly agreed by the representatives of the Government that the press should be accorded full liberty to discuss all political issues, political appointments and arrangements and the conduct of public officers of all descriptions. Consequently, it would be impossible to take a strong stand in the way of restricting the publication of matter criticizing the conduct and actions of Naval or Military officers at Halifax or elsewhere."[4]

Cognizant of his obligation to preserve freedom of the press as much as possible, Chambers nevertheless once more offered his considerable powers of persuasion to try to help ease the situation. He prepared a tactful personal letter to Halifax editors stressing his want of authority or desire to restrict legitimate and reasonable discussion of public affairs but pointing out the problem of undermining naval morale and discipline. Could they frame their comments in such terms as might serve their ends "without impairing the efficiency of the service"?[5] Shown the draft, Kingsmill diplomatically acknowledged that it might accomplish some useful purpose, although he was not very hopeful. Local hostility towards the navy predated the explosion and the inquiry, flamed by such issues as patronage. Moreover, the longstanding enmity of both Senator Dennis and Mayor Martin seemed implacable.[6]

Kingsmill was right about the effect on naval morale and discipline: symptoms appeared almost immediately. Within days of receiving Chambers's appeal, the *Herald* printed a letter from an anonymous naval rating who expressed strong agreement with an earlier article calling for house-cleaning in the Naval Department. The writer stated that it would have to be done "pretty thoroughly in every section of the department if the Canadian taxpayer is to get reasonable value for his money." He went on to condemn the marked inadequacy of the new trawlers and drifters and stated that many sailors were reluctant to take them to sea.[7]

One of the few blessings that had abetted government efforts at damage control had been that its ministers had not yet had to face the newly elected opposition in the House of Commons, however frail it might have been rendered by the Liberals' decisive defeat. The respite would end on 18 March, when an assault on the government might be expected. Thus, a few days after Judge Drysdale's findings were made public, C.C. Ballantyne asked his civil and military officials for a full report on the administration of the port of Halifax, with detailed attention to the role played by the naval authorities. By the time G.J. Desbarats had wrung responses from Admiral Kingsmill's staff and the authorities in Halifax, the minister would be furnished with a thick defence file designed to cover any foreseen question or eventuality.[8]

As has been noted, although the Drysdale Inquiry's findings had been made public, the inquiry itself had provided scant explanation of the rationale that had led to its conclusions. Henry himself seems to have had no real inkling, although his speculations were astute and he clearly recognized that "in the present state of feeling in this community a jury is likely to convict anyone charged with negligence in connection with the explosion." Although he did not say so outright, perhaps Henry was hinting that the committee may indeed have been subject to the same kind of pressure or prejudice.[9] Files of the Departments of Marine and the Naval Service are silent about the motivation of the tribunal. Yet C.C. Ballantyne and Sir Robert Borden appear to have received additional information beyond that made public by the inquiry.

The prime minister's private papers contain two strongly written aides-mémoire that Captain Louis Demers, the dominion wreck commissioner, had prepared for Judge Arthur Drysdale a few days before the commission rendered its findings. Evidently he prepared the two documents on 28 and 29 January, after the last two days of testimony and before commission counsel had presented their summations. Demers had already made up his mind, and his convictions seem to have swayed the findings of the court to a greater degree than any subsequent summation. This suggests that, although Demers had not played a controlling role in the proceedings in the public sense, the crusty sailor's influence was actually paramount in the inquiry's outcome.

The memoranda provide insight into the blame that the court overwhelmingly and unexpectedly attributed to *Mont Blanc*. In reaching his conclusions, Demers rather astonishingly placed moral considerations above rules governing maritime law. To the wreck commissioner's mind, the weighing of evidence required no great efforts of deliberation. Demers's notion was that Captain Le Médec and Pilot Mackey had indefensibly violated the rules of the road in the narrow waters. When *Imo* had sounded her two-blast answer to *Mont Blanc*'s single warning, Demers insisted that the latter should have at once placed her helm to port, sounded a signal of three blasts, and ordered her engines full astern. He also insisted that this obligation to defer immediately to *Imo*'s advertised intentions – normal procedure or no – was *Mont Blanc*'s only proper recourse because only Le Médec and Mackey had knowledge of the very dangerous cargo their ship carried. Demers believed this knowledge carried with it an overriding obligation to take uncommon measures to avoid any prospect of collision. For this reason, although he acknowledged lack of criminal intent, the wreck commissioner was emphatic that *Mont Blanc*'s captain and pilot were to blame and should be punished. Drysdale and Hose were evidently persuaded likewise. Thus, William Henry's subsequent well-reasoned legal observations had been to no avail.[10]

Interestingly, Demers considered *Imo*'s pilot and crew blameless. Pilot Hayes had himself been a victim of the disaster – "he has lost his life, and therefore cannot defend himself" – and Demers would not even blame him for not reporting the ship's departure from Bedford Basin to the naval authorities. Demers would later remark "British fair play is a principle which, for me, is sacred." Rather, he assigned fault to "those who should have seen that the pilots carried out the orders and instructions received [from] the Naval Authorities." Specifically, he directed his scorn towards the carelessness that had been revealed in the administration of the Halifax pilotage, bluntly calling for a uniform system of pilotage controlled by the federal government. Such a finding was not inconsistent with the agenda of the inquiry, but the dominion wreck commissioner had still other opinions.[11]

Initially, Demers was prepared neither to condemn nor condone the actions of those in charge of the traffic in the harbour. To that point he felt that the evidence would not permit logical, fair, or impartial judgments.[12] What had clearly bothered him, however, was the controversy over the letters allegedly submitted to Edward Martin by Frederick Wyatt, complaining about the pilots. When testimony closed on 29 January with the matter still unresolved, an irritated Demers decided to ignore the particular issue. He focused instead "on the admitted fact on the part of both parties, that complaints and conversation had taken place regarding the non-observance of rules by the Pilots."[13]

The wreck commissioner then set his sights squarely on Commander Wyatt. Since the chief examining officer had known the pilots to be an unreliable source of information, it had therefore been his bound duty "to adopt other means to assure himself, and for his own preservation, as well as of lives and property, that when ordering traffic movement, nothing could intervene to prevent or cause interruption or come in conflict with a pre-arranged and determined programme of seeing that the way was absolutely clear for the Mont Blanc's passage from the Harbour to Bedford Basin. He has in this instance shown laxity in the performance of his duties, therefore his mismanagement of traffic is the indirect cause of the collision, and its terrible aftermath."[14] Presumably Demers's conviction on this point was sufficient to withstand the news of Henry's discovery of new evidence to corroborate Wyatt's testimony regarding the letters. Wyatt would be the goat despite Henry's efforts.

Inexplicably, Demers directed no censure towards the dockyard superintendent, Captain Martin. After all, he was the commander on the spot who might reasonably have been expected to provide any necessary supervision in the event of difficulties in the operation of the port. Yet Demers seemed willing to bypass Martin entirely, at the same time directing blame at the dockyard superintendent's superiors in Ottawa. Martin had given evidence that he had reported non-observance of rules by the pilots to authorities in Ottawa. In return, he had been advised to interfere as little as possible with local conditions. Demers was outraged: "On this evidence it is my opinion and belief, that the controlling powers, upon receiving such complaint, should have suggested a remedy, and in their reply to correspondence bearing on the violation of rules, recommended drastic measures to prevent such infringement of regulations. A tolerance of disobedience on the part of the pilots should never have been entertained."[15]

This was dangerous ground, with elements not only of potential embarrassment to the government but of downright scandal. It required action – what some would call careful political damage control and others would label a deliberate cover-up. Certainly the government had hoped to manage the inquiry in the direction of achieving needed reforms to the Halifax Pilotage Commission. Nonetheless, it would not do for it to become public that officials in the Marine Department had held serious concerns about the state of pilotage in the port long before the disaster. Nor would it do to be known that there had been enough truth within the obdurate testimony of Commander Frederick Wyatt and the vague downplay by Captain Martin to apparently corroborate the statement that Ottawa had told naval officials in Halifax to interfere as little as possible in local conditions. Such information would support a view that the government had failed to take necessary action to correct a serious deficiency in the administration of the port, action that might have reduced the likelihood of a disaster. With Demers's memoranda, a senior official of the Marine Department was on record as being in agreement with that view.

Initially, such considerations seem not to have occurred to C.C. Ballantyne. Content that his officials were putting together a defence file for the forthcoming opening of Parliament, he happily passed Demers's comments on to the prime minister, along with addenda to the inquiry report, and took credit for dealing with another matter: "I have already given instructions that Commander Wyatt be dismissed from the Canadian Naval Service. Although it may be possible before this can be done that court martial will have to be held. This matter is now receiving the immediate attention of my technical Naval Officers."[16]

Borden showed no particular interest in the fate of the unfortunate Commander Wyatt, but he was more astute than Ballantyne in immediately seeing grave difficulties in Demers's having alleged "that the authorities in Ottawa knowingly condoned the non-observance of rules by the Pilots." The prime minister's request for a "report ... with regard to the matter" was graciously generic but careful to note Demers's observation that "drastic action" had been called for to enforce the harbour regulations. And he suggested a careful review of Captain Martin's evidence.[17]

Ballantyne was not the only party questioned by the prime minister on problems with non-compliant pilots. He also pursued J.D. Hazen, Ballantyne's predecessor, who had left the government in 1917 to become chief justice of New Brunswick. Hazen was adamant that "no such report was submitted to me from Captain Martin or from anybody else, and if the facts are as stated they never were brought to my attention by the officials of the

Department. Probably Mr. Desbarats or Sir Charles Kingsmill will be able to throw some light upon the matter."[18]

Executive necks were in. Ballantyne's senior officials professed dismay at the interpretation given Captain Martin's evidence by the dominion wreck commissioner. The latter "must be under some misapprehension." Vague in his testimony during the inquiry, Captain Martin was now equally reticent and made every effort not to contribute to the controversy. When questioned by Admiral Kingsmill over the evidence he had provided to the inquiry and what he had meant by it, he professed not to understand how he could have possibly made the statement attributed to him by Demers. His testimony on the issue of Ottawa and the pilotage question had consisted of presenting "only" two letters from his files. The most recent of the letters merely concerned the failure of a pilot to carry out instructions with regard to the berthing of a specific ship in March 1917. The other, from June 1916, was more general and expressed concerns over the failure of the Halifax pilots "to carry out instructions with regard to berthing of ships." Martin played both down, but the reality was that two complaints had indeed been passed to naval service headquarters under his signature, and one of them was quite strongly worded. It stated that Halifax pilots had failed in "many" instances to carry out instructions received from the chief examining officer and had been "persistent" in ignoring these instructions. Martin's letter also reported that there had been several complaints from imperial warships concerning allotted berths being occupied by merchant vessels. Additionally, he reported that, when apprised of the problems, the pilotage commissioners had provided no assurance that disobedience would cease.[19]

The correspondence on this issue survives only in the papers of Sir Robert Borden, which suggests that it was so sensitive that the Department of the Naval Service did not keep copies in its files. Borden's papers show that Martin's initial complaint from Halifax languished for more than three months in Ottawa in-baskets until a brief note from the naval secretary (Acting Staff-Paymaster J.R. Hemsted, RN) advised Martin that the matter had been dealt with in a Department of Marine notice to mariners. In effect, this notice, which would enable the RCN to enforce traffic control directives, had no teeth. The second complaint, which had dealt with a specific violation, had requested instruction upon action to be taken. The reply, again under the hand of the naval secretary, stated (wrongly in fact) that there were no legal powers that would allow action to be taken against the pilot concerned.

It also pointed out (rightly in fact) that the Defence of the Realm Act had no force in Canada. Vague assurances were given of a comprehensive order "now in course of preparation" to deal with the matter, but almost a year later the department had generated no further correspondence on the subject.[20]

Ottawa's reluctance to interfere in Halifax pilotage, despite the complaints from naval officers on the scene, nicely underscores both the degree to which the exercise of RCN and Marine Department responsibilities was subordinated to political considerations of local patronage and the extent to which uniformed or civil officials, with rare exceptions like Captain Demers, were reluctant to rock the boat. It was a classic case in which officials had weighed the seriousness of the situation against the need to avoid controversy and had opted for the latter. Once catastrophe hit, however, the decision began to reek of scandal. It was a fine mess indeed. One can only imagine the outcry and its consequences should the matter have become public. It would be hard to make a case other than to confirm the already widely held belief that the government of Canada, through its Department of the Naval Service, had been criminally negligent in contributing to the collision and, therefore, the ensuing disaster. Perhaps where Senator Dennis had found smoke there had indeed been fire.

Who would have been the likely culprit? Although the replies to the dockyard were traced to the hand of the naval secretary, this staff officer was merely a conduit for the directives of Admiral Kingsmill and George Desbarats, the deputy minister. Given the sailor's absolute subordination to the civil servant, however, and considering that Kingsmill was already a proven enemy of political patronage, it would almost certainly have been Desbarats who took the decision not to interfere in the Halifax pilotage. Yet this decision was indisputably coloured by contact with the Department of Marine and their policy not to interfere in such matters. Teflon had yet to be invented, but the principle was well known.

Whether the prime minister would have supported any pre-explosion initiative to resolve the navy's problems in controlling the pilots in his riding is problematic. After the fact, it was Sir Robert Borden who pointed out to C.C. Ballantyne and his officials that they had been seriously in error with respect to the government's authority over pilotage. It was true that the Defence of the Realm Act had no force in Canada. Yet Canadian legislation – the War Measures Act – provided ample regulatory powers, and the government could have easily dealt with the matter had there been any desire to do so. That these obvious provisions for extraordinary measures in time of war do not seem to have occurred to Canada's apparently inept naval officials reveals how hidebound they had been rendered by the dominance of senior civil servants over senior naval officers, the fuzzy chain of command, and the great weight carried by familiar, long-established British practices and regulations in contrast to newer Canadian ones.[21]

In the face of public wrath, the government was now in some haste to repair the poor state of shipping management in Halifax, which had been confirmed by the explosion inquiry. Indeed, shortly after the hastily organized Royal Commission on Pilotage delivered its not surprising recommendations – these were in the prime minister's hands on 12 March 1918 – the government used the provisions of the War Measures Act to seize authority over the Halifax pilotage for the duration of the war. The order-in-council was issued only two days after the commission's findings were given to Borden, four days before the House was to reconvene. Appropriate regulations for postwar circumstances would follow in due course.[22]

IN HALIFAX, COMMANDER FREDERICK WYATT remained a convenient foil to draw attention away from Ottawa. His sudden arrest by the civil authorities on charges of manslaughter had caught both the former chief examining officer and his boss, Captain Fred Pasco, by surprise. Wyatt understandably challenged his arrest as illegal. The "port being under Naval Authorities and myself responsible to those authorities," any case against him should be considered by the naval disciplinary system. Pasco thought the police should at least have notified him before acting, but he was uncertain enough of his position that he only asked for a copy of the arrest warrant. The response from Ottawa was instantaneous. The civil jurisdiction was indisputable and clearly provided for in naval regulations. Pasco was told to take no action without reference to naval service headquarters.[23] Wyatt was completely on his own, and it was he who would stand trial, not the RCN or the federal government.

Preliminary hearings to consider the charges against Le Médec and Mackey began on 5 February; Wyatt was brought to the court immediately upon his arrest. Held in the same courthouse that had housed the Drysdale Inquiry, the hearing included many of the same participants, although this time a local magistrate, Robert A. McLeod, presided. Andrew Cluney directed the prosecution on behalf of the attorney general of Nova Scotia. The sole victim named in the manslaughter charge was Pilot Hayes of *Imo,* although Magistrate McLeod readily agreed to add additional names of the ship's crew at the conclusion of the proceedings in March. In the prevailing spirit of vindictiveness and grim retribution, the hearings provided few surprises and little doubt but that they would lead to a finding for trial. An exception was the appearance of Mate John Makiny. One of the great oversights of the inquiry had been its failure to call Makiny, who had witnessed the collision and explosion from the deck of the tug *Nereid* alongside the dockyard. Given a chance to testify before the present hearings, he essentially contradicted the findings of the inquiry by suggesting that the collision had been a result of *Imo*'s last change of course. McLeod had little interest in such deviations from received judgment, though, and largely disregarded Makiny's testimony.[24]

The hearing occupied only seven days of court time, but the sessions were intermittent. The finding was not rendered until 6 March. The skipper of HMCS *Canada,* Lieutenant-Commander W.T. Walker, had been sent to the court to observe events on behalf of the RCN. He reported to the new dockyard superintendent, Vice-Admiral Oswald Story, that the magistrate had accepted Cluney's argument that *Imo* should have been detained at her anchorage and more precautions taken. Thus, Wyatt was bound over for appearance at the Supreme Court for a criminal trial, bail being fixed at $6,000. Le Médec and Mackey were to stand trial as well.[25]

The hapless trio of defendants had every reason to fear the worst in the face of the public opinion that had been marshalled against them and the apparent willingness of the legal system to acquiesce. Yet a stratagem employed by Francis Mackey's counsel, Walter O'Hearn, found an unexpectedly sympathetic ear. Because he could not raise bail, Mackey had been kept in custody since his arrest. After his client was remanded for trial, Mackey's lawyer applied for the pilot's release under a writ of habeas corpus (requiring a person to be brought before a judge or into court, usually to investigate the lawfulness of his restraint). The application went before Judge Benjamin Russell of the Nova Scotia Supreme Court, whose later memoirs record that he had serious concerns over the criminal charges against Mackey.[26] O'Hearn argued that there was no evidence to support the charges of criminal negligence; rather, an error of judgment had led to an incorrect manoeuvre.

To determine the question, Judge Russell felt bound to consider the whole of the evidence that had been presented in the preliminary hearing. In contrast to Magistrate McLeod, Russell was much influenced by the credible evidence given by Mate Makiny of *Nereid,* which he felt cast serious doubt on earlier findings. The experienced RNCVR sailor was himself a victim of the disaster, could be assumed to have no partiality for the defence, and, most importantly, had been exceptionally well placed to view the incident. Other accounts at the hearings corroborated the view that *Imo* had been at fault. Thus, Russell concluded, in a judgment published verbatim deep inside the *Halifax Herald,* "I do not think there is anything in all this evidence that tends to substantiate the charge of such negligence as would be a necessary ingredient in the crime of manslaughter. I should go further and be inclined to hold that there is not a single fact proved or even stated in the evidence that is not consistent with the exercise of the highest degree of care and thought on the part of the pilot in charge of the Mont Blanc."[27]

Justice Russell discharged Mackey and applied the ruling to Le Médec as well. *Mont Blanc* had been under the control of the pilot, not her captain. They were both now free. No one knows how much credence the judge gave to affidavits that had been filed by O'Hearn from an American source that *Imo's* helmsman was German-born. Yet Mackey's exoneration provoked a further search for culpability, however far-fetched. The *Herald* played the information to the hilt with screaming headlines asking "Was An Over-Patriotic German at the Steamer Imo's Helm, at the Bottom of the Great Catastrophe of December Sixth?"[28] The absurd conjecture of there having been some intrigue behind the collision continues to the present.

Frederick Wyatt had now become the sole object of blame for the tragedy that had beset Halifax. Now indicted as a result of the hearing, he went before a grand jury on 19 March. Fortunately for Wyatt, Justice Russell again presided, no less disposed to yield to public opinion or abjure his duty. As he later recorded, Russell believed the idea that Wyatt "had anything in the world to do with the disaster was an utterly lunatic notion."[29] He began his charge to the jury with an explanation of why he had disposed of the cases against Mackey and Le Médec under habeas corpus proceedings. Had he entertained any doubts about either case, he would certainly have referred them to another court. His reasons for not doing so were unusually clear-headed: "To imagine that any pilot in charge of a vessel loaded with explosives, as this was known to the pilot to have been, would expose himself and his associates to the risk of instantaneous death by the reckless omission of any precaution or the careless execution of any manoeuvre necessary to his own safety was simply irrational."[30]

Turning to the case against Wyatt, Russell cautioned the jurors against the possibility of using other than legitimate sources to draw their conclusions. They needed to guard against a serious danger of predisposition, Russell warned, not allowing "the injured feelings of the community" to fall upon the naval officer who had been identified as having played a crucial part in the disaster. It was the duty of the grand jury to recognize limitations within which they could properly consider the case: "Whether the defendant had properly discharged the duties devolving upon him as the naval officer in charge of the port was one question. Whether if he had failed to properly discharge the duties devolving upon him he could be indicted for a criminal offense was a different question altogether."

The omnipresent *Herald* reporter recorded the balance of the address. Russell said that

> he would assume for the moment, and for the purpose of his instructions to the jury, that the defendant had violated every regulation made for the safety of the port and in the most reckless and negligent spirit had omitted any and every precaution such as a prudent and diligent official would have taken in the circumstances. The question remained to be considered: could he be held criminally responsible for the ensuing loss of life? His lordship said he had no hesitation in instructing the jury that whatever might be their opinion as to the moral culpability of the defendant, whatever views or feeling they might entertain with reference to his moral accountability for the disaster, howsoever emphatically they might express any judgment to the effect that his official negligence or misperformance of his official duties had prepared the conditions for the happening of a terrible disaster, THE CASE AGAINST HIM NEVERTHELESS FELL SHORT OF THE REQUIREMENTS FOR AN INDICTMENT FOR MANSLAUGHTER.[31]

The following morning the jury disregarded Justice Russell's sage guidance and returned a true bill endorsing the indictment as sustained by the evidence. Community feeling was simply too intense for them to do otherwise.[32]

Negative public opinion continued to be abetted by ongoing controversy over the navy's management of the port. As they had throughout the original inquiry, mishaps continued, always resulting in public outcry far beyond the significance of the individual incidents. In mid-February the SS *Carmania* had become involved in a dangerous situation as a result of sailing against the signals mounted on *Niobo*. The pilot in question had been arrested.[33]

The week before the grand jury, the press had reported on a "steamer laden with high explosives" being allowed to lay in the fairway of the harbour for seven hours. The *Herald*'s front page had exploded into another anti-navy diatribe:

> There is not a man familiar with marine affairs at this port, not a Nova Scotia captain who has gladly given his services to the work of naval patrol, not a master mariner who regularly brings in and takes out his steamer, but what has a story to tell of stupidity, of pigheadedness, of bungling in connection with the affairs of the port and, following up these stories, the trail leads directly to Ottawa and reveals a heterogeneous bunch of incompetents who may know the ways of society, who may be able to judge aright the merits of various blends of wine, but who certainly do not know the ways of ships and are not able to judge the competence of those whom they place in charge.
>
> ...
>
> It took one of the greatest disasters the world has ever known to partially arouse those in authority, but those who were in supreme authority then are still in authority. Britain, France, Italy, the United States all have had a shake up and a betterment of their management of marine affairs. Canada, after appalling evidence of incompetence, is without a shakeup. A Jellicoe was shifted, a Kingsmill reigns supreme.[34]

Admiral John Jellicoe had been dismissed in 1917 as First Sea Lord of the Royal Navy because he had opposed adoption of the convoy system. The *Herald*'s comparison suggested that Kingsmill and others like him were equally redundant and out of date. By implication, the same applied to Frederick Wyatt.

Wyatt's case would go to trial. Events were closing in upon him, and he did not like his chances. When he wrote to Vice-Admiral Story to request that the Department of the Naval Service retain counsel for his defence, he glumly observed that representation was "absolutely indispensable, as every indication shows that I am more than likely to be convicted at my trial by any jury in Nova Scotia, as proved by the Grand Jury finding a true bill."[35]

However much he disapproved of Wyatt's personal conduct, Kingsmill did not hesitate to support his request, advising the deputy minister that the charges were the result of Wyatt's performance as a naval officer and "any action of his must necessarily reflect more or less on the Department." L.A. Lovett, KC, was hired by the federal Justice Department to represent Wyatt, and Thomas Robertson, late counsel to the Pilotage Commission, was retained to "watch the case on behalf of the Department."[36]

Almost a month after the true bill against him, Wyatt's case went to trial on 16 April. It lasted less than a day. Again, Justice Russell presided. When the charge was read, Wyatt entered a plea of not guilty. As the *Herald* account noted, a great deal of challenging for cause and setting aside of jurymen followed before both sides reached agreement on composition. The defence submitted no evidence, "as they considered the case not proven." From the standpoint of the prosecution, even the *Herald* remarked that "no startling evidence was revealed." Interestingly, one of the witnesses called was William Henry "to vouch for evidence given by Commander Wyatt when he appeared before the commission following the disaster on December 6, 1917." Thus, the naval officer finally received a degree of public vindication, though the substance of what he said was unremarked by the news account.[37]

This time, the jury would not disregard the strong charge from Russell "that there was nothing in the eyes of the law to justify the charge of manslaughter." They were out only a few minutes before returning with a verdict for acquittal.[38] "Who Is Guilty?" the *Herald* editorial thundered in frustration the following day.[39] As the *Herald*'s question indicated, this was not the end of attempts to punish scapegoats. Donald Kerr has noted that vengeful local authorities were still trying to indict Mackey and Le Médec as late as October 1918. Of course, the earlier noted civil litigation over which ship had been responsible for the disaster also continued for more than a year.[40]

A few days after Wyatt's brief trial, Rear-Admiral Chambers filed his monthly report to the Admiralty on the state of the port of Halifax. It provides a neat summary of the status of matters some four and a half months after the explosion:

> The "CURACA", one of the vessels sunk in the explosion, has just been raised. She is a terrible wreck, having sustained the full force of the explosion. It is difficult at present to see how she can be again made serviceable; every deck having been beaten in and every excrescence wrenched from its place.
>
> The only vessel now remaining unsalved, is the "IMO", the Belgian relief vessel, the prime cause of the disaster.
>
> Commander Wyatt, the Chief Examining Officer, has stood his trial for manslaughter, and has been acquitted. It remains to be seen whether the matter

will now be dropped, or whether an attempt will be made to bring the responsibility home to Captain Martin, the late Senior Naval Officer.

The weather during the last few weeks has been very fine, and the snow is fast vanishing. With the improved weather, the making good of the explosion damage is proceeding apace.

The Dockyard still shows signs of extensive wreckage, but its renovation is being taken in hand and storehouses etc., are fast being built.[41]

Captain Martin, of course, was now well out of sight, if not entirely out of mind, in faraway Esquimalt. As for Wyatt, Chambers did not have to wait long to see if "the matter" would be dropped. Official Ottawa would certainly have been relieved to hear of Wyatt's acquittal. It meant that the issue could be laid to rest without the further public controversy and embarrassment that might have attended a court martial. Yet Wyatt was still beyond the pale as far as the navy was concerned; it would extend no forgiveness. Informing his minister of events, Kingsmill went on to "submit that this Officer may be informed that his services are no longer required. Commander Wyatt has not only shown himself far from being a very efficient Officer, but his conduct during the Enquiry into the circumstances of the collision between the MONT BLANC and IMO was not at all loyal to his Senior Officer, Captain Martin. I do not consider he is entitled to any sympathy whatever from the Department."[42]

Not surprisingly, C.C. Ballantyne "quite agreed," and Wyatt was quietly sent on leave to await administrative disposition from the Admiralty. As he had no desire for further Canadian or imperial service, and the Admiralty was not "eager to retain his services," Wyatt was Discharged to Shore SNLR (services no longer required) on 3 May. In service terms, the release was administrative rather than punitive; Wyatt was free to go his own way with a war service gratuity.[43] The RCN would turn to the challenge of a new submarine menace in the western Atlantic with one less sea officer.

On the national scene, the dramatic disaster that had befallen Halifax would remain a lasting remembrance, the accounts and myths of which would become embedded in the country's folklore. More immediately, however, the destruction and loss diminished in the face of the continuing sacrifice and anguish of the bitter war. Two days after Parliament assembled on 18 March 1918, the German armies on the western front began the series of desperate offensives that would, over the ensuing weeks, threaten to overwhelm the Allied armies and perhaps end the war on terms favourable to Germany. It precipitated the greatest crisis of the long conflict. In Canada, the worst of the anti-conscription rioting in Quebec occurred that same month, and the nation and government wrestled with the problems of maintaining civil peace and enduring further grim privations. The Halifax disaster faded from the headlines.

By the time Parliament reopened, federal politicians were concerned with other things. The disaster received scant attention from the Opposition, aside from questions on claims, restitution, and relief. The nation looked to continuing problems and to the future. Even when the House assembled in Committee of Supply on 4 April to consider the naval estimates, which asked for $600,000 to provide for the maintenance and upkeep of ships, facilities, dockyards, and the RNCVR, there was no serious trouble except for one sudden veiled attack. It was a sly gambit by Joseph Read, MP, to read into the record one of the *Halifax Herald*'s tirades against the management of the RCN, which had called for a shakeup. Noting that the attack came from "a personal organ of the Prime Minister" and a senator who had obtained his position through the good graces of the present government, Read began to record the editorial but was eventually stopped by the speaker, who ruled the remarks were not relevant to the vote. In the end, the debate over the navy budget emerged as something of a forum for C.C. Ballantyne to promote his plans for naval and marine construction and for individual members to ponder potential benefit to their ridings.[44]

WHAT TO MAKE OF THIS SORRY MESS of apparent intrigue and cover-up? In terms of the scale of the catastrophe at Halifax and the vast human suffering, it is fair to reflect that those responsible should have been held more answerable. Yet the three scapegoats identified by the inquiry had eluded formal punishment. They were nonetheless subjected to lasting resentment and contempt. None of them had been responsible for the circumstances that had brought *Mont Blanc* to Halifax, however. Broadly, accountability extended beyond Canadian jurisdiction, but more in terms of circumstances than individuals. Ultimately, it was the long and deadly war itself that had brought a French ship, loaded with the most extraordinarily explosive cargo, from an American port to a Canadian port for convoy across the Atlantic under a system coordinated by the Royal Navy. Not surprisingly, the federal government acknowledged no legal liability upon the Crown but nor did it claim compensation from Allied powers. Thus it was as "an emergency of the War" that orders-in-council provided for relief and restitution. This effort was coordinated by the Halifax Relief Commission, which was formally mandated on 22 January 1918. The commission spared no pains to come to the aid of the citizens of the unhappy city. It provided the mechanism for claims of indemnity and reconstruction and alleviated any fears that the federal government would not be willing to pay the bills. Ultimately, the dominion government paid out $12 million, another $5 million came from imperial authorities, and donations from other public and private sources brought the total administered by the commission to some $30 million.[45]

As for the controversies surrounding Commander Frederick Wyatt and the behaviour of others in the navy and the government, the reader has been teased with the spectre of intrigue and cover-up. In terms of the rhetoric of journalism and politics in the early twenty-first century, that is unquestionably what it was. Yet, then as now, such simplistic labels are seldom fair in terms of absolute truth. One cannot reasonably infer that the uniformed participants were universally without warts, or that unrelentingly calculating civilians and politicians necessarily connived against them. How the reader views the outcomes of this tale will, to some extent, depend upon his or her own experience and point of view. That said, some conclusions may be drawn from the catastrophe and the way it was handled.

Frederick Wyatt became a pariah not only to Haligonians but also to the navy. Whatever the truth, his stubborn public insistence upon the rightness of his own part in the matter and the blame that he cast upon others, including Captain Edward Martin, had broken the code of loyalty to superiors and to the service. It was not to be expected that the navy would overlook this disloyalty and stand by Wyatt through his ordeal. Yet, with this very obvious exception, the government and the navy had closed ranks – whether to protect the public interest and confidence in the government or to protect personal and career interests is moot. In institutional crisis it has ever been thus.

The same might be said of the evidence on Wyatt and the navy. In the original inquiry, Crown counsel William Henry courageously made the case for those who would regard both the chief examining officer and the navy at large as hapless victims. Henry's convincing closing arguments provide the clearest sense of the injustice done to both the individual and the institution. Yet for those more inclined towards a negative perspective of the uniformed lot or towards the view that some were complicit in their own victimization, there was also grist for the mill. Ultimately, the good and the bad is in the eye of the beholder, but this truism does not absolve the observer from the obligation for a fair and clear-headed examination of the actual facts. Justice is rarely served by the quest for retribution or the grinding of political axes.

Wyatt's reputation was ruined, but his punishment was largely symbolic. Captain Edward Martin kept his neck in and said as little as possible, as any good lawyer would have directed. Admiral Kingsmill protected Martin and others publicly, according to his persuasion of the overall good of the service, while he shifted them out of harm's way. Some would call this good leadership. G.J. Desbarats and his inexperienced political chief, C.C. Ballantyne, moved the appropriate pawns through the crisis, not always surely, to reassure the public, minimize damage, and guard the interests of the government and the country. Some would call this good administration. It included not making public anything that would reflect negatively upon the government or the navy. "Spin" is a new term but not a new concept. Some would defend such action as necessary in war or national crisis, but few would see it congruous with democracy. However interpreted, it can fairly be said that, for the most part, members of the naval family performed well both before and after the explosion. But they also made mistakes, and these were magnified by the crisis. Wyatt was the only major casualty in personal terms, but the reputation of the navy suffered as well.

After his case was dismissed by the Supreme Court of Nova Scotia, Frederick Wyatt judiciously absented himself from Halifax for a time. His naval file shows that he obtained work until the end of the war with the British Ministry of Shipping on the American eastern seaboard. Later he found employment on the steamer *Cacique,* registered in New York. His departure from the RCN marked the end of the allotment from his naval pay to his first wife in England, which had been the initial cause of his falling into disfavour with Admiral Kingsmill. The plea for assistance from the financially compromised first Mrs Wyatt at the beginning of 1919 was not within the Admiral's gift. Kingsmill had no clear idea of her ex-husband's whereabouts at the time and could only inform her solicitors that "any moral suasion with this gentleman is useless." Her fate is unknown. Later entries in Wyatt's file indicate that he returned to Halifax on occasion but he appears to have moved to Boston in 1925. The file records his continued presence there until 1935 as well as the passing of Mate Roland Iceton. From this point, when Wyatt would have been in fifty-seven, the record is silent.[46]

Whatever bitterness and recrimination might have been directed towards and experienced by Frederick Wyatt applied equally for the Royal Canadian Navy in Halifax. Even after the crisis had passed, memories were long. The navy continued its thankless task of safeguarding ports and shipping with its improvised patrol fleet, struggling to cope with the unreliable and difficult trawlers and drifters that were supposed to enhance their operational effectiveness. The submarine incursions into the western Atlantic in 1918 enjoyed some successes against Allied shipping, the fishing fleet suffered the loss of a number of schooners, and a few German mines were laid off the Canadian coast. For their part, the presence of the RCN vessels at vulnerable points kept submarines below the surface and thus restricted their speed and operational range. Such manoeuvres certainly prevented the sinking of a significant number of vessels and represented a notable accomplishment. They did nothing, however, for the public credibility of the navy in the wake of the tragic events at Halifax. Its reputation for incompetence and poor leadership could not be dislodged. The influence of this public disdain on the morale and self-esteem of volunteers in the pursuit of their naval duties is not something that can be precisely measured, but it undeniably had its effect. It is nicely symbolized in an account Michael Hadley and Roger Sarty have rendered of the only recorded encounter of a RCN patrol ship with a surfaced German submarine.

Since appearing in the western Atlantic in late June 1918, *U-156* had stirred up considerable public upset that had also preoccupied and alarmed American and Canadian naval officials. The sub would eventually sink some nine steamships, twenty sailing ships, and a USN armoured cruiser. Although the limited US and Canadian resources available in the area were deployed to counter the threat as best they could, the first vessel to actually have an opportunity to damage the boldly handled submarine was a Canadian merchant tanker sailing in ballast. On 5 August, *Luz Blanca*, which was in the approaches south of Halifax, had been struck by a torpedo fired from *U-156*. When the vessel did not sink, the submarine surfaced to finish the job with her deck gun. With two British naval reservists aboard to man her own inferior twelve-pounder gun, the merchant vessel gamely returned fire, and a running battle ensued. The match, of course, was uneven, and the badly pounded tanker sunk. Most of the crew survived, and it was generally recognized that they had given a good account of themselves.[47]

On 25 August, after further depredations and adventures, *U-156* had fallen among a group of four fishing schooners southwest of the island of St Pierre. As Hadley and Sarty recount, the submarine was finishing the job of destroying the hapless vessels when "a Canadian four-ship patrol (*Cartier, Hochelaga, Trawler 22,* and *Trawler 32*) entered the scene in line abreast at four-mile intervals. Suddenly, HMCS *Hochelaga* sighted two schooners six miles away and left the formation to head due east. Approaching to within four miles, *Hochelaga* glimpsed a submarine, just as one of the schooners mysteriously "disappeared" from view. The U-boat had evidently sunk the vessel and left herself open to counterattack."[48] With her two twelve-pounder guns, *Hochelaga* was at a decided disadvantage to the better-armed submarine. Yet even slight damage to the U-boat so far from its base could have been seriously crippling. The situation called for boldness, but *Hochelaga* promptly turned away, signalling for reinforcements. When these reached the scene, *U-156* had disappeared.[49]

Perhaps there were mitigating circumstances, but a naval court martial convened in October did not agree. The ship of war, however diminutive, had acted with notably less spirit than one of the submarine's civilian targets. Her captain was dismissed from the service for failure to carry out his duty to engage the enemy. His failure to act was a telling symbol of the state of morale in the RCN; it is not likely that the matter remained secret. An opportunity for the navy to begin to reverse its reputation for ineptitude was lost, the results instead further sealing that reputation. The war ended with the RCN apparently discredited and unappreciated.

Unfortunately, the apparent fiascos and failures cloaked some of the navy's modest successes, not only at sea but at the time of the catastrophe in Halifax. As Michael Hadley has already observed in a wider context, "the nascent Royal Canadian Navy of the First World War suffered bad press despite the fact that it actually fulfilled the government's policies, as limited as these were."[50] So did it go in the case of the great disaster in Halifax. Somehow, despite the inadequacies and shortages of personnel and equipment, despite the fuzzy command relationships and political considerations, and despite the destruction wrought within their dockyard, the motley little navy managed to deal with the disaster. Some – Walter Hose, Graham Holloway, and the civilian John Wilson among them – had particularly distinguished themselves in responding to the danger and devastation, bringing the port and its facilities back into operation, and carrying on with the war. Hose would, in the not too distant future, receive the dubious honour of leading the RCN through the difficult years ahead – a task he carried out with distinction and honour. Wilson would distinguish himself in public service vital to the conduct of the Second World War. Other sailors shirked or saw to their families, a universal and normal instinct. The mass of individual officers and sailors, however, did their duty and made their contribution. Some, recognized or not, were heroes. Others, including my grandfather Bert Griffith, suffered ill effects throughout their lives. The combination of slivers of glass in his chest, overwork, and tuberculosis contracted in *Niobe*'s crowded mess decks shortly led to his release from the RCN as unfit for further service. Chronic ill health dogged him to a self-inflicted death in 1945.[51] The war had indeed been brought home, not only to Halifax but to the soldiers and sailors who served there. Some met the test better than others, but most passed, including the unlucky Frederick Wyatt, who, if no saint, was no villain either.

The aftermath of the Halifax explosion would not be the first time that elements of the Canadian military or government departments would be the centre of, and become diminished by, intense public scrutiny and contention, and it would not be the last. Nor would it be the final time that the public, through the media, would demand the punishment of scapegoats who may have shared some degree of culpability or may merely have been in the wrong place at the wrong time. Sheer momentum renders such forces difficult to counter; good news appears contrived, and bad news seemingly confirms ineptitude and incompetence. The level of public outrage against the organization can be disproportionate, as is the sense of grievance and resentment raised among those who serve. Of course, as our own generation has learned, organizations being what they are, few can placate or withstand sustained and strident criticism that takes any allegation as fact. Under such circumstances, they can do no right and can only hunker down and endure until the tumult finally passes. And pass it does, but with effects on morale and efficiency that defy measurement.

The RCN was the subject of widespread controversy from the moment of its establishment and was already the object of ridicule the morning *Mont Blanc* sailed into Halifax Harbour. When military budgets imploded in the postwar cutting, the undistinguished RCN seemed to have few friends and little clout. As well, Canadian sailors were left with their own lasting legacy of bitterness and recrimination. This was largely sub rosa, but the *Halifax Herald* in May 1918 recorded at least one overt symptom. A confrontation between two sailors and the management of a Woolworth store led to their

manhandling and arrest by police. A large mob of sailors and returned soldiers followed the police wagon to the city jail, taunting and jeering the
arresting officers. Increased numbers of servicemen and some civilians gathered to demand the sailors' release. The situation grew increasingly ugly, and
the *Herald* reported that the crowd "smashed up" the city hall and "wrecked"
the police court. Fortunately, cooler heads prevailed, but not before city
authorities had to request assistance from military and naval authorities and
five hundred troops and marines were deployed. It would be some years
before mutual antipathy between some in Halifax and sailors of the RCN
eased. Indeed, the strained relations between the navy and the community
during the Second World War that exploded in the riots of May 1945 may
have had roots in 1917 or even earlier.[52]

Although the navy would survive and ultimately nurture a small but
vital professional corps, the source of the enthusiasm and resolve that would
carry it through the lean years of the Depression and into another war would
be the network of small reserve units that Walter Hose sagely spread across
the interior with the RCN's tiny financial allocations. These inland commu-
nities had been the source of much of the manpower that had brought the
navy to a strength of more than 5,500 officers and men operating some one
hundred vessels by the end of 1918. By such means, however much it may
have suffered, the navy retained sufficient profile to earn a place for a solitary
sailor among the magnificently portrayed hard-toiling soldiers, nurses, and
airmen that graced a new national war memorial unveiled in Ottawa in 1939
by King George VI. The lone sailor wears the tally of HMCS *Stadacona,* one
of the ships of Walter Hose's Patrol Service. Today the sculpture also sym-
bolizes the sacrifices at sea that were yet to come. That monument would
have made my grandfather very proud.

Notes

Introduction: Through Sailors' Eyes

1 For example, a major magazine feature on Canada at the millennium by historians Jack Granatstein and Norman Hillmer calls it one of the twenty-five events that shaped our century. See "The Halifax Explosion Brought the War Home," in "Canada's Century: *Maclean's* Presents the 25 Events That Shaped Canada in the Past 100 Years," *Maclean's*, 1 July 1999, 25.

2 See Robert Craig Brown and Ramsay Cook, *Canada 1896-1921: A Nation Transformed* (Toronto: McClelland and Stewart, 1974); Robert Bothwell, Ian Drummond, and John English, *Canada, 1900-1945* (Toronto: University of Toronto Press, 1987); Desmond Morton and J.L. Granatstein, *Marching to Armageddon: Canadians and the Great War, 1914-1919* (Toronto: Lester and Orpen Dennys, 1989). See also Robert Craig Brown, *Robert Laird Borden: A Biography,* vol. 2 (Toronto: Macmillan, 1980), 121-2.

3 Sir Andrew MacPhail, *Official History of the Canadian Forces in the Great War, 1914-19: The Medical Services* (Ottawa: King's Printer, 1925), 327.

4 Desmond Morton, *A Military History of Canada: From Champlain to the Gulf War* (Toronto: McClelland and Stewart, 1992), 160-1.

5 Gilbert N. Tucker, *The Naval Service of Canada: Its Official History,* vol. 1 (Ottawa: King's Printer, 1952), 229-233.

6 Michael L. Hadley and Roger Sarty, *Tin-Pots and Pirate Ships: Canadian Naval Forces and German Sea Raiders: 1880-1918* (Montreal: McGill-Queen's University Press, 1991), 203-4.

7 Marc Milner, *Canada's Navy: The First Century* (Toronto: University of Toronto Press, 1999).

8 Samuel Henry Prince, *Catastrophe and Social Change: Based upon a Sociological Study of the Halifax Disaster* (New York: Columbia University, 1920).

9 For a representative selection see Alan Ruffman and Colin D. Howell, eds., *Ground Zero: A Reassessment of the 1917 Explosion in Halifax Harbour* (Halifax: Nimbus, 1994).

10 Janet Kitz, *Shattered City: The Halifax Explosion and the Road to Recovery* (Halifax: Nimbus, 1989); Robert Macneil, *Burden of Desire* (New York: N.A. Talese/Doubleday, 1992).

Chapter 1: The RCN in Halifax – December 1917

1 Roger F. Sarty, "Silent Sentry: A Military and Political History of Canadian Coast Defence, 1860-1945" (PhD dissertation, University of Toronto, 1982), 275.

2 "Responsibility of the Navy at Halifax in Time of War," n.d. (probably January-February 1918), National Archives of Canada (hereinafter NAC), RG 24, vol. 6197, NS 1001-13-1.

3 For details of the evolution and development of Halifax defences see Sarty, "Silent Sentry." For composition of the garrison see "Active Militia (Garrison Duty)," ff. 78, and "In Garrison – C.E.F.," ff. 79, of main Militia Headquarters subject file on Halifax Explosion, HQ 71-26-99, vol. 2, NAC, RG 24, vol. 6355. Also see Sir Andrew MacPhail, *Official History of the Canadian Forces in the Great War, 1914-19: The Medical Services* (Ottawa: King's Printer, 1925), 327-8.

4 Research has revealed only the existence of this school and that it was "new" in post-explosion correspondence. None has so far been conducted into RCN communications in the First World War era. See Naval 700 to Navyard, 9 December 1917, NSS 37-25-3, NAC, RG 24, vol. 5635.

5 Macphail, *Official History,* 239.

6 Marilyn Gurney Smith, *The King's Yard: An Illustrated History of the Halifax Dockyard* (Halifax: Nimbus, 1985), 36-9, and D.R. Moore, *History of H.M.C. Dockyard, Halifax, N.S.* (Halifax: privately printed for Queen's Harbourmaster, 1967), 54-8.

7 Captain Superintendent to Secretary Naval Service, 18 December 1917, NSS 37-25-3, NAC, RG 24, vol. 5635.

8 Captain Superintendent, HMC Dockyard, to Secretary Naval Service, 15 March 1918, NSS 37-25-7, NAC, RG 24, vol. 5635.

9 Michael Hadley and Roger Sarty, *Tin-Pots and Pirate Ships: Canadian Naval Forces and German Sea Raiders, 1880-1918* (Montreal: McGill-Queen's University Press, 1991), 210.

10 Kingsmill to Deputy Minister, 30 October 1917, NSC 1017-10-3, NAC, RG 24, vol. 3832.

11 Sarty, "Silent Sentry," 304, 308-9.

12 Ibid., 306.

13 General Officer Commanding Military District No. 6 (Halifax) (hereinafter GOC MD6), circular letter to editors of Halifax area newspapers, 28 October 1917, HQS-66-Vol 10, NAC, RG 24, vol. 2323.

14 Captain Superintendent, HMC Dockyard, to Secretary Naval Service, 12 September 1917, NSS 1001-19-4, NAC, RG 24, vol. 6197.

15 Naval Service, Confidential Weekly Orders, No. 993, 21 November 1917; Captain Superintendent HMC dockyard to Secretary Naval Service, 28 July and 6 November 1917, NSS 1001-19-4, NAC, RG 24, vol. 6197. For information on tugboats, see NSS 58-45-1, NAC, RG 24, vol. 5661. Of particular interest on this same file, Chief of Naval Staff to Deputy Minister, 18 February 1933, details the consequences of employing civilians on operational service, particularly in the case of *Musquash*, which suffered casualties in the Halifax explosion.

16 Sweeping operations are documented at Ships Logs, *PV-V* and *PV-VII*, November-December 1917, NAC, RG 24, vols. 7760 and 7761.

17 Hadley and Sarty, *Tin-Pots and Pirate Ships*, 119-22.

18 Ibid., 72.

19 See individual listings in Ken Macpherson and John Burgess, *The Ships of Canada's Naval Forces, 1910-1981* (Toronto: Collins, 1981). Officially, Ottawa designated the auxiliary patrol ships as APS, i.e., APS *Lady Evelyn*, and *Grilse* as a torpedo boat destroyer (TBD), and ordered this nomenclature rather than the traditional HMCS. This was largely ignored in the fleet, where sentiment prevailed. I have adopted the use of HMCS as it better reflects actual usage. See NSS 58-53-1, NAC, RG 24, vol. 5662, *passim*, including copy of Naval Service, Confidential Weekly Orders, No. 995, Classification of Vessels.

20 Macpherson and Burgess, *Ships of Canada's Naval Forces*; J.O.B. LeBlanc, Assistant Naval Secretary, "Historical Synopsis of Organization and Development of the R.C.N.," 1937, National Defence Headquarters, Directorate of History and Heritage (hereinafter DHH), 87/93. *Acadia* survives as part of Halifax's Maritime Museum of the Atlantic.

21 Captain of Patrols to Secretary Naval Service, 8 and 27 November 1917, NSS 1001-19-4, NAC, RG 24, vol. 6197.

22 Ibid., 8 November 1917. Admiral Kingsmill's direction to use *Acadia* as a base for control of neutral shipping appears to have been misinterpreted as an order to pay her off, which was not corrected until 18 January 1918, when the director of the naval service (DNS) was obliged to order her "recommissioned immediately and to remain under orders of Senior Officer Patrols, and placed at service of Control Officer." See Kingsmill to Navyard Halifax, 18 January 1918, NSS 58-35-1, vol. 1, NAC, RG 24, vol. 5660.

23 Most of the new drifters were not intended for Canadian service; indeed, fifteen had been turned over to the RN by January 1918 before the British agreed to alter their allocations to meet the growing Canadian need. Hadley and Sarty, *Tin-Pots and Pirate Ships*, 211.

24 The exception was *CD-21*, broken down in Charlottetown, where she was obliged to spend the winter. Naval to Collector of Customs, Charlottetown, 8 December 1917, and Naval to Admiralty, London, 10 December 1917, NSS 29-16-1, NAC, RG 24, vol. 5604. This file also records efforts to move the vessels down the St Lawrence in the face of winter's onset. Six of the voyages, which were carried out by RCN crews sent from Halifax, are recorded in varying degrees of detail in surviving ships logs: *CD-24* at vol. 7164, *CD-25* at vol. 7165, *CD-26* at vol. 7167, *CD-27* at vols. 7168-9, *CD-29* at vol. 7170, and *CD-53* at vols. 7178-9. Identifying the three trawlers safely at Halifax proved something of a challenge:

St Julien: Navyard 309 to Naval, 2 November 1917, NSS 58-129-1, NAC, RG 24, vol. 5665; *Messines* and *Ypres*: HMCS *Margaret* log, 28 November 1917, NAC, RG 24, vol. 7494.

25 Captain of Patrols to Secretary Naval Service, 8 November 1917, NSS 1001-19-4, NAC, RG 24, vol. 6197.

26 Captain Superintendent, HMC Dockyard Halifax, to Secretary Naval Service, 6 November 1917, NSS 1001-19-4, NAC, RG 24, vol. 6197.

27 Hadley and Sarty, *Tin-Pots and Pirate Ships*, 89-90.

28 Despite the difficulties, the crews, who had of necessity accumulated considerable technical expertise, had performed well in spite of this duress, and they were roundly commended by the senior Halifax and Bermuda naval authorities. Report of HMCS *Shearwater* to Captain Superintendent, HMC Dockyard Halifax, 17 October 1917, and C-in-C [Commander in Chief] North America and West Indies to Director Naval Service, 15 October 1917, NS 45-2-12, NAC, RG 24, vol. 3595.

29 Admiralty 180 to Naval, Ottawa, 28 October 1917, NS 45-2-12, NAC, RG 24, vol. 3595.

30 Joint Officers, HMC Dockyard, to Captain Superintendent, 17 October 1917, and Director Naval Service to Deputy Minister, 30 October 1917, NS 45-2-12, NAC, RG 24, vol. 3595

31 Navinet 494 to Naval, Ottawa, 15 November 1917, NSC 1947-19-8, NAC, RG 24, vol. 3969.

32 Maps in such popular works as Michael Bird, *The Town That Died* (Toronto: McGraw-Hill Ryerson, 1962) suggest the *Niobe* was berthed somewhat farther south, in the vicinity of Piers 3 or 4. These piers were in use for other purposes, however, and *Niobe*'s true position can be verified from photographs at DHH, *Niobe* Permanent Record File (hereinafter PRF). Also see A.H. Wickens to E.C. Russell, 16 November 1955, DHH, HMCS Niobe 8000, vol. 2, p. 7.

33 Letter from P.F. Newcombe, 20 March 1918, NSS 37-25-7, NAC, RG 24, vol. 5635.

34 "Brief History of HMCS *Niobe*," DHH, *Niobe* PRF and HMCS *Niobe* 8000 file. The latter includes an interesting account of life aboard the depot ship; see A.H. Wickens to E.C. Russell, 16 November 1955. As to the presence of Royal Marines on *Niobe*, no official source detailing this unusual arrangement has been found. Wickens's account attests to their presence, however, as does *CD-53* log, 2 December 1917, NAC, RG 24, vol. 7179.

35 "Responsibility of the Navy at Halifax in Time of War," n.d., and "Port of Halifax, N.S., Public Traffic Regulations," 19 February 1918, copies at file NS 1001-13-1, NAC, RG 24, vol. 6197. This material was consolidated for preparation of a report to the minister of the Naval Service on the RCN's part in the Halifax explosion. The term McNab's Island is now in general usage in Halifax. According to researchers at the National Defence HQ Directorate of History and Heritage, however, the island was named after the Macnab family. That is also the name that appears on Admiralty charts of the period (National Map Collection, Halifax Harbour, 1918, no. 163989) and that is used in this account.

36 Wyatt to Kingsmill, 27 April 1915, F. Wyatt Personal File, NAC, RG 24, ACC 1992-93/169, vol. 233.

37 Corbett to Kingsmill, c. 17 August 1915, and accompanying minutes, F. Wyatt Personal File, NAC, RG 24, ACC 1992-93/169, vol. 233.

38 Director Naval Service to Secretary Admiralty, 17 January 1916, F. Wyatt Personal File, NAC, RG 24, ACC 1992-93/169, vol. 233.

39 From Hose "for the consideration of the Department," plus minuted comments, 1 September 1917; Captain of Patrols to Secretary Naval Service, 4 September 1917; Hazen to McCurdy (Parliamentary Secretary Militia Department), 12 September 1917, and Kingsmill 780 to Naval, Ottawa, 21 September 1917, NSS 58-53-24, vol. 1, NAC, RG 24, vol. 5662. Despite suggestions that the refinery was still in active production at the time of the Halifax explosion, Rear-Admiral Chambers and officials in Ottawa believed that all or part of the property had been closed for some time. See Hazen to McCurdy 12 September 1917; Anonymous [Rear-Admiral B.M. Chambers], "Halifax explosion," *Naval Review* 7, 1 (1920): 449-50; James Mahar and Rowena Mahar, *Too Many to Mourn: One Family's Tragedy in the Halifax Explosion* (Halifax: Nimbus, 1998), 55; Janet Kitz, "The Explosion Mortuary Artifacts: A Look at the Victims," in *Ground Zero: A Reassessment of the 1917 Explosion in Halifax Harbour*, ed. Alan Ruffman and Colin Howell (Halifax: Nimbus, 1994), 19-20.

40 See Hadley and Sarty, *Tin-Pots and Pirate Ships,* 190-1, 207.

41 See [Chambers], "Halifax Explosion."

42 *The Royal Navy List or Who's Who in the Navy: A Book of Reference Relating to the Personnel of the Navy, Both Active and Retired ... Special War Supplement ...* (London: Witherby, 1917), 61.

43 Hadley and Sarty, *Tin-Pots and Pirate Ships,* 202.

44 Paraphrase of cypher telegram from Mr Long to Governor General, 19 November 1917, attached to Kingsmill to Deputy Minister, Naval Service, 21 November 1917, NSS 1048-48-1, vol. 1, NAC, RG 24, vol. 3773.

45 Kingsmill to Deputy Minister, 21 November 1917, NSS 1048-48-1, vol. 3, NAC, RG 24, vol. 3773.

46 Deputy Minister Naval Service to Under-Secretary of State External Affairs, 23 November 1917, NSS 1048-48-1, vol. 3, NAC, RG 24, vol. 3773.

47 Paraphrase of Cypher Telegram from Mr Long to the Governor General, 8 December 1917, NSS 1048-48-1, vol. 3, NAC, RG 24, vol. 3773.

48 *Morning Chronicle* (Halifax), 1 January 1918.

49 For an example of this antipathy see Kingsmill to Chambers, 14 February 1918, File 350, NAC, RG 6 E, vol. 621.

50 *Calgary Eye Opener,* 22 September 1917, copy attached to NSHQ Chief of Staff to Chief Press Censor, NSC 1029-6-14, vol. 1, NAC, RG 24, vol. 3883.

Chapter 2: Towards the Unthinkable

1 Shipping arrivals for the port of Halifax can be tracked with relative precision at NSS 1048-48-8, National Archives of Canada (hereinafter NAC), RG 24, vol. 3774. There are details of convoy sailings and composition at NSS 1048-48-2, NAC, RG 24, vol. 3773.

2 HMCS *Laurentian* log, 29 November-5 December 1917, NAC, RG 24, vol. 7450.

3 HMCS *Stadacona* log, 28 November-7 December 1917, NAC, RG 24, vol. 7870.

4 HMCS *Niobe* log, 5 December 1917, NAC, RG 24, vol. 7686, and HMCS *Grilse* log, 5 December 1917, NAC, RG 24, vol. 7371. No log of *Hochelaga* can be located for this period; thus, the assertion that she would have taken on coal on 6 December is presumption. As noted at a later point and different context and in her log, *Niobe's* crew worked the coaling sheds until late afternoon.

5 *PV-V* log, 3-6 December 1917, NAC, RG 24, vol. 7760.

6 HMCS *Margaret* log, 3 November-5 December 1917, NAC, RG 24, vol. 7494, and CO *Margaret* to Captain of Patrols, 15 November 1917, NSS 58-16-6, NAC, RG 24, vol. 5659.

7 HMCS *Grilse* log, 5 December 1917, NAC, RG 24, vol. 7371. Designation "special patrol" from Captain Superintendent HMC Dockyard, General Orders, 14 September 1917, NSS 1001-13-1, NAC, RG 24, vol. 6197.

8 HMCS *Grilse* log, 5 December 1917, NAC, RG 24, vol. 7371. Many ships' logs have not survived. This is one example of using a different ship's log for information. *Margaret, Lady Evelyn,* and *Grilse* are particularly helpful in this respect.

9 HMCS *Margaret* log, 28 November 1917, NAC, RG 24, vol. 7494.

10 No surviving documentation confirms the location or status of *St Julien* and *Ypres.* See Captain Arthur Darby, Engineer Captain, RN, Consulting Naval Engineer to Director Naval Service, 14 November 1917, NSS 58-134-1, NAC, RG 24, vol. 5665 (non-delivery of evaporators and distillers in trawlers built in Montreal), and NSS 13-7-1, NAC, RG 24, vol. 3602, *passim* (Director of Ship Construction – Correspondence). Also see Michael Hadley and Roger Sarty, *Tin-Pots and Pirate Ships: Canadian Naval Forces and German Sea Raiders, 1880-1918* (Montreal: McGill-Queen's University Press, 1991), 187, 220-1.

11 Navyard 414 to Naval, 10 November 1917, NSC 1047-19-8, NAC, RG 24, vol. 3969.

12 All logs at NAC, RG 24: *CD-24,* vol. 7164; *CD-25,* vol. 7165; *CD-26* vol. 7167; *CD-27,* vol. 7169; *CD-29,* vol. 7170; *CD-53,* vol. 7179. Drifters mentioned in HMCS *Niobe* log, NAC, RG 24, vol. 7686 are *CD-14,*

19 November; *CD-52, CD 64,* and *CD 43,* 21 November, and *CD-16,* 24 November. HMCS *Grilse* log, 3 December 1917, NAC, RG 24, vol. 7371, records a minor collision with *CD-73,* which slightly damaged the larger ship's stern. The presence of *CD-73* and the experiences of Herbert Whitehead, her master, are extensively documented in the Wreck Commissioner's Inquiry, NAC, RG 42, vol. 596/7 (hereinafter Inquiry). A post-disaster photo documents the presence of *CD-74.* See *Niobe* PRF, National Defence Headquarters, Directorate of History and Heritage (hereinafter DHH).

13 Documentation estimating numbers as of January 1918 suggests the presence of approximately twenty-two. See Hadley and Sarty, *Tin-Pots and Pirate Ships,* 211.

14 Testimony of Herbert Whitehead, RNCVR, 25 January 1918, Inquiry, and *CD-53* log, 1 December 1917, NAC, RG 24, vol. 7179.

15 *CD-53* log, 14 November-5 December 1917, NAC, RG 24, vol. 7179.

16 *CD-26* log, 24 November-5 December 1917, NAC, RG 24, vol. 7167, and *CD-27* log, 24 November-5 December 1917, NAC, RG 24, vol. 7169.

17 HMCS *Niobe* log, 5 December 1917, NAC, RG 24, vol. 7686, and L.B. Griffith to Dorothy Helen Griffith, 21 December 1917, author's files.

18 HMCS *Grilse* log, 5 December 1917, NAC, RG 24, vol. 7371.

19 HMCS *Canada* log, 5 December 1917, NAC, RG 24, vol. 7128. The reference to the anchorage position is estimated from the official map of "HM Naval Yard, Hospital & Admiralty House, Halifax, 1900," NAC, National Map Collection, NMC 0034329.

20 HMCS *Lady Evelyn* log, 5 December 1917, NAC, RG 24, vol. 7444.

21 Some detail of employment, cargo, and scheduling of armed merchant cruisers may be found at NSS 1048-48-2, NAC, RG 24, vol. 3773. Navyard 792 to Naval, 5 December 1917, same file, outlines proposals of the Commander in Chief (C-in-C) North America and West Indies for escort requirements at time of Halifax explosion.

22 C-in-C North America and West Indies to Naval, 5 December 1917, NSS 1048-48-2, NAC, RG 24, vol. 3773.

23 Bermuda 643 to Naval, 5 December 1917, NSS 1048-48-2, NAC, RG 24, vol. 3773.

24 Navinet 597 to Naval, 23 November 1917, NSS 1048-48-8, NAC, RG 24, vol. 3774. As recently as 1998, some writers have wrongly implied that USS *Old Colony* was a fully equipped hospital ship. For example, see James Mahar and Rowena Mahar, *Too Many to Mourn: One Family's Tragedy in the Halifax Explosion* (Halifax: Nimbus, 1998), 8, and Janet Kitz, *Shattered City: The Halifax Explosion and the Road to Recovery* (Halifax: Nimbus, 1989), 60.

25 Navinet 659 to Naval, 26 November 1917, and Naval to Admiralty, 27 November 1917, NSS 1048-48-5, NAC, RG 24, vol. 3774; James L. Mooney, ed., *Dictionary of American Naval Fighting Ships* (Washington, DC: Naval Historical Center, 1981), 149.

26 Admiralty to Naval, 28 November 1917; Navyard to Naval, 4 and 17 December 1917, NSS 1048-48-5, NAC, RG 24, vol. 3774. As detailed in the same file, the USN eventually authorized the work to be done in Halifax.

27 Mooney, ed., *Dictionary of American Naval Fighting Ships,* 436-7.

28 HMCS *Lady Evelyn* log, 5 December 1917, NAC, RG 24, vol. 7444.

29 For a summary of how shipping traffic in the harbour was regulated, see Admiral Superintendent to Secretary Naval Service, 4 March 1918, NSS 37-25-8, NAC, RG 24, vol. 5635.

30 The reserve rank is vaguely equivalent to the regular naval rank of petty officer. Spelling of Freeman's name varies. This account takes the Wreck Commissioner's Inquiry, 1152, as authority. Also see Bird, *The Town That Died,* 19, and *Halifax Herald,* 24 January 1918.

31 Naval Report of Halifax Explosion, n.d. (early February 1918), p. 7, NSS 37-25-9, NAC, RG 24, vol. 5635. This includes copies of applicable regulations. Report also at NS 1001-13-1, NAC, RG 24, vol. 6197.

32 Michael J. Bird, *The Town That Died* (Toronto: McGraw-Hill Ryerson, 1967), 16-21, and David Simpson and Alan Ruffman, "Explosions, Bombs, and Bumps: Scientific Aspects of the Explosion," in

Ground Zero: A Reassessment of the 1917 Explosion in Halifax Harbour, ed. Alan Ruffman and Colin D. Howell (Halifax: Nimbus, 1994), 275-6. These events are also covered in excruciating detail in the testimony of Lieutenant Terrence Freeman, Aimé Le Médec, Francis Mackey, and others in the inquiry conducted by the Dominion Wreck Commissioner of the Department of Marine, chaired by Justice Arthur Drysdale. See NAC, RG 42, vols. 596/597.

33 Testimony of Lieutenant Terrence Freeman, ibid. To illustrate how entrenched bureaucratic routine can become once it has been established, it is interesting to note that Halifax naval intelligence authorities released a telegram to Naval Service Headquarters early on 7 December 1916 reporting the previous day's shipping arrivals, including *Mont Blanc,* which was reported as arriving at 0830 from New York. No mention is made of the explosion, which took place less than an hour later. See Navinet 808 to Naval Ottawa, 7 December 1917, NSS 1048-48-8, NAC, RG 24, vol. 3774.

34 Bird, *The Town That Died,* 20-1. Also see DNS Extract from Confidential Weekly Orders, 14 November 1917, 978 "Belgian Relief Ships – Dates of Arrival," NSS 1048-36-3, NAC, RG 24, vol. 3757.

35 HMCS *Lady Evelyn* log, 5 December 1917, NAC, RG 24, vol. 7444.

36 Weather observations were posted every four hours, HMCS *Grilse* log, 5-6 December 1917, NAC, RG 24, vol. 7371.

37 HMCS *Margaret* log, 5-6 December 1917, NAC, RG 24, vol. 7494.

38 HMCS *Niobe* log, 6 December 1917, NAC, RG 24, vol. 7686.

39 Ibid. The *Grilse* crew called at 6:15, HMCS *Grilse* log, 6 December 1917, NAC, RG 24, vol. 7371. *Canada*'s crew called at 6:30, HMCS *Canada* log, 6 December 1917, NAC, RG 24, vol. 7128. Clearly, the *Grilse* log was written after the fact: it recorded some measure of the larger events and the damage done to Halifax.

40 A.H. Wickens to E.C. Russell, 16 November 1955, DHH, HMCS Niobe 8000, vol. 2, p. 6.

41 P. Willet Brock, "Commander E.A.E. Nixon and the Royal Naval College of Canada, 1910-1922," in *The RCN in Retrospect, 1910-1968,* ed. James A. Boutilier (Vancouver: University of British Columbia Press, 1982), 37-8, and Captain H. Kingsley, RCN (Ret.), "Notes from a Naval Scrapbook," *Victoria Colonist,* 9 December 1951.

42 Minesweeping trawler *PV-VII* log, 6 December 1917, NAC. RG 24, vol. 7761.

43 Testimony of Edward Renner, 21 January 1918, Inquiry, 905-22. See the discussion at Chapter 7.

44 The movements of *Mont Blanc* and *Imo* are analyzed in painstaking and painful detail in testimony, although with some variances at the Wreck Commissioner's Inquiry, NAC, RG 42, vol. 596/7 and subsequent litigation.

45 Testimony of Captain Frederic C.C. Pasco, 23 January 1918, Inquiry, p. 1040. Also see Anonymous [Rear-Admiral B.M. Chambers], "Halifax Explosion," *Naval Review* 7, 1 (1920): 445.

46 Bird, *The Town That Died,* 26-7.

47 J.C.B. LeBlanc, Assistant Naval Secretary, "Historical Synopsis of Organization and Development of the RCN," Formerly in Minister's Office, DHH 87/93.

48 No. 29., Evidence of William Nickerson, 2nd Mate of *Stella Maris,* Direct Examination by Mr Henry K.C. (Counsel to Department of Marine), Exchequer Court of Canada, Nova Scotia Admiralty District, NAC, RG 42, vol. 597 (hereinafter cited as Appeal Book). Also see No. 38., Evidence of Walter Brannen, Mate of *Stella Maris,* and son of its captain. RCN records confuse Horatio Brannen with an Arthur W. Brannen, who commanded the tug in May 1917. Horatio can be traced to the tug *Deliverance,* until June 1917, when it sunk. His name is found associated with *Stella Maris* after that time. The surname has also been found spelled as Brannan and Brennan. The spelling used in this account is believed correct and is found both in RCN records of the charter and the inquiry. See Eagar to Gray, 31 May 1929, NSS 58-13-20, and Brannen to O i/c Fleet Auxiliaries, 16 June 1917, NAC, RG 24, vol. 5659. Bird, *The Town That Died,* 51 [Brannan], and *McAlpine's Halifax City Directory* (1918), List of Dead [Brennan].

49 No. 62, Statement of Thomas Roberts, Yeoman of Signals, on board HMS *Highflyer,* 10 December 1917, Appeal Book, p. 743.

50 No. 61, Statement of Lieutenant R.D. Woolams, RNR, on board HMS *Highflyer*, 10 December 1917, Appeal Book, p. 742.

51 Subject file for *Nereid*, NSS 58-13-15, NAC, RG 24, vol. 5658.

52 No. 7, Testimony of John L. Makiny, 1 April 1918, Appeal Book, p. 12.

53 Ibid., pp. 12-26.

54 Testimony given at the subsequent Wreck Commissioner's Inquiry covers these last moments in both elaborate and confusing detail, as survivors and witnesses struggle to remember precise aspects and lawyers endeavour to discredit accounts unfavourable to their retainers. See NAC, RG 42, vol. 596/7, Nevertheless, the evidence of Aimé Le Médec and Francis Mackey provides a generally reliable sequence of events. For learned evaluation of the process and the reliability of witness accounts, see Judgment of the Lords of the Judicial Committee of the Privy Council, delivered 22 March, 1920, Privy Council Appeals Nos. 129 and 130 of 1919 from the Supreme Court of Canada, copy at Canada Department of Transport, File 9704-244 pt. 3, NAC, RG 12, vol. 2827. For recent and expert discussion of the Collision Regulations and the case from the standpoint of both ships see Donald A. Kerr, "Another Calamity: The Litigation," in *Ground Zero*, ed. Ruffman and Howell, 365-8. Contemporary discussion of rules for the prevention of collision at sea is in R.G. Marsden, *A Treatise on the Law of Collisions at Sea*, 7th ed. (London: Stevens, 1919), 377. This edition contains no reference to the *Mont Blanc-Imo* collision, possibly due to the continuing litigation.

55 Testimony of Herbert Whitehead, RNCVR, 25 January 1917, Inquiry, 1383-6.

56 Judgment of the Lords of the Judicial Committee of the Privy Council, delivered 22 March, 1920, Privy Council Appeals Nos. 129 and 130 of 1919 from the Supreme Court of Canada, copy at Canada Department of Transport, File 9704-244 pt. 3, NAC, RG 12, vol. 2827. Other reliable accounts are more accessible. See Kerr, "Another Calamity," 365-8, and Bird, *The Town That Died*, 30-3.

57 Testimony of Herbert Whitehead, RNCVR, 25 January 1917, Inquiry, 1389.

58 Testimony of Aimé Le Médec, 13 December 1917, Inquiry, 11-A22.

59 Testimony of George Abbott, 22 January 1918, Inquiry, 970-81.

60 Testimony of Herbert Whitehead RNCVR, 25 January 1918, Inquiry, 1390.

61 Testimony of George Abbott, 22 January 1918, Inquiry, 971.

62 Testimony of Herbert Whitehead RNCVR, 25 January 1918, Inquiry, 1390-1, 1402.

63 Ibid., 1403-4.

64 No. 29, Evidence of William Nickerson, Appeal Book, 373-4; No. 38, Evidence of Walter Brannen, Appeal Book, 484-6; Testimony of Herbert Whitehead, 25 January 1918, Inquiry, 1406-8; Captain H.N. Garnett, RN, HMS *Highflyer*, to Senior Naval Officer Halifax, 7 December 1917, Public Records Office (hereinafter PRO), ADM 1/8507/273.

65 CO *Niobe* to Captain Superintendent, 21 January 1918, NSS 37-25-2, vol. 3, NAC, RG 24, vol. 5634. Surprisingly, there is no mention of the steam pinnace that day in the HMCS *Niobe* log, NAC, RG 24, vol. 7686.

66 Undated list of men who lost their lives on 6 December at Halifax (Steam boat's crew), ff. 79, NSS 37-25-2, vol. 3, NAC, RG 24, vol. 5634.

67 Bird, *The Town That Died*, 59. Although this book describes itself as a novel, it is generally accurate. Thus, it is most unfortunate that Bird did not document his sources other than to indicate a wide range of valuable interviews with witnesses and participants who were still living at the time, including *Mont Blanc*'s pilot.

68 No. 29, Evidence of William Nickerson, Appeal Book, 373-4; No. 38, Evidence of Walter Brannen, Appeal Book, 484-6, and Bird, *The Town That Died*, 59.

69 Testimony of Herbert Whitehead RNCVR, 25 January 1918, Inquiry, 1393.

70 Ibid., 1392-4, 1409-10, 1415.

71 Testimony of Frederick Wyatt, 24 January 1918, Inquiry, 1249.

72 L.B. Griffith to Dorothy H. Griffith, 8 December 1917, author's files. Griffith's three letters provide the

basis for John G. Armstrong, "Letters from Halifax: Reliving the Halifax Explosion through the Eyes of My Grandfather, a Sailor in the Royal Canadian Navy," *Northern Mariner/Le Marin du nord* 8, 4 (1998): 55-74.

73 Brock, "Commander E.A.E. Nixon," 38-9; Captain H. Kingsley, RCN (Ret.), "Notes from a Naval Scrapbook," *Victoria Colonist*, 9 December 1951, copy at DHH 89/22.

74 HMCS *Margaret* log, 6 December 1917, NAC, RG 24, vol. 7494.

75 Commanding Officer *Niobe* to Captain Superintendent, 18 December 1917, NSS, 37-25-2, vol. 3, NAC, RG 24, vol. 5634.

76 Julie H. Ferguson, *Through a Canadian Periscope: The Story of the Canadian Submarine Service* (Toronto: Dundurn Press, 1995), 82. The source appears to be an interview in the *Victoria Colonist* of unknown date, with the former coxswain of *CC-2*.

77 Testimony of Captain F.C.C. Pasco, 23 January 1918, Inquiry, 1038-9, NAC, RG 42, v. 596/7.

78 Written accounts vary widely as to the exact time of the explosion. HMCS *Niobe*'s log records it as 9:07 (NAC, RG 24, vol. 7686). Alan Ruffman and David Simpson found seismographic records from Dalhousie College that established the time given here. See Alan Ruffman and David Simpson, "Realities, Myths, and Misconceptions of the Explosion," in *Ground Zero*, ed. Ruffman and Howell, 301-6.

Chapter 3: Halifax Tide

1 Written by Bruce Grinstead and Pat Bourke, 1995. Available at Dacre Mountain Productions, RR#2, Arnprior, ON, K7S 3G8.

2 H.L. Bronson, PhD, F.R.S.C., "Some Notes on the Halifax Explosion," *Transactions of the Royal Society of Canada,* series 3, vol. 12 (June 1918, talk given in May), section 3, pp. 33, 31. Partial transcription at NSS 37-25-1, NAC, RG 24, vol. 5634. For a more recent and detailed scientific analysis, see David Simpson and Alan Ruffman, "Explosions, Bombs, and Bumps: Scientific Aspects of the Explosion," in *Ground Zero: A Reassessment of the 1917 Explosion in Halifax Harbour,* ed. Alan Ruffman and Colin D. Howell (Halifax: Nimbus, 1994), 275-99. The authors also trace through discrepancies in various accounts over the years in the amount of explosives, citing those given on the original New York City manifest and shipper's export declarations.

3 Ships destroyed or significantly damaged are named at Navyard 974 to Naval, 19 December 1917, NSS 37 25-1, National Archives of Canada (NAC), RG 24, vol. 5634. Some details of casualties suffered by merchant vessels can be found in NSS 37-25-2, NAC, RG 24, vol. 5634.

4 CO *Niobe* to Secretary Naval Service, 20 January 1918, NSS 37-25-2, vol. 3, NAC, RG 24, vol. 5634.

5 Report of Captain H.N. Garnett, RN, 7 December 1917, Public Records Office (PRO), ADM 1/8507/273.

6 No. 29, Evidence of William Nickerson, Exchequer Court of Canada, Nova Scotia Admiralty District, NAC, RG 42, vol. 597 (hereinafter Appeal Book), 373-4; No. 38, Evidence of Walter Brannen, Appeal Book, 485; Navyard 974 to Naval, 19 December 1917, NSS 37-25-1, NAC, RG 24, vol. 5634, and extract from letter to the Deputy Minister from C.H. Harvey, 12 December 1917, File 39796, NAC, RG 42, vol. 274. Futile efforts to obtain compensation from the RCN on behalf of the crew would continue for years. See Secretary Halifax Harbour Commission to Deputy Minister, 13 September 1934, NSS 58-27-1, NAC, RG 24, vol. 5659.

7 Testimony of Herbert Whitehead RNCVR, 25 January 1918, Wreck Commissioner's Inquiry, 1394-6, NAC, RG 42, vol. 596/7 (hereinafter Inquiry), and Navyard 974 to Naval, 19 December 1917, NSS 37-25-1, NAC, RG 24, vol. 5634.

8 L.B. Griffith to Dorothy H. Griffith, 8 December 1917, author's files.

9 Alan Ruffman, David Greenberg, and Tad Murty, "The Tsunami from the Explosion in Halifax Harbour," in *Ground Zero*, ed. Ruffman and Howell, 327-44.

10 L.B. Griffith to Dorothy H. Griffith, 8 December 1917, author's files.

11 For other personal descriptions see Jack Stotesbury, Letters 7-10 December 1917, National Defence

Headquarters, Directorate of History and Heritage (DHH), HMCS Niobe (Cruiser) 8000 and Reuben Hamilton, transcript of interview, unspecified date in 1950s, DHH Biographical File.

12 CO HMCS *Niobe* to Secretary Naval Service, 20 January 1918, NAC, RG 24, NSS 37-25-2, vol. 3; Accounts Officer HMCS *Niobe* to Naval, 8 December 1917, and Wilson to Desbarats, 9 December 1917, NSS 37-25-1, NAC, RG 24, vol. 5634.

13 L.B. Griffith to Dorothy H. Griffith, 8 December 1917, author's files.

14 CO HMCS *Niobe* to Captain Superintendent HMC Dockyard, 18 December 1917, NSS 37-25-2, vol. 3, NAC, RG 24, vol. 5634.

15 See "Brief History of HMCS *Niobe*," DHH, *Niobe* Permanent Record File (PRF), and HMCS *Niobe* log, 6 and 7 December 1917, NAC, RG 24, vol. 7686.

16 Fred Longland, "The Great Halifax Disaster of December 1917," NAC, MG 30 E 183.

17 Navyard 833 to Naval, 9 December 1917, NSS 37-25-1, NAC, RG 24, vol. 5634; CO *Niobe* to Secretary Naval Service, 20 January 1918, NSS 37-25-2, NAC, RG 24, vol. 5634.

18 CO HMCS *Niobe* to Captain Superintendent, 19 December 1917, NSS 37-25-2, vol. 3, NAC, RG 24, vol. 5634.

19 CO *Niobe* to Captain Superintendent, 18 December 1917, ibid.

20 Captain H. Kingsley, RCN (Ret.), "Notes from a Naval Scrapbook," *Victoria Colonist*, 9 December 1951.

21 P. Willet Brock, "Commander E.A.E. Nixon and the Royal Naval College of Canada, 1910-1922," in *The RCN in Retrospect, 1910-1968*, ed. James A. Boutilier (Vancouver: University of British Columbia Press, 1982), 38.

22 Kingsley, "Notes from a Naval Scrapbook."

23 College to Naval, 7 December 1917, NSS 37-25-2, vol. 1, NAC, RG 24, vol. 5634.

24 Michael Bird, *The Town That Died* (Toronto: McGraw-Hill Ryerson, 1967), 69-70.

25 Kingsley, "Notes from a Naval Scrapbook,"and Brock, "Commander E.A.E. Nixon," 39.

26 E.A.E. Nixon, "Account of the Explosion at Halifax," E.A.E. Nixon papers, DHH, 74/689.

27 Philip Weatherbe, W.B.Cb.B., F.A.C.S, Description of injuries, Commander Nixon, 25 January 1918, NSS 37-25-2, vol. 3, NAC, RG 24, vol. 5634.

28 Director of Stores to Deputy Minister, 24 December 1917, NSS 37-25-1, vol. 1, NAC, RG 24, vol. 5634, and Desbarats to Burrows, 7 January 1918, NSS 37-25-3, NAC, RG 24, vol. 5635.

29 Photographic evidence at NSS 37-25-12, NAC, RG 24, vol. 5635. Damage to the YMCA is also discussed in L.B. Griffith to Dorothy Helen Griffith, 8 and 16 December 1917, author's files.

30 Fleet Wireless Officer to Naval, 8 December 1917, NSS 37-25-3, NAC, RG 24, vol. 5635, and Fleet Wireless Officer to Captain Superintendent, 20 December 1917, NSS 37-25-2, vol. 3, NAC, RG 24, vol. 5634.

31 Director of Stores to Deputy Minister, 24 December 1917, NSS 37-25-1, vol. 1, NAC, RG 24, vol. 5634, and Duicock to Beausoleil, 14 December 1917, NSS 37-25-3, NAC, RG 24, vol. 5635.

32 *Ottawa Citizen*, 13 December 1917, copy filed at NSS 37-25-11, NAC, RG 24, vol. 5635.

33 Captain Superintendent to Secretary Naval Service, 24 January 1918, NSS 37-25-2, vol. 3, NAC, RG 24, vol. 5634; Long to Devonshire, 8 April 1918, NSS 37-25-10, NAC, RG 24, vol. 5635; and *Ottawa Citizen*, 13 December 1917.

34 Desbarats to Burrows, 7 January 1918, NSS 37-25-3, NAC, RG 24, vol. 5635.

35 Testimony of Captain F.C.C. Pasco, 23 January 1918, Inquiry, 1041.

36 Ibid., 1042.

37 No. 61, Testimony of John L. Makiny, 1 April 1918, Appeal Book, 23.

38 Makiny to Chief Examining Officer, 7 May 1918, accompanying minutes and Charter Party, good tug *Nereid*, 23 July 1917; NSS 58-13-15, NAC, RG 24, vol. 5658.

39 *PV-V* log, 6-8 December 1917, NAC, RG 24, vol. 7760.

40 Captain of Patrols to Secretary Naval Service, 10 January 1918, NSS 37-25-6, NAC, RG 24, vol. 5635

41 HMCS *Margaret* log, 6 December 1917, NAC, RG 24, vol. 7494.

42 HMCS *Grilse* log, 6 December 1917, NAC, RG 24, vol. 7371. The injuries to Walker were recorded at

Captain Superintendent to Secretary Naval Service, 24 January 1918, NSS 37-25-2, vol. 3, NAC, RG 24, vol. 5634.

43 This account was found by Julie H. Ferguson and presented in her history of the Canadian submarine service, *Through a Canadian Periscope: The Story of the Canadian Submarine Service* (Toronto: Dundurn Press, 1995), 82-3. The bracketed names and initials were verified from *The Canadian Navy List*, January 1918 (Ottawa: King's Printer, 1917).

44 Ibid., 83.

45 Bird, *The Town That Died*, 8-9; 90 (presumably sourced by documents on PRO, ADM1/8507/273), and L.B. Griffith to Dorothy H. Griffith, 8 December 1917, author's files.

46 Captain Superintendent to Secretary Naval Service, 24 January 1918, NSS 37-25-2, vol. 3, NAC, RG 24, v. 5634.

47 Ibid. No other injuries are recorded; however, on 11 December, an exchange between the captains of *Grilse* and *Canada* is recorded in *Canada*'s log but unremarked in that of *Grilse*. As has been mentioned, Walker's face had been injured. *Canada*'s log indicates that Wood of *Canada* was visited by doctor from *Highflyer* on 9 December and by another from HMS *Donegal* on the 10th (*Donegal* arrived on 9 December). Logs of HMCS *Grilse* and HMCS *Canada*, 7-11 December 1917, NAC, RG 24, vols. 7371 and 7128.

48 Abstract, ff. 8, NSS, 37-25-6, NAC, RG 24, vol. 5635.

49 HMCS *Canada* log, 6 December 1917, NAC, RG 24, vol. 7128.

50 *CD-53* log, 6 December 1917, NAC, RG 24, vol. 7179. *CD-27* log, vol. 7169.

51 *CD-26* log, NAC, RG 24, vol. 7167.

52 *CD-27* log, NAC, RG 24, vol. 7169.

53 Anonymous [Rear-Admiral B.M. Chambers], "Halifax Explosion," *Naval Review* 7, 1 (1920): 417-18.

54 *PV-VII* log, 6 December 1917, NAC, RG 24, vol. 7761.

55 HMCS *Lady Evelyn* log, 6 December 1917, NAC, RG 24, vol. 7444.

Chapter 4: Through the Grim Day

1 Personal memoirs of A.H. Wickens in A.H. Wickens to E.C. Russell, 16 November 1955, National Defence Headquarters, Directorate of History and Heritage (DHH), HMCS *Niobe* 8000, vol. 2, p. 8. Wickens's account is repeated in the ship's unofficial history ("Brief History of HMCS *Niobe*," DHH, *Niobe* Permanent Record File [PRF]), but no other references to the incident have been found thus far in Naval Service records. The reference to the *Birkenhead* is obscure but was traced with the gruff assistance of Mr Don Graves, then of the staff of DHH. *Birkenhead* was a paddle-wheel troopship proceeding to the Cape of Good Hope in 1851 carrying detachments or drafts from the depots of ten regiments, "accompanied by the proportion of wives and children usually permitted to attend soldiers going to a colony." After the ship struck a rock and was sinking, the women and children aboard were despatched to the safety of shore in the ship's only cutter, while the soldiers and sailors maintained their discipline and went down with the ship. Four hundred and eighty died in the disaster. See William O.S. Gilly, *Narratives of Shipwrecks of the Royal Navy between 1793 and 1857* (London: Longman, Green, 1864), 348-57.

2 Admiral Superintendent to Secretary Naval Service, 4 March 1918, NSS 37-25-8, National Archives of Canada (NAC), RG 24, vol. 5635.

3 CO HMCS *Niobe* to Captain Superintendent, 19 December 1917, NSS 37-25-2, vol. 3, NAC, RG 24, vol. 5634.

4 Navyard 813 to Naval, 6 December 1917 (not received until the 8th), NSS 37-25-3, vol. 1, NAC, RG 24, vol. 5634.

5 Testimony of Captain F.C.C. Pasco, 23 January 1918, Wreck Commissioner's Inquiry, 1042, NAC, RG 42, vol. 596/7 (hereinafter Inquiry) and Captain Superintendent to Director Naval Service, 14 December 1917, NSS 37-25-3, NAC, RG 24, vol. 5635.

6 OC 1st Depot Battalion Nova Scotia Regiment to Assistant Adjutant General (hereinafter AAG), Military District No. 6 (Halifax), 17 January 1918, MD6 86-2-1, NAC, RG 24, vol. 4548. Regrettably, neither the Officer Commanding nor the staff officer who prepared the consolidated report of services rendered by the Militia garrison troubled to note the sergeant-major's name.

7 To Marie Putnam, 7 December 1917, Ms 84660, Papers of Carl Moulton, folder 1, at the Connecticut Historical Society, Hartford, CT, copy at Public Archives of Nova Scotia (hereinafter PANS), reel 10,921.

8 Admiral Superintendent to Secretary Naval Service, 4 March 1918, NSS 37-25-8, NAC, RG 24, vol. 5635; CO HMCS *Niobe* to Captain Superintendent, 18 December 1917, NSS 37-25-2, vol. 3, NAC, RG 24, vol. 5634, and L.B. Griffith to Dorothy H. Griffith, 8 December 1917, author's files. Also see "Brief History of HMCS *Niobe*," DHH, *Niobe* PRF.

9 J. Stotesbury, Letters 7-10 December 1917, DHH, HMCS *Niobe* (cruiser) 8000.

10 To Marion [surname unknown], 9 December 1917, Ms 84660, Papers of Carl Moulton, folder 1, at the Connecticut Historical Society, Hartford, CT, copy at PANS, reel 10,921.

11 General Officer Commanding Military District No. 6 (Halifax) (hereinafter GOC MD6) to Secretary Militia Council, 15 December 1917, MD6 86-2-1, NAC, RG 24, vol. 4548.

12 Ibid. This file also contains detailed reports of the responses and activities of units and subunits other than medical. The main Militia HQ subject file on the explosion is HQ 71-26-99. The Militia HQ subject file on medical aspects of the explosion is HQ 71-26-99-3.

13 Sir Andrew MacPhail, *Official History of the Canadian Forces in the Great War, 1914-19: The Medical Services* (Ottawa: King's Printer, 1925), 327.

14 GOC MD6 (Halifax) to Secretary Militia Council, 15 December 1917, MD6 86-2-1, NAC, RG 24, vol. 4548.

15 Report of Lieutenant C.A. McLennan, n.d., MD6 86-2-1, NAC, RG 24, vol. 4548.

16 See reports of Captain H.J. Wilcox, RN, Lieutenant-Commander F.H. Drake-Clarke, RNR, and Lieutenant F.B. Thompson, RNR from HMS *Changuinola*, Public Records Office (PRO), ADM 1/8507/273 (portions published in Michael J. Bird, *The Town That Died* [Toronto: McGraw-Hill Ryerson, 1967]), 99-101, 103-4.

17 Report of Lieutenant C.A. McLennan, n/d, MD6 86-2-1, NAC, RG 24, vol. 4548.

18 McLennan learned the cause of the panic only later from the sentries who had been stationed nearby and who had seen the civilians take flight. Report of Lieutenant C.A. McLennan, n/d, MD6 86-2-1, NAC, RG 24, vol. 4548.

19 *Ottawa Citizen*, 12 December 1917.

20 Bird, *The Town That Died*, 68-9, presumably based on interview with P. Willet Brock.

21 Report of Lieutenant C.A. McLennan, n.d., MD6 86-2-1, NAC, RG 24, vol. 4548.

22 Reports of Captain H.J. Wilcox, RN, Lieutenant-Commander F.H. Drake-Clarke, RNR, and Lieutenant F.B. Thompson, RNR from HMS *Changuinola*, PRO, ADM 1/8507/273.

23 Julie H. Ferguson, *Through a Canadian Periscope: The Story of the Canadian Submarine Service* (Toronto: Dundurn Press, 1995), 83.

24 Captain Superintendent to Director Naval Service, 14 December 1917, NSS 37-25-3, NAC, RG 24, vol. 5635.

25 Testimony of Captain F.C.C. Pasco, 23 January 1918, Inquiry, 1042.

26 Anonymous [Rear-Admiral B.M. Chambers], "Halifax Explosion," *Naval Review* 7, 1 (1920): 446. This literate account is largely an edited and considered version of Chambers's reports to the Secretary of the Admiralty of 6 and 9 December 1917, at PRO, ADM 1/8507/273. The primary documents and the review article are of equal value, but the latter is cited as more generally available in military and other libraries. A copy of this Admiralty subject file was acquired in 1998 by the DHH. According to Michael Bird's account, Rear-Admiral Chambers received a report of the collision and fire at home and, as "one of the few men who knew the nature of the French freighter's cargo he immediately

realised the terrible danger to the city." Bird, *The Town That Died*, 89. These statements are not correct, as the account in the text makes clear.

27 [Chambers], "Halifax Explosion," 446.

28 Ibid., 446.

29 Port Convoy Officer to Secretary of the Admiralty, 6 December 1917, PRO, ADM 1/8507/273.

30 Bird, *The Town That Died*, 56-62.

31 Captain H.N. Garnett, RN, HMS *Highflyer* to Senior Naval Officer Halifax, 7 December 1917, PRO, ADM 1/8507/273.

32 [Chambers], "Halifax Explosion," 446-8.

33 Ibid.

34 Report of Surgeon H.G. Brown, RN, HMS *Changuinola*, 7 December 1917, PRO, ADM 1/8507/273.

35 [Chambers], "Halifax Explosion," 447.

36 Report of Vice-Admiral E.R. Le Marchant, 9 December 1917, PRO, ADM 1/8507/273.

37 Port Convoy Officer to Secretary of Admiralty, 6 December 1917, PRO, ADM 1/8507/273.

38 [Chambers], "Halifax Explosion," 448.

39 Admiral Superintendent to Secretary Naval Service, 4 March 1918, NSS 37-25-8, NAC, RG 24, vol. 5635.

40 Long (Admiralty) to Devonshire (GG), 8 April 1918, NSS 37-25-10, NAC, RG 24, vol. 5635. For a more complete description see report of Captain Garnett, *Highflyer*, 7 December 1918, PRO, ADM 1/8507/273.

41 Naval Transport Officer to Captain Superintendent, 19 December 1917, NSS 37-25-2, NAC, RG 24, vol. 5634, and Bird, *The Town That Died*, 95.

42 [Chambers], "Halifax Explosion," 449.

43 Kingsmill to Chambers, 7 December 1917, NSS 37-25-2, vol. 1, NAC, RG 24, vol. 5634, and [Chambers], "Halifax Explosion," 449.

44 USS *Tacoma*, James L. Mooney, ed., *Dictionary of American Naval Fighting Ships* (Washington, DC: Naval Historical Center, 1981). HMCS *Lady Evelyn* log, 6 December 1917, NAC, RG 24, vol. 7444.

45 Commanding Officer USS *Tacoma* to Commander Squadron Two, Cruiser Force, 11 December 1917, microfilm reel 15125, PANS, MG 27, vol. 2, #31.

46 HMCS *Lady Evelyn* log, 6 December 1917, NAC, RG 24, vol. 7444.

47 *Kronprinz Wilhelm* had achieved a certain notoriety, mostly in Latin American waters, where she had destroyed just under 56,000 tons of Allied shipping. This seventy-two-day stint had been ended upon failing to replenish her coal supply. USS *Von Steuben*, in Mooney, ed., *Dictionary of American Naval Fighting Ships*. This source states that the two American ships had been bound for Halifax. This is contradicted by Rear-Admiral Chambers's report of conversations held with the two officers in his article in *Naval Review* 7, 1 (1920): 452.

48 CO *Tacoma* to Commander Squadron Two, Cruiser Force, 11 December 1917, and Medical Officer to Commanding Officer USS *Tacoma*, 9 December 1917, microfilm reel 15125, PANS, MG 27, v. 2, #31. This correspondence confuses the identity of *Old Colony* by also referring to a ship named USS *Old Glory*. Mooney lists no such ship in *Dictionary of American Naval Fighting Ships*, nor has any entry been found in port records (or for that matter in any other primary source) reporting the arrival or departure of a ship of that name. I believe that no such ship existed. The confusion is attributed to typographical error and/or transcription of the infamous handwriting of physicians. Certainly, my own poor hand makes the two names look identical.

49 Medical Officer USS *Tacoma* to Commanding Officer, 9 December 1917, microfilm reel 15125, PANS, MG 27, v. 2, #31.

50 [Chambers], "Halifax Explosion," 451, and Chambers to Secretary Admiralty, 6 December 1917, PRO, ADM 1/8507/273.

51 Halifax City Council, Minutes, 6 December 1917, PANS, reel 12426, and GOC MD6 (Halifax) to Secretary Militia Council, 15 December 1917, MD6 86-2-1, NAC, RG 24, vol. 4548.

52 R.A. 803 to Naval, 6 December 1917, NSS 1048-48-1, vol. 3, NAC, RG 24, vol. 3773.

53 [Chambers], "Halifax Explosion," 452, and Commanding Officer USS *Tacoma* to Commander Squadron Two, Cruiser Force, 11 December 1917, microfilm reel 15125, PANS, MG 27, vol. 2, #31.

54 CO *Tacoma* to Commander Squadron Two, Cruiser Force, 11 December 1917, microfilm reel 15125, PANS, MG 27, vol. 2, #31. Chambers also records meeting *Tacoma*'s captain. See "Halifax Explosion," 452.

55 Pasco to Director Naval Service, 14 January 1918, NSS 37-25-2, NAC, RG 24, vol. 5634 and Pasco to Secretary Naval Service, 10 December 1917, NSS 37-25-3, NAC, RG 24, vol. 5634.

56 Navyard 804 to Naval, 6 December 1917, NSS 37-25-3, NAC, RG 24, vol. 5634.

57 See J. Castell Hopkins, ed., *The Canadian Annual Review, 1917* (Toronto: annual review publishing co., 1918), 467, and Charles E. Tanner to A.W. Blount, 7 December 1917, Sir Robert Borden Papers, NAC, MG 26 H1, vol. 89.

58 Comments of Mr Hayes, General Manager Canadian Government Railways, meeting held in Board of Trade Rooms, 8 December 1917, NSS 37-25-1, vol. 1, NAC, RG 24, vol. 5634, and [Chambers], "Halifax Explosion," 451. Plans and development of the new terminal facilities can be followed from the perspective of the Halifax business community in PANS, Micro 12400, Reports of the Halifax Board of Trade, 1912-18.

59 Bird, *The Town That Died,* 148-9.

60 CO *Niobe* to Captain Superintendent, 18 December 1917, NSS 37-25-2, vol. 3, NAC, RG 24, vol. 5634, and HMCS *Niobe* log, 6 December 1917, NSS 37-25-2, NAC, RG 24, vol. 7686.

61 [Chambers], "Halifax Explosion," 452-3; HMCS *Grilse* log, 6 December 1917, NAC, RG 24, vol. 7371; and HMCS *Canada* log, 6 December 1917, NAC, RG 24, vol. 7128.

62 HMCS *Lady Evelyn* log, 6 December 1917, NAC RG 24, vol. 7444.

Chapter 5: Reaction and Recovery

1 Diary, 6 December 1917, G.J. Desbarats Papers, National Archives of Canada (NAC), MG 30, E 89, vol. 5; Deputy Minister Naval Service to Minister, 19 November 1917, NS 14-4-2, vol. 2, NAC, RG 24, vol. 3603.

2 Robert Craig Brown and Ramsay Cook, *Canada, 1896-1921: A Nation Transformed* (Toronto: McClelland and Stewart, 1974), 272, and H.J. Morgan, ed., *The Canadian Men and Women of the Time* (Toronto: William Briggs, 1912), 56.

3 Diary, 1 January 1918, Desbarats Papers, NAC, MG 30 E 89, vol. 5.

4 L.B. Griffith to Dorothy H. Griffith, 21 December 1917, author's collection.

5 *Halifax Herald,* 3 December 1917, and Halifax *Morning Chronicle,* 5 December 1917.

6 The Censor, Halifax, to Deputy Chief Censor, Ottawa, 12 December 1917, and Curran to Chambers (personal letter), 12 December 1917, File 353, NAC, RG 6 E, vol. 621.

7 Morgan, ed., *Canadian Men and Women,* 218-19, and Arnold W. Thomas, ed., *The Canadian Almanac and Miscellaneous Directory* (Toronto: Copp Clark, 1917), 303.

8 For a brief but not entirely sympathetic discussion, see W.H. Kesterton, *A History of Journalism in Canada* (Toronto: McClelland and Stewart, 1967), 246-7.

9 Chambers to Knowles, Canadian Press, 6 December 1917, File 350, NAC, RG 6 E, vol. 621.

10 E.J. Chambers, Memorandum for Office File, 6 December 1917, ff. 10, File 350, NAC, RG 6 E, vol. 621.

11 Ibid., ff. 11, File 350, NAC, RG 6 E, vol. 621.

12 Ibid., ff. 12, File 350, NAC, RG 6 E, vol. 621.

13 Quote from Naval to McGillivray, Camperdown, 6 December 1917. Other messages referred to are Naval to Navyard 659, and Naval to Transport, Saint John, all 6 December 1917, NSS 37-25-1, NAC, RG 24, vol. 5634.

14 Director of Stores to Deputy Minister, 24 December 1917, NSS 37-25-1, NAC, RG 24, vol. 5634. The J.A. Wilson Papers, NAC, MG 30 E 243, contain biographical information and details of his distinguished

career as a pioneer administrator of Canadian aviation. Unfortunately, they provide no insight into his remarkable contribution to the RCN in dealing with the situation created by the Halifax explosion.

15 Director of the Naval Service to Senior Naval Officer (hereinafter SNO) Halifax, NSS 37-25-2, vol. 1, NAC, RG 24, vol. 5634.

16 North Sydney Radio Station to Naval Ottawa, 6 December 1917, NSS 37-25-3, NAC, RG 24, vol. 5635.

17 Transport Saint John 640 to Naval Ottawa, 6 December 1917, NSS 37-25-1, NAC, RG 24, vol. 5634.

18 E.J. Chambers, Memorandum for Office File, 6 December 1917, ff 12, File 350, NAC, RG 6 E, vol. 621.

19 Naval to SNO Halifax, very urgent, 6 December 1917, NSS 37-25-1, NAC, RG 24, vol. 5634.

20 A. Johnston to SNO Halifax, 6 December 1917.

21 Chief of General Staff (hereinafter CGS) 9650 to General Officer Commanding Military District No. 6 (Halifax) (hereinafter GOC MD6), 6 December 1917, HQ 71-26-99, vol. 1, NAC, RG 24, vol. 6358.

22 CGS to GOC MD7 (Saint John), MD6 (Halifax), and MD5 (Quebec), HQ 71-26-99, vol. 1, NAC, RG 24, vol. 6358.

23 GOC MD6 (Halifax) to CGS, 7 December 1917, HQ 71-26-99, vol. 1, NAC, RG 24, vol. 6358.

24 The response of Militia HQ can be traced at the multivolume file HQ 71-26-99, NAC, RG 24, vol. 6358-9. The HQ medical file dealing with the disaster is HQ 71-26-99-3, NAC, RG 24, vol. 6359. Copies of Militia HQ reports on the disaster are also in Sir Robert Borden Papers, NAC, MG 26 H 1 (a), vols. 89-90.

25 Kingsmill to Curren, 7 December 1917, NSS 37-25-1, NAC, RG 24, vol. 5634.

26 E.J. Chambers, Memorandum for Office File, 7 December 1917, ff. 14, and Chambers to McMillan, Manager CPR Telegraph, Montreal, 7 December 1917, File 350, NAC, RG 6 E, vol. 621.

27 Kingsmill to Chambers, 7 December 1917, NSS 37-25-2, NAC, RG 24, vol. 5634.

28 Director Naval Service to Captain Superintendent, 7 December 1917, NSS 37-25-3, NAC, RG 24, vol. 5635.

29 G.J. Desbarats, diary, 7 December 1917, NAC, MG 30 E 89, vol. 5.

30 Kingsmill to E.J. Chambers, 20 December 1917, File 350, NAC, RG 6 E, vol. 621.

31 Desbarats, diary, 7 December 1917, NAC, MG 30 E 89, vol. 5.

32 HMCS Lady Evelyn log, 7 December 1917, NAC, RG 24, vol. 7444 and HMCS Laurentian log, 7 December 1917, vol. 7450.

33 HMCS Laurentian log, 7 December 1917, NAC, RG 24, vol. 7450.

34 Weather observations in the harbour are from HMCS Margaret log, 7-8 December 1917, NAC, RG 24, vol. 7494, and HMCS Grilse log, 7-8 December 1917, NAC, RG 24, vol. 7371. The report on the weather at sea, where the wind rose to Force 9, is from HMCS Lady Evelyn log, 7-8 December 1917, NAC, RG 24, vol. 7444. Also see Anonymous [Rear-Admiral B.M. Chambers], "Halifax Explosion," Naval Review 7, 1 (1920): 453.

35 Navyard 813 to Naval, 7 December 1917, NSS 37-25-2, NAC, RG 24, vol. 5634.

36 Commanding Officer USS Tacoma to Commander Squadron Two, Cruiser Force, 11 December 1917, microfilm reel 15125, Public Archives of Nova Scotia (hereinafter PANS), MG 27, vol. 2, #31.

37 HMCS Margaret log, 7 December 1917, NAC, RG 24, vol. 7494, and HMCS Canada log, 7 December 1917, NAC, RG 24, vol. 7128.

38 Censor Halifax to Deputy Chief Censor Ottawa, 12 December 1917, File 350, NAC, RG 6 E, vol. 621.

39 HMCS Niobe log, 7 December 1917, NAC, RG 24, vol. 7686. Other activities are recorded in the logs of HMCS Grilse (vol. 7371), Canada (vol. 7128), and Margaret (v. 7494).

40 [Chambers], "Halifax Explosion," 453-4.

41 SNO (British), (circular) Memorandum Z/2, 7 December 1917, MD6 86-2-1 CONF, NAC, RG 24, vol. 4548.

42 [Chambers], "Halifax Explosion," 453.

43 Ibid.; SNO (British), (circular) Memorandum Z/2, 7 December 1917, MD6 86-2-1 CONF, NAC, RG 24, vol. 4548.

44 Naval Stores Officer to J.A. Wilson, Ottawa, 7 December 1917, NSS 37-25-3, NAC, RG 24, vol. 5635, and Wilson to Deputy Minister, 24 December 1917, NSS 37-25-1, NAC, RG 24, vol. 5634.

45 Laurie to Wilson, 7 December 1917, NSS 37-25-3, NAC, RG 24, vol. 5635.

46 Laurie to Wilson, 8 December 1917, NSS 37-25-1, NAC, RG 24, vol. 5634.

47 Director of Stores to Deputy Minister, 24 December 1917, NSS 37-25-1, NAC, RG 24, vol. 5634.

48 L.B. Griffith to Dorothy H. Griffith, 16 December 1917, author's collection.

49 L.B. Griffith to Dorothy H. Griffith, 8 December 1917, author's collection.

50 Commanding Officer USS *Tacoma* to Commander Squadron Two, Cruiser Force, 11 December 1917, microfilm reel 15125, PANS, MG 27, vol. 2, #31.

51 Navyard 809 and 810 to Naval, 7 December 1917, NSS 37-25-2, NAC, RG 24, vol. 5634.

52 RN College of Canada to Naval Ottawa, 7 December 1917, NSS 37-25-1, NAC, RG 24, vol. 5634; identity of sender not shown.

53 Kingsmill to Mrs Kingsmill, 8 December 1917, NSS 37-25-2, NAC, RG 24, vol. 5634.

54 HMCS *Lady Evelyn* log, 8 December 1917, NAC, RG 24, vol. 7444.

55 HMCS *Canada* log, NAC, RG 24, vol. 7128.

56 HMCS *Lady Evelyn* log, 8 December 1917, NAC, RG 24, vol. 7444.

57 [Chambers], "Halifax Explosion," 453-4.

58 Ibid., 454.

59 Ibid.

60 Summary of file HQ 60-P-30, Captain F.C.C. Pasco, National Defence Headquarters, Directorate of History and Heritage (hereinafter DHH), 4000-100/14.

61 Navyard 813 to Naval, 8 December 1917, NSS 37-25-1, NAC, RG 24, vol. 5634.

62 Navyard 828 to Naval, 8 December 1917, NSS 37-25-1, NAC, RG 24, vol. 5634.

63 Intermediate Medical Report of Lieutenant-Colonel F. McKelvey Bell, under cover Bell to Director General Medical Service (hereinafter DGMS), 25 January 1918, HQ 71-26-99-3, vol. 1, NAC, RG 24, HQ 71-26-99-3, vol. 5369. Also see remarks [Chambers], "Halifax Explosion," 454, and Commanding Officer USS *Tacoma* to Commander Squadron Two, Cruiser Force, 11 December 1917, microfilm reel 15125, PANS, MG 27, vol. 2, #31. Also see Michael J. Bird, *The Town That Died* (Toronto: McGraw-Hill Ryerson, 1967), 144-58.

64 Intermediate Medical Report of Lieutenant-Colonel F. McKelvey Bell, under cover Bell to DGMS, 25 January 1918, HQ 71-26-99-3, vol. 1, NAC, RG 24, HQ 71-26-99-3, vol. 5369.

65 Ibid. An edited version of the report was later printed and circulated as a general statement of interest to the public. See Department of Militia and Defence, Extracts from an Intermediate Medical Report re the Halifax Disaster, December 6th, 1917, MD2 22-1-245, NAC, RG 24, vol. 4273. The report does not appear to have been found by the historians who have most recently investigated medical aspects of the disaster. See T.J. Murray, "Medical Aspects of the Disaster: The Missing Report of Dr David Fraser Harris," and Neena Abraham, "Medical Memories of the 1917 Explosion" both in *Ground Zero: A Reassessment of the 1917 Explosion in Halifax Harbour*, ed. Alan Ruffman and Colin D. Howell (Halifax: Nimbus, 1994), 229-44, 245-50.

66 Intermediate Medical Report of Lieutenant-Colonel F. McKelvey Bell, under cover Bell to DGMS, 25 January 1918, HQ 71-26-99-3, vol. 1, NAC, RG 24, vol. 6359.

67 Commanding Officer USS *Tacoma* to Commander Squadron Two, Cruiser Force, 11 December 1917, microfilm reel 15125, PANS, MG 27, vol. 2, #31.

68 Director of Stores to Deputy Minister, 24 December 1917, NSS 37-25-1, NAC, RG 24, vol. 5634.

69 Wilson to Desbarats, 9 December 1917, NSS 37-25-1, NAC, RG 24, vol. 5634.

70 Naval records are silent as to Wyatt's service since his arrival at the dockyard on the 6th, other than that he had carried out "no other duties" than his continued role as CXO. Admiral Superintendent to Secretary Naval Service, 4 March 1918, NSS 37-25-8, NAC, RG 24, vol. 5635.

71 Meeting Held in Board of Trade Rooms, 8 December 1917, NSS 37-25-1, NAC, RG 24, vol. 5634.

72 The disaster receives only a short paragraph in Borden's memoirs; however, his papers show that his office maintained active watching files on events, including the important daily situation reports from

MHQ. See Heath Macquarrie ed., *Robert Laird Borden: His Memoirs* (Toronto: McClelland and Stewart, 1969), 2:113, and Sir Robert Borden Papers, NAC, MG 26 H, vols. 89-90, 233, 236.

73   Meeting Held in Board of Trade Rooms, 8 December 1917, NSS 37-25-1, NAC, RG 24, vol. 5634.

74   Ibid.

75   Ibid.; CPR Circular Letter, 5 December 1917, and Maughan to LCdr Morres, 7 December 1917, NSS 1048-45-2, vol. 8, NAC, RG 24, vol. 3768. Since April 1917, and in great secrecy, large drafts of closely guarded coolies from China had been arriving in Vancouver and moved via the Canadian Pacific Railroad to Halifax, where they were loaded onto ships for delivery to France. In all, some 25,000 Chinese were transported. See multivolume RCN coordination and tracking files at 1048-45-1 and 1048-45-2, NAC, RG 24, vols. 3767-9.

76   Meeting Held in Board of Trade Rooms, 8 December 1917, NSS 37-25-1, NAC, RG 24, vol. 5634.

77   Ibid.

78   Ibid.

79   Ibid.

80   Ibid.

81   Ibid.; [Chambers], "Halifax Explosion," 453; Director of Stores to Deputy Minister, 24 December 1917, NSS 37-25-1, NAC, RG 24, vol. 5634. These committees should not be confused with the "Reconstruction" subcommittee embodied in the Halifax Relief Commission. The latter was not concerned with operation of the port.

82   HMCS *Lady Evelyn* log, 9 December 1917, NAC, RG 24, vol. 7444, and HMCS *Grilse* log, 9 December 1917, NAC, RG 24, vol. 7371.

83   [Chambers], "Halifax Explosion," 454.

84   Director of Stores to Deputy Minister, 24 December 1917, NSS 37-25-1, NAC, RG 24, vol. 5634.

85   Navyard (Wilson) to Naval, 9 December 1917, NSS 37-25-3, NAC, RG 24, vol. 5634: Wilson to Desbarats, 11 December 1917, and Director of Stores to Deputy Minister, 24 December 1917, NSS 37-25-1, NAC, RG 24, vol. 5634.

86   Director of Stores to Deputy Minister, 24 December 1917, and Meeting Held in Board Room Board of Trade, 9 December 1917, NSS 37-25-1, NAC, RG 24, vol. 5634.

87   Director of Stores to Deputy Minister, 24 December 1917, NSS 37-25-1, NAC, RG 24, vol. 5634, Wilson to Desbarats, 11 December 1917, and Desbarats to Wilson, 14 December 1917, NSS 37-25-3, NAC, RG 24, vol. 5635. Additional minutes detailing reconstruction activities may be found in these files.

88   GOC MD6 (Halifax) to Secretary Militia Council, 15 December 1917, MD6 86-2-1, NAC, RG 24, vol. 4548, and Assistant Adjutant General (hereinafter AAG) MD6 to McIlreith, 9 December 1917, MD6 86-4-1, vol. 1, NAC, RG 24, vol. 4549.

89   Lieutenant-Colonel R.B. Simmonds (66th Regt) to DAA & QMG (Deputy Assistant Adjutant and Quarter-Master General) MD6 (Halifax), 12 January 1918, MD6 86-4-1, vol. 1, NAC, RG 24, vol. 4549.

90   Commanding Officer USS *Tacoma* to Commander Squadron Two, Cruiser Force, 11 December 1917, microfilm reel 15125, PANS, MG 27, vol. 2, #31.

91   HMCS *Lady Evelyn* log, 9 December 1917, NAC, RG 24, vol. 7444.

92   Commanding Officer USS *Tacoma* to Commander Squadron Two, Cruiser Force, 11 December 1917, microfilm reel 15125, PANS, MG 27, vol. 2, #31.

93   Chambers circular to Naval Ottawa, Admiralty, C-in-C North America and West Indies, 9 December 1917, NSS 1048-48-1, vol. 3, NAC, RG 24, vol. 3773.

94   Naval to Navyard, 10 December 1917, NSS 1048-48-1, vol. 3, NAC, RG 24, vol. 3773.

95   Navyard 830 to Naval, 8 December 1917, NSS 1048-45-2, vol. 8, NAC, RG 24, vol. 3768.

96   Naval to "Britannia," Bermuda, 10 December 1917, NSS 1048-48-1, vol. 3, NAC, RG 24, vol. 3773; Naval to A.H. Harris, CPR, 10 December 1917, NSS 1048-45-2, vol. 8; Naval to Guthrie, New York, 7 December 1917, NSS 1048-45-2, vol. 7, NAC, RG 24, vol. 3768.

97   Diary, 15 December 1917, Desbarats Papers, NAC, MG 30, E 89, vol. 5.

98 Kingsmill to Chambers, 14 February 1918, File 350, NAC, RG 6 E, vol. 621.

99 P. Willet Brock, "Commander E.A.E. Nixon and the Royal Naval College of Canada, 1910-1922," in *The RCN in Retrospect, 1910-1968*, ed. James A. Boutilier (Vancouver: University of British Columbia Press, 1982), 39.

100 Diary, 15 December 1917, Desbarats Papers, NAC, MG 30, E 89, vol. 5.

101 Kingsmill to Atwood and others, 12 December 1917, NSS 37-25-3, NAC, RG 24, vol. 5635.

102 Ibid.

103 Fleet Wireless Officer to Naval, 8 December 1917, NSS 37-25-3, NAC, RG 24, vol. 5635.

104 Naval 700 to Navyard (for Fleet Wireless Officer), 9 December 1917; Navyard 849 to Naval, 10 December 1917; Naval 733 to Navyard, 13 December 1917, all NSS 37-25-3, NAC, RG 24, vol. 5635.

105 Meeting of Subcommittee, 10 December 1917, NSS 37-25-1, NAC, RG 24, vol. 5634.

106 Meeting of Subcommittee, 10 December 1917, and Subcommittee to Hensley, 11 December 1917, NSS 37-25-1, NAC, RG 24, vol. 5634.

107 Wilson to Desbarats, 11 December 1917, NSS 37-25-1, NAC, RG 24, vol. 5634.

108 Navyard to Naval, 11 December 1917, NSS 37-25-3, NAC, RG 24, vol. 5635.

109 [Chambers], "Halifax Explosion," 454, and Williams to Gainings, 13 December 1917, NSS 1048-48-3, vol. 1, NAC, RG 24, vol. 3773. The latter includes names of all ships in the convoy.

110 HMCS *Margaret* log, 11 December 1917, NAC, RG 24, vol. 7494, and HMCS *Lady Evelyn* log, 11 December 1917, NAC, RG 24, vol. 7444.

111 *Ottawa Citizen*, 13 December 1917.

112 Ibid.

113 Ibid. Naval and militia records listed twenty sailors and twenty-two soldiers as either killed or missing. Due to the general confusion in the aftermath – there being a foggy chain of command, disrupted administrative capability, and no central naval hospital – naval sources are vague on the numbers injured. Only some thirty-nine sailors are identified as "injured," and, if the experience of L.B. Griffith is any example, sailors well enough to stay on duty were not included in the list. See NSS 37-25-2, NAC, RG 24, vol. 5634, *passim*. By contrast, the comprehensive militia report of casualties by units lists 502 injured, over 400 of them on the Wellington Barracks property north of the dockyard and closer to the blast. See MD6 file 86-1-3-1, District Musketry Instructor to General Staff Officer MD6 (Halifax), 10 January 1918, NAC, RG 24, vol. 4548.

114 HMCS *Lady Evelyn* log, 11 December 1917, NAC, RG 24, vol. 7444.

115 Wilson to Desbarats, 15 December 1917, NSS 37-25-3, NAC, RG 24, vol. 5635.

116 Wilson to Naval, 18 December 1917, NSS 37-25-3, NAC, RG 24, vol. 5635.

117 Captain Superintendent to Secretary Naval Service, 18 December 1917, NSS 37-25-3, NAC, RG 24, vol. 5635.

118 Ibid.

119 L.B. Griffith to Dorothy H. Griffith, 16 December 1917, author's files.

120 Kenneth P. Kirkwood Papers, Journals and Diaries, Reminiscences of wartime experiences (1930), NAC, MG 27 III E3, vol. 1. Kirkwood went on to a distinguished career in the Department of External Affairs, including service as high commissioner to Pakistan and New Zealand and ambassador to Egypt.

Chapter 6: Of Sailors, Lawyers, Goats, and Newspapers

1 L.B. Griffith to Dorothy H. Griffith, 8 December 1917, author's files.

2 See John G. Armstrong, "Canadian Home Defence, 1914-1917: and the Role of Major-General Willoughby Gwatkin" (MA thesis, Royal Military College of Canada, 1982). For additional material drawn from the perspective of Canadian coastal defence see Roger F. Sarty, "Silent Sentry: A Military and Political History of Canadian Coast Defence 1860-1945" (PhD dissertation, University of Toronto, 1982).

3 *Halifax Herald,* 10 December 1917.

4 Ibid., 8 December 1917.

5 Ibid., 22 January 18.

6 Address to the Court by C.J. Burchell, KC, Counsel for SS *IMO,* prior to testimony of Johan Johansen, 21 January 1918, Wreck Commissioner's Inquiry, 773-4, National Archives of Canada (NAC), RG 42, vol. 596/7 (hereinafter Inquiry). Also see Affidavit of C.J. Burchell, Exchequer Court of Canada, Nova Scotia Admiralty District, NAC, RG 42, vol. 597 (hereinafter Appeal Book), Exhibits, M.B.R./19, 22-26; *Halifax Herald,* 21 December 1917; and account in Michael J. Bird, *The Town That Died* (Toronto: McGraw-Hill Ryerson, 1967), 167-8. Beyond Burchell's veiled suggestion, no further claim was made during the inquiry that Johansen had actually been beaten by his guards, nor has any other supporting evidence been found.

7 *Halifax Herald,* 5 December 1917.

8 Ibid., 21 December 1917.

9 Janet Kitz, *Shattered City: The Halifax Explosion and the Road to Recovery* (Halifax: Nimbus, 1989), 151.

10 CO *Tacoma* to Commander Squadron Two, Cruiser Force, 11 December 1917, microfilm reel 15125, Public Archives of Nova Scotia (hereinafter PANS), MG 27, vol. 2, #31.

11 Senior Naval Officer (hereinafter SNO) (British) Halifax to C-in-C North America and West Indies, 13 December 1917, Public Records Office (PRO), ADM 1/8507/273.

12 CO 63rd Regt. to Assistant Adjutant General (hereinafter AAG) Military District No. 6 (MD6) (Halifax), 21 January 1918, MD6 86-2-1, NAC, RG 24, vol. 4548.

13 SNO (British) Halifax to C-in-C North America and West Indies, 13 December 1917, PRO, ADM 1/8507/273.

14 *Halifax Herald* and *Halifax Chronicle,* 11 December 1917; SNO (British) Halifax to C-in-C North America and West Indies, 13 December 1917, PRO, ADM 1/8507/273. The latter is also quoted at length in Bird, *The Town That Died,* 156-7.

15 Halifax City Council Minutes, 11 December 1917, PANS, reel 12426 (copies in Navyard 279 to Naval, 11 January 1918, NSS 37-25-1, NAC, RG 24, vol. 5634).

16 Navyard 279 to Naval, 11 January 1918, NSS 37-25-1, NAC, RG 24, vol. 5634.

17 E.J. Chambers Memorandum for Office File, 11 December 1917, and Chambers to Gwatkin, 18 December 1917, File 350, both NAC, RG 6 E, vol. 621.

18 E.J. Chambers Memorandum for Office File, 11 December 1917 File 350, NAC, RG 6 E, vol. 621.

19 H.J. Morgan, ed., *The Canadian Men and Women of the Time* (Toronto: William Briggs, 1912), 314.

20 Ibid., 347. The organization and salaries of the Admiralty Division and the Nova Scotia courts at the time are briefly sketched at Arnold W. Thomas, ed., *The Canadian Almanac* (Toronto: Copp Clark, 1917), 321, 362.

21 Johnston to Henry, 6 December 1917, 9704-244, Pt. 1, NAC, RG 12, vol. 2827.

22 Johnston to Grant, 6 December 1917, 9704-244, Pt. 1, NAC, RG 12, vol. 2827.

23 Dominion Wreck Commissioner to Deputy Minister Marine, 19 April 1919, 9704-244, Pt. 3, NAC, RG 12, vol. 2827.

24 Burnett to Deputy Minister, 29 March 1919, File 45247, NAC, RG 42, vol. 282.

25 Burnett to Deputy Minister, 29 November 1916, File 34747, NAC, RG 42, vol. 218.

26 Johnston to Secretary Pilotage Commissioners, 9 December 1917, 9704-244, Pt. 1, NAC, RG 12, vol. 2827.

27 Morgan, ed., *Canadian Men and Women,* 527.

28 Henry to Johnston, 22 December 1917, 9704-244, Pt. 1, and Statement of Account attached to Henry to Johnston, 12 February 1918, 9704-244, Pt. 2, both NAC, RG 12, vol. 2827.

29 Borden to Ballantyne, 8 December 1917, Sir Robert Borden Papers, NAC, MG 26H, reel C-4325, 46382.

30 *Halifax Herald* and Halifax *Morning Chronicle,* 11 December 1917.

31 W.H. Kesterton, *A History of Journalism in Canada* (Toronto: McClelland and Stewart, 1967), 132-3.

32 Halifax *Morning Chronicle,* 11 December 1917.

33 Morgan, ed., *Canadian Men and Women,* 317.

34 Kingsmill to Chambers, 14 February 1918, File 350, NAC, RG 6 E, vol. 621, reel T-102.

35 See brief note about the *Globe* in Kesterton, *A History of Journalism,* 133.

36 *Halifax Herald,* 10 December 1917.

37 Ibid., 12 December 1917.

38 Henry to Johnston, 12 February 1917, 9704-244, Pt. 2, NAC, RG 12, vol. 2827.

39 Donald A. Kerr, "Another Calamity: The Litigation," in *Ground Zero: A Reassessment of the 1917 Explosion in Halifax Harbour,* ed. Alan Ruffman and Colin D. Howell (Halifax: Nimbus, 1994), 369.

40 *Who's Who* (Toronto 1936).

41 Kerr, "Another Calamity," 369.

42 Henry to Johnston, 22 December 1917, 9704-244, Pt. 1, NAC, RG 12, vol. 2827.

43 Henry to Johnston, 22 December 1917, Ballantyne to Borden, 15 January 1918, 9704-244, Pt. 1, and Henry to Johnson, 4 February 1918, 9704-244, Pt. 2, all in NAC, RG 12, vol. 2827. Halifax *Morning Chronicle,* 22 December 1917. Donald A. Kerr lists inquiry and appeal documents available from various sources in Halifax in "Another Calamity," 475-6 n.2. The inquiry cited appears to be incomplete, however, as it does not include the vital two days of summation on 30 and 31 January 1918. Thus, I believe that the only complete copy of the inquiry exists among the consolidated proceedings that were held by the Department of Marine and later the Department of Transport. They are now maintained, in three volumes, with a copy of the Appeal Book and exhibits, at NAC, RG 42, vol. 596/7.

44 E.J. Chambers to Gwatkin, 18 December 1917, File 350, NAC, RG 6 E, vol. 621, reel T-102.

45 Ibid.

46 Ibid. Also see *Halifax Herald,* 21 December 1917, p. 2.

47 Ibid., 17 December 1917.

48 Ibid., 21 December 1917, p. 2. Kayford's testimony, along with that of his shipmate, Thomas Johnston, commences at Inquiry, p. K64.

49 *Halifax Herald,* 21 December 1917, p.2.

50 Halifax *Morning Chronicle,* 20 December 1917.

51 Ibid.

52 Ibid.

53 City Clerk to Borden, BPP, NAC, MG 26H, reel C-4325, 46714-15.

54 Johnston to Drysdale (Telegram), 18 December 1917, 9704-244, Pt. 1, NAC, RG 12, vol. 2822.

55 Johnston to Drysdale (letter), 18 December 1917, 9704-244, Pt. 1, NAC, RG 12, vol. 2822.

56 Drysdale to A/M Marine, 14 January 1918, 9704-244, Pt. 1, NAC, RG 12, vol. 2827.

57 *Halifax Herald,* 24 and 26 December 1917.

58 R.A. 986 circular to Naval, Admiralty, C-in-C North America and West Indies, Commodore Gaunt, Washington, 20 December 1917, NSS 1048-48-1, vol. 3, NAC, RG 24, vol. 3773.

59 Henry to Johnston, 22 December 1917, 9704-244, Pt. 1, NAC, RG 12, vol. 2827.

60 Ibid.

61 No documentation of initiation of these measures has been found until the later point when NSHQ requested details. See Harris to Chief of Staff, Naval HQ, 3 January 1918 (noting measures in existence), and Kingsmill to Pasco, 18 January 1918 (report procedures in effect), both NSC 1048-17-30, NAC, RG 24, vol. 3713.

62 Harris 1406 to Transports Admiralty, 26 December 1917, and Harris to Chief of Staff, NSHQ, 3 January 1918, NSC 1048-17-30, NAC, RG 24, vol. 3713.

63 Chambers 335 to Naval, 14 January 1918, NSC 1048-17-30, NAC, RG 24, vol. 3713, and Chambers to Secretary Admiralty, 5 January 1918, PRO, ADM 137/1620.

64 *Halifax Herald,* 27 and 28 December 1917. The level of care and accuracy of the *Herald's* reportage may be inferred by its mistake in referring to Captain Hose as "Charles," not Walter.

65 Dennis to Yates, 28 December 1917, BPP, NAC, MG 26H, reel C-4325, 46728-30.

66 *Halifax Herald*, 29 December 1917. Unrecorded in Desbarats's office diary, where there are no entries for the dates 26-31 December 1917. See G.J. Desbarats Papers, NAC, MG 30, E 89, vol. 5.

67 *Halifax Herald*, 29 December 1917.

68 Munshull to Ballantyne, 8 January 1918, 9704-244, Pt. 1, NAC, RG 24, vol. 2827. Also see Halifax *Morning Chronicle*, 28 December 1917.

69 Halifax *Morning Chronicle*, 31 December 1917.

70 Ibid.

71 Chambers to Secretary Admiralty, 5 January 1918, PRO, ADM 137/1620.

72 *Halifax Herald*, 31 December 1917.

73 *Ottawa Journal*, 3 January 1918.

74 Henry to Johnston, 2 January 1918, and Johnston to Drysdale, 15 January 1918, 9704-244, Pt. 1, NAC, RG 12, vol. 2827.

75 Henry to Johnston, 2 January 1918, 9704-244, Pt. 1, NAC, RG 12, vol. 2827.

76 Ibid.

77 Ibid.

78 Ibid.

79 *Halifax Herald*, 4 January 1918.

80 Munshull to Ballantyne, 8 January 1918.

81 [Illegible signature on Archives National du Canada stationery], personal letter to Borden, 7 January 1918, BPP, MG 26H, reel C-4325, 46752.

82 Reid to Borden, 2 January 1918, BPP, MG 26H, reel C-4325, 46737-8. Imperial practice at the time, however, was that the Crown, without admitting liability was "in the habit of granting compensation *ex gratia* [as an act of grace, without acceptance of liability] in such cases." Colonial Office to Governor General, 18 January 1918, BPP, MG 26H, reel C-4325, 46813-6.

83 Halifax *Morning Chronicle*, 15 January 1918.

84 Johnston to Desbarats, 9 January 1917; Desbarats to Johnston, 11 January 1918; Pasco to Secretary Naval Service, 14 January 1918; Pasco 438 to Kingsmill, 21 January 1918; and Naval 170 to Captain Superintendent, 23 January 1918, all NSS 37-25-1, NAC, RG 24, vol. 5634.

85 [Illegible signature on Archives National du Canada stationery], personal letter to Borden, 7 January 1918, BPP, MG 26H, reel C-4325, 46752.

86 For example, *Halifax Herald*, 12 January 1918.

87 Ibid., 10 January 1918.

88 Pasco 306 to Kingsmill, 12 January 1918, NSS 37-25-2, NAC, RG 24, vol. 5634.

89 Kingsmill to Pasco, 13 January 1918, NSS 37-25-2, NAC, RG 24, vol. 5634. Also see Captain Superintendent to Director of the Naval Service, 14 January 1918, ibid.

90 Martin to Borden, 13 January 1918, 9704-244, Pt. 1, NAC, RG 12, vol. 2827.

91 Diary, 14-27 January 1918, Desbarats Papers, NAC, MG 30, E 89, vol. 5.

92 Ballantyne to Borden, 15 January 1918, 9704-244, Pt. 1, NAC, RG 12, vol. 2827, copy also on BPP, NAC, MG 26, vol. 233, 130313-6, reel C-4411.

93 Borden to Martin, 17 January 1918, BPP, NAC, MG 26, vol. 233, 130317, reel C-4411.

94 Unsigned memo, probably from Naval Secretary to Captain Superintendent, 21 January 1918, NSS 37-25-2, NAC, RG 24, vol. 5634.

95 Ballantyne to Kingsmill, 21 January 1918, 36984, NAC, RG 42, vol. 252.

96 Kingsmill to Ballantyne, 22 January 1918, Cameron Stanton (A/DM Marine), Memorandum Re Harbour Master, Halifax, 24 January 1918, both 36984, NAC, RG 42, vol. 252.

97 Naval 95 to Navyard, 16 January 1918; Navyard 379 to Naval, 17 January 1918; Kingsmill 117 to Pasco, 18 January 1918; and Pasco 402 to Kingsmill, 18 January 1918, NSC 1048-17-30, NAC, RG 24, vol. 3713.

98 Pasco 463 to Kingsmill, 22 January 1918, NSC 1048-17-30, NAC, RG 24, vol. 3713.

99 Kingsmill to Pasco, 22 January 1918, NSC 1048-17-30, NAC, RG 24, vol. 3713.

100 Navyard 435 to Naval, 21 January 1918, NSC 1048-17-30, NAC, RG 24, vol. 3713.

101 Port Convoy Officer to Secretary Admiralty, 29 January 1918, PRO, ADM 137/1620, and Navyard 435 to Naval, 21 January 1918, NSC 1048-17-30, NAC, RG 24, vol. 3713.

102 Port Convoy Officer to Secretary Admiralty, 29 January 1918, PRO, ADM 137/1620.

Chapter 7: Goats to the Slaughter

1 Opening remarks by Judge Drysdale, 21 January 1918, Wreck Commissioner's Inquiry, 773-4, National Archives of Canada (NAC), RG 42, vol. 596/7 (hereinafter Inquiry) and *Halifax Herald*, 22 January 1918.

2 Inquiry, 21 January 1918, and *Halifax Herald*, 22 January 1918.

3 Testimony of Edward Renner, 21 January 1918, Inquiry, 905-22.

4 Navinet 808 to Naval, 7 December 1917, NSC 1048-48-8, NAC, RG 24, vol. 3774, and Lloyd's *Shipping Registry*, 1918-19.

5 Testimony of Willard C. Cope, Chemist, and Norman A. Currie, Government Steamship Inspector, Inquiry, 26 January, 1500-42 and 24 January, from 1337.

6 Inquiry, 25 January 1918, 1382.

7 Ibid., 22 January 1918, 970-81.

8 Testimony of Herbert Whitehead, 25 January 1918, Inquiry, 1383-1418.

9 Henry to Johnston, 12 February 1918, 9704-244, Pt. 2, NAC, RG 12, vol. 2827.

10 Testimony of F.G. Rudolf, 22 January 1918, Inquiry, 923-54, and *Halifax Herald*, 23 January 1918.

11 Ibid.

12 Testimony of F.C.C. Pasco, 23 January 1918, Inquiry, 1043.

13 Ballantyne to MacGillivray, 29 January 1918, 9704-244, Pt. 1, NAC, RG 12, vol. 2827.

14 Testimony of F.C.C Pasco, 23 January 1918, Inquiry, 1037-90.

15 Ibid., 1043.

16 Ibid., 1044, and Halifax *Morning Chronicle*, 25 January 1918.

17 Testimony of F.C.C. Pasco, 23 January 1918, Inquiry, 1059-61.

18 Ibid., 1057-8.

19 Ballantyne to MacGillivray, 29 January 1918, 9704-244, Pt. 1, NAC, RG 12, vol. 2827; CXO to Captain Superintendent, 26 January 1918, F. Wyatt Personal File, NAC, RG 24, ACC 1992-93/169, vol. 233, and Naval Report of Halifax Explosion (undated), NSS 37-25-9, p. 50, NAC, RG 24, vol. 5635.

20 *Halifax Herald*, 24 January 1918; Halifax *Morning Chronicle*, 25 January 1918.

21 Testimony of F.E. Wyatt, 23 January 1918, Inquiry, 1091-8.

22 Examination by W.A. Henry and Testimony of F.E. Wyatt, 23 January 1918, Inquiry, 1095-6. Regulations stated at Chief Examining Officer to Secretary Pilots' Office, 4 May 1917, Exchequer Court of Canada, Nova Scotia Admiralty District, NAC, RG 42, vol. 597 (hereinafter Appeal Book), Exhibit R./67, p. 57.

23 Examination by Mr Bell and Testimony of F.E. Wyatt, 23 January 1918, Inquiry, 1095-7.

24 Testimony of T.V. Freeman, 23 January 1918, Inquiry, 1152-66, and Halifax *Morning Chronicle*, 25 January 1918.

25 Testimony of James Hall, 23 January 1918, Inquiry, 1167-79, and Halifax *Morning Chronicle*, 25 January 1918.

26 Ballantyne to MacGillivray, 29 January 1918, 9704-244, Pt. 1, NAC, RG 12, vol. 2827, and Testimony of Roland Iceton, 25 January 1918, Inquiry, 1452-55. The time of the incident taken from a question by Mr Burchell, 24 January 1918, Inquiry, 1219. The Naval Report of Halifax Explosion (undated), which was prepared for Ballantyne after the inquiry, in anticipation of questions when the House of Commons resumed, wrongly states that Wyatt had not known that *Galileo* was still in port and that Wyatt did not change the signal until he had returned from court. See NSS 37-25-9, p. 50, NAC, RG 24, vol. 5635, and Ballantyne to Desbarats, 8 February 1918, NSS 37-25-8, NAC, RG 24, vol. 5635.

27   Testimony of Frederick Wyatt, 28 January 1918, Inquiry, 1681.

28   Questions by Mr Henry and Testimony of Frederick Wyatt, 24 January 1918, Inquiry, 1197-8.

29   Chief Examining Officer to Secretary Pilots' Office, 4 May 1917, Appeal Book, Exhibit R./67, p. 57.

30   Testimony of F. Wyatt, 24 January 1918, Inquiry, 1209.

31   CXO to Captain Superintendent, 21 June 1917, and 1 August 1917, Appeal Book, Exhibits R./103 and R./104.

32   CXO to Captain Superintendent, 15 September 1917, Exhibit R. /105, as published in Halifax *Morning Chronicle,* 28 January 1918. Document undated but confirmed at question by Captain Demers, 26 January 1918, Inquiry, 1613. Inexplicably, the exhibit is not entered in the Appeal Book.

33   Questions by Mr Burchell and testimony of F. Wyatt, 24 January 1918, Inquiry 1217-18.

34   Ibid., 1218.

35   Ibid., 1263-6.

36   Question by Mr Burchell, 24 January 1918, Inquiry, 1213.

37   Testimony of F. Wyatt, 24 January 1918, Inquiry, 1213-15

38   Question by Mr Burchell and testimony of F. Wyatt, 24 January 1918, Inquiry 1215.

39   Testimony of James Creighton, 24 January 1918, Inquiry, 1300-19, and Edward Beazley, 28 January 1918, 1665-75; *Halifax Herald,* 29 January 1918.

40   Questions by Mr Burchell and Testimony of F. Wyatt, 24 January 1918, Inquiry, 1218.

41   Testimony of G.R. Smith, Pickford and Black, 24 January 1918, Inquiry, 1323-4.

42   Martin to Pasco, 24 January 1918, 9704-244, Pt. 1, NAC, RG 12, vol. 2827.

43   Henry to Johnston, 12 February 1918, 9704-244, Pt. 2, NAC, RG 12, vol. 2827.

44   *Halifax Herald,* 25 and 26 January 1918.

45   Statement by Judge A. Drysdale, 26 January 1918, Inquiry 1499.

46   *Halifax Herald,* 25 January 1918.

47   Dennis to Borden, 24 January 1918, 9704-244, Pt. 1, NAC, RG 12, vol. 2827.

48   Williams and Graham to Borden, 28 January 1918, 9704-244, Pt. 1, NAC, RG 12, vol. 2827.

49   Kingsmill to Pasco, "Very Urgent," 25 January 1918, NSC 1048-17-30, NAC, RG 24, vol. 3713.

50   Captain Superintendent to CXO, 23 January 1918, F. Wyatt Personal File, NAC, RG 24, ACC 1992-93/169, vol. 233.

51   Questions by Mr Burchell and testimony of F. Wyatt, Inquiry, 1219-21.

52   CXO to Captain Superintendent, 23 January 1918, F. Wyatt Personal File, NAC, RG 24, ACC 1992-93/169, vol. 233.

53   Pasco 517 to Kingsmill, 25 January 1918, NSC 1048-17-30, NAC, RG 24, vol. 3713.

54   Pasco to Martin, 25 January 1918, Minutes of Halifax Board of Control, 29 January 1918, Public Archives of Nova Scotia (PANS), RG 35-102, Series 2A, vol. 9, 725-39. Investigation included in Naval Report of Halifax Explosion (undated), NSS 37-25-9, pp. 51-2, NAC, RG 24, vol. 5635.

55   Pasco 518 to Kingsmill, 25 January 1918, NSC 1048-17-30, NAC, RG 24, vol. 3713.

56   Pasco 521 to Kingsmill, 25 January 1918, NSC 1948-17-30, NAC, RG 24, vol. 3713.

57   CXO to Captain Superintendent, 26 January 1918, F. Wyatt Personal File, NAC, RG 24, ACC 1992-93/169, vol. 233.

58   Pasco 534 and 536 to Kingsmill, 26 January 1918, NSC 1048-17-30, NAC, RG 24, vol. 3713.

59   Testimony of Roland Iceton, 25 January 1918, Inquiry, 1450-1460, and *Halifax Herald,* 26 January 1918.

60   Testimony of Captain Edward H. Martin, 26 January 1918, Inquiry, 1575.

61   Question by W.A. Henry, 26 January 1918, Inquiry, 1598.

62   Questions by Mr Henry and Testimony of E.H. Martin, 26 January 1918, Inquiry, 1593.

63   Halifax *Morning Chronicle,* 28 January 1918, and Testimony of Edward Martin, 26 January 1918, Inquiry, 1590-1.

64   *Morning Chronicle,* 28 January 1918.

65   Questions by Mr Cluney and Testimony of E.H. Martin, 26 January 1918, Inquiry 1609.

66 Ibid., 1610.

67 Ibid., 1610-11.

68 Questions by Captain Demers and Testimony of E.H. Martin, 26 January 1918, 1613-14.

69 Ibid., 1614-15, and Halifax *Morning Chronicle*, 28 January 1918.

70 Kingsmill to Wyatt, 25 June 1917, and Wyatt to Kingsmill, 2 July 1917, F. Wyatt Personal File, NAC, RG 24, ACC 1992-93/169, vol. 233.

71 Questions by Mr Burchell and Testimony of E.H. Martin, 26 January 1918, Inquiry, 1627.

72 Questions by Mr Henry and Testimony of E.H. Martin, 26 January 1918, Inquiry, 1629.

73 Questions by Captain Demers and Testimony of E.H. Martin, 26 January 1918, Inquiry, 1630.

74 *Halifax Herald*, 28 January 1918.

75 Henry to Johnston, 12 February 1918, 9704-244, Pt. 2, NAC, RG 12, vol. 2827.

76 Testimony of R.H. Price, 28 January 1918, Inquiry, 1649-56.

77 Testimony of C. McGannon, 28 January 1918, Inquiry, 1657-60.

78 Questions by Mr Henry and Testimony of F.E. Wyatt, 28 January 1918, Inquiry, 1676-8.

79 Ibid., 1679.

80 Ibid., 1680-1.

81 Questions by Captain Demers and Testimony of Frederick Wyatt, Inquiry, 1685-6.

82 Port Convoy Officer to Secretary Admiralty, 29 January 1918, Public Records Office (PRO), ADM 137/1629.

83 Henry to Johnston, 28 January 1918, 9704-244, Pt. 1, NAC, RG 12, vol. 2827.

84 Halifax *Morning Chronicle*, 27 January 1918.

85 Henry to Johnston, 12 February 1918, 9704-244, Pt. 2, NAC, RG 12, vol. 2827.

86 Navinet 559 to Naval, 28 January 1918, NSC 1048-17-30, NAC, RG 24, vol. 3713.

87 As related in Halifax *Morning Chronicle*, 1 February 1918.

88 Discussions of Judge and Counsel, 29 January 1918, Inquiry, 1742-5.

89 *Halifax Herald*, 29 January 1918.

90 Wyatt to Captain Superintendent, 29 January 1918, and attached minutes of Pasco and Kingsmill, 30 January and 2 February 1918, F. Wyatt Personal File, NAC, RG 24, ACC 1992-93/169, vol. 233.

91 Port Convoy Officer to Secretary Admiralty, 29 January 1918, PRO, ADM 137/1620.

92 Ibid.; Naval Report of Halifax Explosion, NSS 37-25-9, 52-4, NAC, RG 24, vol. 5635; Martin to Borden, and Martin to Ballantyne, 29 January 1918, 9704-244, Pt. 1, NAC, RG 12, vol. 2827; Navyard 568 to Naval, 29 January 1918, and Naval 249 to Navyard, 30 January 1918, NSC 1948-17-30, NAC, RG 24, vol. 3713; *Halifax Herald*, 30 January 1918.

93 Halifax *Morning Chronicle*, 30 January 1918.

94 *Halifax Herald*, 30 January 1918, (italics in original).

95 Ibid. Kingsmill had been captain of the battleship HMS *Dominion* during a visit to Montreal in August 1906. The ship had struck rocks in the Bay de Chaleur and suffered embarrassing damage. *Montreal Gazette*, 17 August 1906.

96 *Halifax Herald*, 31 January 1918.

97 Ibid.

98 Drysdale to Ballantyne, 4 February 1918, 9704-244, Pt. 2, NAC, RG 12, vol. 2827.

99 C.E. Kingsmill, Memorandum for the Minister, 18 January 1918, W.O. Story Personal File, NAC, RG 24, ACC 1992-93/169, vol. 204.

100 "By Way of Farewell to Captain Martin," *Halifax Herald*, 13 February 1918. Mentions her loss as "bitterness of deep personal sorrow ... a lady whose gentleness and sweetness of nature won all who knew her." The article is in curious contrast to the *Herald*'s attacks on the RCN, a generous tribute to a man of qualities "which not only win, but – which retain friends."

101 C.E. Kingsmill, Memorandum for the Minister, 18 January 1918, W.O. Story Personal File, NAC, RG 24, ACC 1992-93/169, vol. 204.

102 Ibid., and Michael L. Hadley and Roger Sarty, *Tin-Pots and Pirate Ships: Canadian Naval Forces and German Sea Raiders, 1880-1918* (Montreal: McGill-Queen's University Press, 1991), 91, 202.

103 Kingsmill to Nixon, 30 January 1918, E.A.E. Nixon Papers, Folder A, File 6, National Defence Headquarters, Directorate of History and Heritage (hereinafter DHH), 74/69.

104 Martin 548 to Director of the Naval Service, 27 January 1918, NSC 1048-17-30, NAC, RG 24, vol. 3713. The offer was evidently made by private telegram with no copies kept, as was the case with the Wyatt matter. Martin's reply merely states "in reply to your telegram will accept."

105 Kingsmill 211 to Pasco, 26 January 1918, ff. 89, NSC 1948-17-30, NAC, RG 24, vol. 3713; and *Halifax Herald,* 4 February 1918.

106 Ballantyne to MacGillivray, 29 January 1918, 9704-244, Pt. 1, NAC, RG 12, vol. 2827.

107 Ibid.

108 *Halifax Herald,* 31 January 1918.

109 Summation by Mr Burchell, 30 January 1918, Inquiry, 1875.

110 Ibid., 1826.

111 Ibid., 1771-1910.

112 Donald A. Kerr, "Another Calamity: The Litigation," *Ground Zero: A Reassessment of the 1917 Explosion in Halifax Harbour,* ed. Alan Ruffman and Colin D. Howell (Halifax: Nimbus, 1994), 369.

113 Summation by Mr Mellish, 31 January 1918, Inquiry, 1983.

114 Summation by Mr Robertson, 31 January 1918, Inquiry, 2025.

115 Summation by Mr Cluney, 31 January 1918, Inquiry, 2077.

116 Ibid., 2079.

117 Ibid., 2081-2.

118 Ibid., 2082-95.

119 Summation by Mr Henry, 31 January 1918, Inquiry, 2099.

120 Ibid., 2116, 2108.

121 Ibid., 2118.

122 Ibid., 2128.

123 Naval 215 to Navyard, 28 January 1918, NSC 1048-17-30, NAC, RG 24, vol. 3713.

124 Summation by Mr Henry, 31 January 1918, Inquiry, 2123.

125 Ibid., 2124-5.

126 Ibid., 2127.

127 Ibid., 2129-30.

128 Ibid., 2131-2.

129 Ibid., 2132.

130 Ibid., 2135.

131 Ibid., 2136-40.

132 *Halifax Herald,* 1 and 2 February 1918.

133 Henry to Johnston, 4 February 1918, 9704-244, Pt. 2, NAC, RG 12, vol. 2827.

134 Report of Justice L.J.A. Drysdale, 4 February 1918, Inquiry. Copy also at NSS 80-5-13, NAC, RG 24, vol. 5671.

135 *Halifax Herald,* 5 February 1918.

Chapter 8: Covering the Tracks

1 Henry to Johnston, 4 February 1918, 9704-244, Pt. 2, National Archives of Canada (NAC), RG 12, vol. 2827 and Judgment of the Lords of the Judicial Committee of the Privy Council, 22 March 1920, 9704-244, Pt. 3, NAC, RG 12, vol. 2827. For additional details of the subsequent litigation process and sources see Donald A. Kerr, "Another Calamity: The Litigation," in *Ground Zero: A Reassessment of the 1917 Explosion in Halifax Harbour,* ed. Alan Ruffman and Colin D. Howell (Halifax: Nimbus, 1994), 365-76.

2 Henry to Johnston, 4 February 1918, 9704-244, Pt. 2, NAC, RG 12, vol. 2827.

3 Ottawa *Evening Journal,* 5 February 1918.

4 Chambers to Kingsmill, 12 February 1918, File 350, NAC, RG 6 E, vol. 621, reel T-102.

5 E.J. Chambers Circular Letter to Halifax editors, 13 February 1918, File 350, NAC, RG 6 E, reel T-102.

6 Kingsmill to Chambers, 14 February 1918, File 350, NAC, RG 6 E, vol. 621, reel T-102.

7 Letter from "Sub Rosa," *Halifax Herald,* 19 February 1918.

8 Ballantyne to Desbarats, 8 February 1918, and Deputy Minister to Director Naval Service, 12 February 1918, NSS 37-25-8, NAC, RG 24, vol. 5635. The process of consolidating the information may be followed in this file and NSS 37-25-7 ("Particulars of Officers at Halifax Dockyard") for "Naval Report of Halifax Explosion," see NSS 37-25-9.

9 Henry to Johnston, 4 February 1918, 9704-244, Pt. 2, NAC, RG 12, vol. 2827.

10 Demers to Drysdale, 28 and 29 January 1918, Sir Robert Borden Papers, NAC, MG 26H, vol. 90, reel C-4325, 46874-6. Demers also felt that *Imo*'s intentions were determined by her encounter with the "tramp" American ship (*Clara*), which had demanded the port side of the harbour coming up the channel before *Mont Blanc.*

11 Demers to Drysdale, 28 January 1918, Borden papers, NAC, MG 26H, vol. 90, reel C-4325, 46874-6.

12 Ibid.

13 Demers to Drysdale, 28 January 1918, Borden Papers, NAC, MG 26H, vol. 90, reel C-4325, 46877-8.

14 Ibid.

15 Ibid.

16 Ballantyne to Borden, 12 February 1918, Borden Papers, NAC, MG 26H, vol. 90, reel C-4325, 46885.

17 Borden to Ballantyne, 18 February 1918, Borden Papers, NAC, MG 26H, vol. 90, reel C-4325, 46899.

18 Hazen to Borden, 25 February 1918, Borden Papers, NAC, MG 26H, vol. 90, reel C-4325, 46913.

19 Ballantyne to Borden, 21 February 1918 and 1 March 1918; Martin to Kingsmill, 24 February 1918; Captain Superintendent to Secretary Naval Service, 16 June 1916 and 7 March 1917, all in Borden Papers, NAC, MG 26H, vol. 90, reel C-4325, 46906, 46908-10, 46912.

20 H.C. Pinsent to Captain Superintendent, 30 September 1916, and J.R. Hemsted to Captain Superintendent, 24 March 1917, Borden Papers, NAC, MG 26H, vol. 90, reel C-4325, 46910-11.

21 Borden to Ballantyne, 4 March 1918, and PM Secretary to Ballantyne, 12 March 1917, Borden Papers, NAC, MG 26H, vol. 90, reel C-4325, 46918, 46945.

22 Order-in-Council P.S. 607, 14 March 1918, Johnston to Lindsay, 10 April 1918, and Masters, Seamen and Pilotage Branch to Deputy Minister of Marine, 29 March 1919, File 45247, NAC, RG 42, vol. 282.

23 Navyard 670 and 673 to Naval; Naval 301 to Navyard, 6 February 1918, F. Wyatt Personal File, NAC, RG 24, ACC 1992-93/169, vol. 233.

24 Good accounts of the criminal proceedings have already been published. For a colourful narrative that emphasizes the role played by Judge Benjamin Russell see "Assigning the Blame," in Dean Jobb, *Crime Wave: Con Men, Rogues and Scoundrels from Nova Scotia's Past* (Lawrencetown Beach, NS: Pottersfield Press, 1991), 57-66. Close professional analysis is provided by lawyer Donald A. Kerr in a lengthy footnote (12) to "Another Calamity," 476-8).

25 Walker to Admiral Superintendent, 7 March 1918, F. Wyatt Personal File, NAC, RG 24, ACC 1992-93/169, vol. 233.

26 Benjamin Russell, *Autobiography* (Halifax: Royal Print & Litho, 1932), 271, and Jobb, "Assigning the Blame," 63-4.

27 Russell, *Autobiography,* 63-4, and *Halifax Herald,* 16 March 1918. Explained in greater detail in 20 March edition.

28 *Halifax Herald,* 16 March 1918, 1.

29 Russell, *Autobiography,* 270.

30 *Halifax Herald,* 20 March 1918.

31 Ibid. Emphasis in the original.

32 *Halifax Herald,* 21 March 1918.

33 Captain A.H. Rostron to Senior Naval Officer Halifax, 14 March 1918, and Admiral Superintendent to Secretary Naval Service, 18 March 1918, NSS 37-25-8, NAC, RG 24, vol. 5635.

34 *Halifax Herald,* 12 March 1918.

35 Wyatt to Admiral Superintendent, 23 March 1918, F. Wyatt Personal File, NAC, RG 24, ACC 1992-93/169, vol. 233.

36 Kingsmill to Deputy Minister, 2 April 1918, and Naval Secretary to Deputy Minister, Department of Justice, 16 April 1918, F. Wyatt Personal File, NAC, RG 24, ACC 1992-93/169, vol. 233.

37 *Halifax Herald,* 18 April 1918.

38 Ibid.

39 Ibid., 19 April 1918.

40 Kerr, "Another Calamity," 365-76.

41 Port Convoy Officer to Secretary Admiralty, 22 April 1918, Public Records Office (PRO), ADM 137/1620, 123562.

42 Kingsmill to Ballantyne, 18 April 1918, F. Wyatt Personal File, NAC, RG 24, ACC 1992-93/169, vol. 233.

43 Chief Accountant, "Particulars of Service ...," 17 May 1918, Department of the Naval Service, F. Wyatt Personal File, NARC, RG 150, Box 233, ACC 1992-93/169.

44 Canada, House of Commons, First Session – 13th Parliament, V of CXXII, 4 April 1918, 362-82, and *Halifax Herald,* 12 March 1918. The extensive RCN aides-mémoire on the disaster and other disaster-related documents were gradually moved into government file cabinets. Some were kept close at hand in the office of the deputy minister of marine, however, until after it was merged into the Department of Transport in 1936. See File 970-4-244 (3 vols.), NAC, RG 12, c. 2827.

45 J. Castell Hopkins, ed., *The Canadian Annual Review, 1917* (Toronto: annual review publishing co., 1918), 651-2.

46 F. Wyatt Personal File, NAC, RG 24, ACC 1992-93/169, vol. 233.

47 Michael L. Hadley and Roger Sarty, *Tin-Pots and Pirate Ships: Canadian Naval Forces and German Sea Raiders, 1880-1918* (Montreal: McGill-Queen's University Press, 1991), 248-59.

48 Ibid., 268.

49 Ibid., 268-9.

50 Michael L. Hadley, "The Popular Image of the Canadian Navy," in *A Nation's Navy: In Quest of Canadian Naval Identity,* ed. Michael L. Hadley, Rob Huebert, and Fred W. Crickard (Montreal: McGill-Queen's University Press, 1996), 36.

51 John G. Armstrong, "Letters from Halifax: Reliving the Halifax Explosion through the Eyes of My Grandfather, a Sailor in the Royal Canadian Navy," *Northern Mariner/Le Marin du nord* 8, 4 (1998): 55-74.

52 *Halifax Herald,* 27 and 28 May 1918. Also see R.H. Caldwell, "The VE Day Riots in Halifax, 7-8 May 1945," *Northern Mariner/Le Marin du nord* 10, 1 (2000): 3-20.

Bibliography

This account relies heavily on archival documents from Canada, Britain, and the United States. These are cited in full in the notes, as are extracts from contemporary newspapers. To avoid needless repetition they are not included here. Rather, the bibliography comprises only a selected list of the published material that I have consulted.

Anonymous. *The Royal Navy List, or, Who's Who in the Navy: A Book of Reference Relating to the Personnel of the Navy, Both Active and Retired ...* London: Witherby, 1917.

Anonymous [Rear-Admiral Bertram M. Chambers]. "Halifax Explosion." *Naval Review* 7, 1 (1920): 445-57.

Armstrong, John G. "Canadian Home Defence, 1914-1917: and the Role of Major-General Willoughby Gwatkin." MA thesis, Royal Military College of Canada, 1982.

–. "Letters from Halifax: Reliving the Halifax Explosion through the Eyes of My Grandfather, a Sailor in the Royal Canadian Navy." *Northern Mariner/Le Marin du nord* 8, 4 (1998): 55-74.

Beed, Blair. *1917 Halifax Explosion and American Response.* Halifax: Dtours Visitors and Convention Service, 1998.

Bird, Michael J. *The Town That Died.* Toronto: McGraw-Hill Ryerson, 1962.

Bothwell, Robert, Ian Drummond, and John English. *Canada, 1900-1945.* Toronto: University of Toronto Press, 1987.

Brock, P. Willet. "Commander E.A.E. Nixon and the Royal Naval College of Canada, 1910-1922." In *The RCN in Retrospect, 1910-1968,* ed. James A. Boutilier, 33-43. Vancouver: University of British Columbia Press, 1982.

Bronson, H.L. "Some Notes on the Halifax Explosion." *Transactions of the Royal Society of Canada,* series 3, vol. 12 (June 1918), section 3, 31-5.

Brown, Robert Craig. *Robert Laird Borden: A Biography.* 2. vols. Toronto: Macmillan, 1980.

Brown, Robert Craig, and Ramsay Cook. *Canada, 1896-1921: A Nation Transformed.* Toronto: McClelland and Stewart, 1974.

Caldwell, R.H. "The VE Day Riots in Halifax, 7-8 May 1945." *Northern Mariner/Le Marin du nord* 10, 1 (2000): 3-20.

Ferguson, Julie H. *Through a Canadian Periscope: The Story of the Canadian Submarine Service.* Toronto: Dundurn Press, 1995.

Gilly, William O.S. *Narratives of Shipwrecks of the Royal Navy: Between 1793 and 1857.* London: Longman, Green, 1864.

Hadley, Michael L. "The Popular Image of the Canadian Navy." In *A Nation's Navy: In Quest of Canadian Naval Identity,* ed. Michael L. Hadley, Rob Huebert, and Fred W. Crickard, 35-56. Montreal: McGill-Queen's University Press, 1996.

Hadley, Michael L., and Roger Sarty. *Tin-Pots and Pirate Ships: Canadian Naval Forces and German Sea Raiders, 1880-1918.* Montreal: McGill-Queen's University Press, 1991.

Hopkins, J. Castell, ed. *The Canadian Annual Review, 1917.* Toronto: annual review publishing co., 1918.

–. *The Canadian Annual Review, 1918.* Toronto: annual review publishing co., 1919.

Jobb, Dean. *Crime Wave: Con Men, Rogues and Scoundrels from Nova Scotia's Past.* Lawrencetown Beach, NS: Pottersfield Press, 1991.

Kesterton, W.H. *A History of Journalism in Canada.* Toronto: McClelland and Stewart, 1967.

Kitz, Janet. *Shattered City: The Halifax Explosion and the Road to Recovery.* Halifax: Nimbus, 1989.

LeBlanc, J.O.B. Ass't Naval Sect., "Historical Synopsis of Organization and Development of the R.C.N." Briefing/fact book, 1937. National Defence Headquarters, Directorate of History and Heritage, CHH 8//93.

MacPhail, Sir Andrew. *Official History of the Canadian Forces in the Great War, 1914-19: The Medical Services.* Ottawa: King's Printer, 1925.

Macpherson, K., and J. Burgess. *The Ships of Canada's Naval Forces 1910-1981.* Toronto: Collins, 1981.

Macquarrie, Heath, ed. *Robert Laird Borden: His Memoirs.* Toronto: McClelland and Stewart, 1969.

Mahar, James, and Rowena Mahar. *Too Many to Mourn: One Family's Tragedy.* Halifax: Nimbus, 1998.

Milner, Marc. *Canada's Navy: The First Century.* Toronto: University of Toronto Press, 1999.

Mooney, James L., ed. *Dictionary of American Naval Fighting Ships.* Washington, DC: Naval Historical Center, 1981.

Moore, D.R. *History of H.M.C. Dockyard, Halifax, N.S.* Halifax: Privately printed for Queen's Harbourmaster, 1967.

Morgan, H.J., ed. *The Canadian Men and Women of the Time.* Toronto: William Briggs, 1912.

Morton, Desmond. *A Military History of Canada: From Champlain to the Gulf War.* Toronto: McClelland and Stewart, 1992.

Morton, Desmond, and J.L. Granatstein. *Marching to Armageddon: Canadians and the Great War, 1914-1919.* Toronto: Lester and Orpen Dennys, 1989.

Prince, Samuel Henry. *Catastrophe and Social Change: Based upon a Sociological Study of the Halifax Disaster.* New York: Columbia University, 1920.

Ruffman, Alan, and Colin D. Howell, eds. *Ground Zero: A Reassessment of the 1917 Explosion in Halifax Harbour.* Halifax: Nimbus, 1994.

Russell, Benjamin. *Autobiography.* Halifax: Royal Print & Litho, 1932.

Sarty, Roger F. "Silent Sentry: A Military and Political History of Canadian Coast Defence 1860-1945." PhD dissertation, University of Toronto, 1982.

Smith, Marilyn Gurney. *The King's Yard: An Illustrated History of the Halifax Dockyard.* Halifax: Nimbus, 1985.

Thomas, Arnold W., ed. *The Canadian Almanac and Miscellaneous Directory.* Toronto: Copp Clark, 1917.

Tucker, Gilbert N. *The Naval Service of Canada: Its Official History.* Ottawa: King's Printer, 1952.

Index

Abbott, George (Able Seaman), 36, 142
Acadia, HMCS, 18, 26, 36, 51, 65, *80*
Acadia Sugar Refinery, 21, 42, 95
Adams, Arthur (Lieutenant, RNVR), 163
Admiralty House, 11, 14
AMC. *See* Canadian Army Medical Corps
American Red Cross, 97
Ames, SS, 94
Anstey (Sergeant-Major, AMC), 97
Appalache, SS, 147
Armitage, J.A. (Captain, British Expeditionary Force), 55
Armstrong, B.R. (Lieutenant Colonel, CGA), 99, 101
Army. *See* Canadian Militia; Department of Militia and Defence
Atwood, Arthur (Commander, RN [Ret.]), 106

Baddeley, Allan (Temporary Lieutenant-Commander, RCN), 54, 56-7
Baleine, tugboat, 16-17, 32, 52
Ballantyne, Charles Colquhoun (Minister of Naval Service): and cabinet subcommittee on Halifax explosion, 130; and clean-up of Halifax Harbour, 136; defence of Captain Hose on panel of public inquiry, 137; on discharge of Wyatt from navy, 202; discussion with Kingsmill about Edward Martin, 171-2; guarding of government interests during Halifax crisis, 205; insistence on changes in naval command in Halifax, 173; lack of naval experience, 83; letter to Judge Drysdale regarding Captain Hose, 141; passing of Demers' comments on to Borden, 193; and preparations for public inquiry, 119; reassurances to Halifax population, 132; on reconstruction of storehouses, 104; and regulations for munitions ships, after explosion, 138; report on second *Picton* fire, 169; request for information of *Galileo* and *Picton* incident, 154; request for report on naval administration of port of Halifax, 190; on responsibility for port of Halifax, 131-2; and royal commission into pilotage system, 128, 167; and suspension of Wyatt, 173; use of naval budget to promote naval and marine construction, 203
Barrat, H. (Captain, PAMC), 97
Beazley, Edward, 152
Bell, F.C., 122
Bell, Frank McKelvey (Lieutenant-Colonel,

Militia): 96, 97, 104; and testimony of Frederick Wyatt, 145-6
Benson, Thomas (Major-General, Militia): briefing by Rear-Admiral Chambers on dockyard, 68; and chain of command after explosion, 66; and chief press censor on help with media at inquiry, 116, 124, 125; and complaint regarding lack of fire precautions around *Picton*, 153; and fire in Wellington Barracks magazine, 59; and Halifax Relief Committee, 104; on military activity after explosion, 57; offer of help from US Navy, 93; reply to Gwatkin's offer of assistance, 87; report on relief efforts to Militia Council, 69; request for American patrols against looting, 70
Bernier, Serge, xi
Bird, Michael, J., 4, 62
Borden, Robert (Sir): and cabinet subcommittee on Halifax explosion, 130; coalition government of, 83; at 8 December meeting organized by Rear-Admiral Chambers, 99, 101; and Demers's notes foreshadowing inquiry's judgment, 190-2; and implications of Demers's comments on Halifax pilotage, 193; offer of federal assistance after explosion, 99-100; and preparations for public inquiry, 119; and question of indemnity for damage due to explosion, 135; re-election of, 109, 125; report on second *Picton* fire, 169; request for naval information on Halifax Harbour management, 138; and retention of Captain Hose on public inquiry, 137; and universal military service, 125
Boutin, Alice M.(Nursing Sister, RCN), 48
Brannen, Horatio H., 33, 38, 42
Brannen, Walter, 43
British Expeditionary Force, 55
British Navy. *See* Royal Navy (RN)
Brock, P. Willet (Rear-Admiral, RCN), 46
Bronson, Howard L., 41, 43
Brookfield, John W., 100
Brown, Horace G., 64
Browning, M.C. (Vice-Admiral, RN), 172
Burchell, Charles J.: on collision of *Imo* and *Mont Blanc*, 175; as counsel for *Imo*, 122; discrediting of *Mont Blanc* witnesses, 124; final summations for public inquiry, 174-5; and "mystery ship" that preceded *Imo*, 141; and testimony of Edward Martin, 162; and testimony of Frederick Wyatt, 147-52; and

testimony of Herbert Whitehead, 142; and testimony of Terrence Freeman, 146
Burnett, Mr., 47
Burnett, Rodney O., 37

Cadets. *See* Royal Naval College of Canada
Calgarian, HMS, 115
Calonne, SS, 25, 96, 124, 125
CAMC. *See* Canadian Army Medical Corps (CAMC)
Canada, HMCS: explosion casualties, 51; location before explosion on 5 December, 27-8; photograph, *76*; report of ships adrift after explosion, 90; as rescue ship after explosion, 54-5; during storm of 7 December, 94; as training ship, 18; view of initial fire on *Mont Blanc* from deck of, 40
Canada Shipping Act, 117, 133
Canada Steamship Lines, 18
Canadian Army. *See* Canadian Army Medical Corps (CAMC); Canadian Militia
Canadian Army Medical Corps (CAMC), 97
Canadian Expeditionary Force (CEF), 11
Canadian Government Railway, 62, 65, 101
Canadian Militia: credit for efforts after Halifax explosion, 6; garrison in Halifax, 10-11; medical assistance after explosion, 57-8; relief efforts by, 104; underrepresentation in military history of Halifax explosion, 5. *See also* Department of Militia and Defence
Canadian Pacific Railway, telegraph services, 84
Canadian War Museum, ix-x, xiii
Cann, Malcolm, 14
Carmania, SS, 199
Cartier, HMCS, 18, 27, 207
Carvell, F.B. (Minister of Public Works), 104, 130
Casualties, of Halifax explosion: dockyard, 47-8, 95, 96, 100; military funerals, 108-9; ships' crews, 51, 65, 68, 93, 125
CC-1, Canadian submarine, 19, *77*
CC-2, Canadian submarine, 19, 50, *77*
CD-26, coastal drifter, 27, 51
CD-27, 27, 51
CD-53, 27, 51
CD-73: attempt to rescue *Mont Blanc* sailors after collision, 36; effects of explosion on, 43; testimony of skipper at inquiry, 142; view of collision of *Mont Blanc* and *Imo* from, 34-5; view of initial fire on *Mont Blanc* from deck of, 36, 38
CD-74, 79
CEF. *See* Canadian Expeditionary Force (CEF)
Censorship, wartime, and public inquiry, 124-5
Chambers, Bertram M. (Rear-Admiral, RN): assistance to Canadian Navy after explosion, 95; biography, 22; on casualties of explosion, 65; and convoys, resumption after explosion, 108; and convoys, suspension of, 71; on dismissal of Frederick Wyatt, 167; and early information about explosion, 65-6, 88, 89; experience of explosion, 60-2; and fire aboard *Picton,* 115, 116; inspection of explosion damage, 63-4, 94-5; letter to Halifax press, 189; meeting of 8 December on reconstruction efforts, 91, 99, 100, 102, 105; meeting with Lieutenant Governor Grant, 68-9; meeting with William Henry regarding public inquiry, 119; and naval chain of command, 22, 136, 172; operational responsibility of, after explosion, 63; on permission for *Mont Blanc* to enter harbour, 128; report on manslaughter trial of Wyatt, 201-2; and second fire on *Picton,* 169; on transportation lines, after explosion, 101; on unconfirmed ship's fire, 132; on US munitions ships in Halifax Harbour, 128; on weather, after explosion, 90, 102
Chambers, Ernest J. (chief press censor): and news reports on Halifax explosion, 84-5, 88; public inquiry, and wartime censorship requirements, 116, 124-5
Changuinola, HMS: and aftermath of explosion, 63, 64; effects of explosion on, 50; location before explosion on 5 December, 28; medical assistance to explosion victims, 55, 64; rescue efforts by crew of, 58-9
Chief examining officer (CXO): role of, 20. *See also* Wyatt, Frederick Evan (Acting Commander, RCN) (Chief Examining Officer)
Clara, SS, 141, 185
Clove, SS, 90
Cluney, Andrew: assigning of blame in final summation to inquiry, 176-7; inquiry about safety of *Picton,* 144; at manslaughter trial of Wyatt, Le Médéc, and Mackey, 196; representative of attorney general of Nova Scotia at inquiry, 122; and testimony of Edward Martin, 158-60
Coastal Drifters (CD) (patrol boats), *78*
Colchester and Hants Rifles, 58
Communications: after Halifax explosion, 84, 85-6; interference by storm of 7 December, 90. *See also* Radio; Telegraph services
Compagnie Générale Transatlantic, 141
Conscription: anti-conscription sentiment in Quebec, 114, 203; Borden election victory and universal military service, 125; coverage by *Halifax Herald,* 121; as election issue, 83; national service appeals, presided by Judge Drysdale, 123
Convoys, shipping: Convoy Office, survived

explosion, 69; economic value of exports, from Halifax, 23; merchant ships damaged in explosion, 91; organized from Halifax Harbour, 17; as responsibility of Royal Navy, 22; resumption, after explosion, 105-6, 107-8; ships in Halifax Harbour on 5 December, 25; suspension of, following explosion, 70, 71

Creighton, James, 151, 152

Critch, W.G. (Able Seaman, RCN), 45

Cunard Lines, 30

CXO. *See* Chief examining officer (CXO); Wyatt, Frederick Evan (Acting Commander, RCN) (Chief Examining Officer)

Dangerous cargo: aboard *Mont Blanc*, 30, 36, 62-3, 114, 123; lack of procedures for, in Public Traffic Regulations, 30. *See also* Munitions ships

Defence of the Realm Act, 150, 195

Demers, Louis Auguste (Captain): and judgment of inquiry, 187; as member of inquiry, 117, 118, 121; notes to Robert Borden foreshadowing inquiry's judgment, 190-2; on pilot Frank Mackey, 147; and testimony of Edward Martin, 160-1, 162; and testimony of Frederick Wyatt, 165-7; and testimony of Herbert Whitehead, 142

Dennis, William: critique of public inquiry, 130; meeting with C.C. Ballantyne regarding public inquiry, 130-1; and political patronage, 120; request for Frederick Wyatt's dismissal, 154. *See also Halifax Herald*

Department of Marine and Fisheries: building, in dockyard, 14; at 8 December meeting organized by Rear-Admiral Chambers, 99; launch of investigation into Halifax explosion, 117-20; on pilotage as topic for public inquiry, 127-8; request for naval information on Halifax Harbour management, 138

Department of Militia and Defence: competent handling of rescue efforts, 87-8; and naval service, working relationship, 83. *See also* Canadian Militia

Department of the Naval Service: and reconstruction of storehouses, 103; request for naval information on Halifax Harbour management, 138. *See also* Desbarats, George Joseph (Deputy Minister for Naval Service); Kingsmill, Charles E. (Admiral, RCN); Royal Canadian Navy (RCN)

Department of Public Works, 103, 104, 109

Department of Railways and Canals: at 8 December meeting organized by Rear-Admiral Chambers, 99; and reconstruction of storehouses, 103, 104, 109

Desbarats, George (Cadet), 93

Desbarats, George Joseph (Deputy Minister for Naval Service): as advisor of C.C. Ballantyne, 83; and cabinet subcommittee on Halifax explosion, 130; decision not to interfere with Halifax pilotage, 195; as father of cadet at Royal Naval College, 85, 89; guarding of government interests during crisis, 205; as portrayed in media, 171; and ranking of Rear-Admiral Chambers (RN), 22; and reconstruction of storehouses, 103, 104; report on naval administration of port of Halifax, 190

DeWolf, James, 99

Divers: during initial fire on *Mont Blanc*, 39-40; rescue, after explosion, 44-5; resumption of services on 7 December, 90

Dockyard, HMC (Halifax): activity, before explosion on morning of 6 December, 32; casualties, 47-8, 96, 100; under command of Edward Martin, 14; effects of explosion on, 43, 47-9, *79, 81*, 98, 100; labour force, 14; plan of, *15*; records, destruction in fire of 18 November, 14, 110; repairs to, 11, 100, 108

Donegal, HMS, 105

Dry dock, condition after explosion, 95, 100

Drysdale, Arthur (Hon.): appointment to inquiry into Halifax explosion, 117; on Captain Hose as member of inquiry, 140-1; and judgment of inquiry, 187; meeting with William Henry regarding inquiry, 119; notes prepared by Louis Demers foreshadowing inquiry's judgment, 190-2; and physical setting of inquiry, 122

Dynes, Russell R., 4

Edwardes, G.H.S. (Lieutenant, RNCVR), 50

Edwards, Bob, *Calgary Eye Opener,* 23

Eldridge, George (Captain, RN [Ret.]), 66, 89, 125, 163, 167

Election, federal: and conscription, 83, 125; coverage by *Halifax Herald,* 121; re-election of Robert Borden, 109, 125

Electricity, after explosion, 71

Evening Journal (Ottawa), on naval ineptitude, 188-9

Examination Office: anchorage of *Mont Blanc* on 5 December, 30; ignoring of reports on ships' movements, 151-2, 156; query regarding sailing of *Imo,* 152-3; and role of chief examining officer, 20. *See also* Wyatt, Frederick Evan (Acting Commander, RCN)(Chief Examining Officer)

Exchequer Court of Canada, Admiralty Division, 117

Federal government: cabinet subcommittee on Halifax explosion, 130-3; restitution of Halifax explosion, 135. *See also* Borden, Robert (Sir); Election, federal; names of specific departments

Fleet Wireless School, 11, 107

Freeman, Terrence (Mate, RNCVR), 30, 146

Furness Withy & Company (ship owners), 99

Gainings, Mr., 91, 103

Galileo, SS: in Cluney's summation to inquiry, 177; fire in coal bunker, 139; incident, at departure on 23 January, 143, 144, 147, 151, 154; testimony of Frederick Wyatt, 155-6; testimony of Roland Iceton, 156; in William Henry's summation to inquiry, 184

Gammon, John T. (Acting Gunner, RCN), 39, 44-5

Garnett, H.N. (Captain, RN), 37, 63, 64, 67, 69, 91

Gas supply, after explosion, 71

Gaunt (Commodore, RN), 96, 99

Germany: explosion assumed result of German enemy action, 112-13. *See also* Submarines

Good Hope, HMS, 14

Gopher, tugboat, 16-17

Gordon (Captain), 63, 64

Grant, J. McCallum (Lieutenant Governor, Nova Scotia): briefing on explosion, 69; and public inquiry, 118, 119

Grant, W.L. (Vice-Admiral, RN), 172

Great North Western, telegraph services, 84, 88

Griffith, Lambert (Bert) Barron (Able Seaman, RNCVR): on dockyard work parties, 92-3; on effects of explosion, 43, 112; family, news of explosion, 84; injuries, xi, 208; as part of relief effort, 44; photograph, 73; on resumption of regular duties after explosion, 110; view of initial fire on deck of *Mont Blanc,* 39

Grilse, HMCS: effects of explosion on, 50; location before explosion on 5 December, 26; photograph, 76; role in, 17; weather reports, after explosion, 72, 89, 102

Groves, Jean, 48

Gwatkin, Willoughby (Major-General, CGS Canadian Militia) and censorship and security during public inquiry, 124; and delay of news of explosion, 85; offer of military assistance after explosion, 87; request to Ernest Chambers for help with Halifax media, 116-17

Hadley, Michael L., 4, 14, 172, 206, 207

Halifax (city): blackout, 16; Board of Control, 116, 127; economic prosperity, due to war, 23;

fires, after explosion, 63-4; geography, 10; history of, 10; as military port, 10; population, 10; as principal base of Royal Canadian Navy, 5; representation at public inquiry, 122. *See also* Halifax explosion; Martin, P.F. (Mayor of Halifax)

Halifax Board of Trade: at 8 December meeting organized by Rear-Admiral Chambers, 99; meeting with cabinet subcommittee on Halifax explosion, 131-2

Halifax Commercial Club, 131, 134

Halifax dockyard. *See* Dockyard, HMS (Halifax)

Halifax explosion: assumption of German enemy action, 112-13; as disaster, and military response, 69; early news of, 84-5; effects of, 49, 50, 63-4; injuries and mortality due to, 3, 41, 47-8, 65, 68, 93, 95, 96; in literature, 4; medical assistance after, 64, 68, 87-8, 96-7; military funerals, 108-9; news reports, 84, 86; official report of, 70-1; patrols, against looting, 70; relief efforts, 69, 104; rescue efforts, 45, 54-5, 56-7, 64, 65, 66, 72, 87-8; second (false alarm, steam from Wellington Barracks magazine), 59-60; strength of, 41-2; and tsunami, 43-4, 49, 51; underrepresentation in Canadian military history, 3-4; utilities, interruption of, 71; weather, on day of, 72; in William Henry's summation for inquiry, 181-2. *See also* Halifax Harbour; *Imo,* SS; *Mont Blanc,* SS

Halifax Fire Department, 38

Halifax Harbour: clean-up, after explosion, 135-6; damage, as result of explosion, 110-11; map of, 12, 13; naval protection of, 16-17; reconstruction plans, 99-100; regulations, media critique of, 130; resumption of shipping, after explosion, 105-6, 108; traffic control problems, 151-2. *See also* Halifax explosion; Pilotage services; Royal Canadian Navy (RCN)

Halifax Herald: coverage of Frederick Wyatt's inquiry testimony, 153-4; coverage of inquiry into explosion, 120, 121, 125-6, 127, 128, 129-30, 134, 136, 137-8, 142, 156; coverage of manslaughter trial of Wyatt, 199, 201; critique of Charles Kingsmill, 170-1; critique of William Henry's final summation to inquiry, 184; on fire aboard *Picton,* 115; on "Gallic cowardice" and "British gallantry," 114; on incompetence of navy, 199, 200; on inconsistencies in Martin's and Wyatt's testimony, 162-3; on military assistance during Halifax relief efforts, 121; on responsibility for Halifax explosion, 170; on suspicion of German enemy action, 113; on transfer of Admiral Story, 174

Halifax Ladies' College, 97

Halifax *Morning Chronicle*. See *Morning Chronicle*

Halifax Pilotage Commission: investigation into, 133; legal counsel at inquiry, 122, 176; political implications of naval policies, 192-5; relationship with Examination Office, 152; testimony at inquiry, 146-7, 151, 152, 163. *See also* Pilotage services

Halifax Relief Commission: accusations of mismanagement, 130; creation of, 129; disbursement of compensation funds by, 204; and visit of cabinet subcommittee, 133

Halifax Relief Committee: creation of, on 9 December, 104; critique of, 134; sanction of military medical assistance under Bell, 97-8; work of, 104

Hall, James, 146

Hanson, Francis (Lieutenant, RNCVR), 60

Hardy, J.J. (Assistant Surgeon, USN), 68

Harris Abattoir Company, 107

Harrison, James W. (Captain [merchant]), 99, 101, 102, 108

Hathaway, John, 14

Hayes, Charles A., 101

Hayes, R.M. (Medical Officer, USN), 68

Hayes, William (pilot): cited as victim of manslaughter in Wyatt trial, 197; guiding of *Imo* into Halifax Harbour on 6 December, 32-3; in testimony of Wyatt, 146, 148

Hazen, J.D., 193

Hemsted, J.R. (Acting Staff-Paymaster, RN), 194

Henry, William Alexander: on behaviour of Charles Burchell, 183; as crown counsel in inquiry, 87, 118, 122; and delay in beginning of inquiry, 121; on excesses of media, 182, 183; final summation to inquiry, 177-84; on first round of hearings, 123; on *Imo*'s movements and collision with *Mont Blanc*, 178; on issues regarding munitions ships in Halifax Harbour, 128-9, 179; on letters to Edward Martin by Frederick Wyatt, 182-3; meetings with witnesses, 163; on pilotage service, 167, 181, 183; preparations for inquiry, 119-20; request to Martin for additional testimony, 167-8; and speculation of pressure on inquiry, 190; testified at manslaughter trial of Wyatt, 201; and testimony of Edward Martin, 162; on testimony of Herbert Whitehead, 142; on testimony of *Mont Blanc* witnesses, 178; and testimony of Terrence Freeman, 143; and testimony of Walter Pasco, 143-4; view of navy, 204; on Wyatt's blame for collision, 187-8

Hensley, George W., 99, 101, 102

Herald. See *Halifax Herald*

Highflyer, HMS: attempt by whale boat crew to tow *Mont Blanc* from Pier 6, 37-8; casualties, during explosion, 125; effects of explosion on, 42, 50-1; escort to first convoy after explosion, 108; location before explosion on 5 December, 28; medical assistance to explosion victims, 55, 65; photograph, *81*; position, during collision of *Mont Blanc* and *Imo*, 33-5; repairs to, 91; report of *Mont Blanc-Imo* collision, 40, 62, 63; signal flags after explosion, 63; and survey of explosion damage, 64

Hilford, tugboat, 64, 65

Hochelaga, HMCS, 18, 26, 51, 91, 207

Holloway, Graham (Acting Commander, RNR): authority over docking of overseas transport ships, 108; on berth space for military transport, after explosion, 100-1; at 8 December meeting organized by Rear-Admiral Chambers, 99, 102; distinguished service of, 207; inspection of *Picton* after fire, 155; notification of *Mont Blanc-Imo* collision, 40; and rescue efforts, 65; and resumption of convoys, 105

Holme, Hugh E. (Commander, RCN), 155

Hose, Walter (Acting Captain, RCN): as acting superintendent of naval dockyard, 131; on assistance by Royal Navy, 95; on assistance by US Navy, 95; biography, 17; as Captain of Patrols, 17-18, 21; command post for ships' orders, after explosion, 49; at 8 December meeting organized by Rear-Admiral Chambers, 99; distinguished service of, 207-8, 209; and judgment of inquiry, 187; as member of inquiry, 118, 130, 136, 137, 171; official report of explosion, 70-1; reporting to Kingsmill, 21; reports on harbour ships during 7 December storm, 89; rescue efforts after explosion, 64, 66; and retrieval of AWOL crew of *Niobe*, 54; on shipping regulations, 101-2; telegraph on Halifax explosion to Kingsmill, 88

Hovland, SS, 25, *81*, 95, 100

Iceton, Roland (Mate), 144, 147, 156, 183, 205

ICR (Intercolonial Railway). See Canadian Government Railway

Imo, SS: absolved of blame in collision by Louis Demers, 191; collision with *Mont Blanc*, 3, 34-5, 197; crew, on deck after collision with *Mont Blanc*, 37; crew, testimony at public inquiry, 124; effects of explosion on, 42; helmsman, as witness at inquiry, 113, 141; movement, before explosion on 6 December,

30-1, 32-3, 34; ruled equally to blame for collision by Privy Council, 187; telephone call about movements of, 156; in William Henry's final summation for inquiry, 178-9. *See also* Johansen, Johan (*Imo* helmsman)

Intercolonial Railway. *See* Canadian Government Railway

J.A. McKie, SS, 96

Jellicoe, John (Admiral, RN), 200

Johansen, Johan (*Imo* helmsman): German origins of, cited as possible issue in collision, 198; testimony at public inquiry, 113, 124, 141

Johnston, Alexander (Deputy Minister of Marine and Fisheries), 87; and cabinet sub-committee on Halifax explosion, 130; on clean-up of Halifax Harbour, 135-6; letter from William Henry on harbour regulations, 187; meeting with Judge Drysdale, 133; on pilotage as topic for public inquiry, 119, 127-8; and public inquiry into Halifax explosion, 118

Kayford, Alfred, 125-6

Kerr, Donald A., 121-2, 201

King, William (Chief Petty Officer, RCN)(Royal Naval College), 39, 46

King Edward, SS. *See Laurentian*, HMCS.

Kingsley, Harry (Captain [Ret.], RCN), 39, 45

Kingsmill, Charles E. (Admiral, RCN): appointment of counsel for Wyatt's manslaughter trial, 200-1; attack on, in media, 170-1; attempts at information on Halifax explosion, 85, 86, 88; aversion to political patronage, 23, 106, 120, 195; distress on negative publicity about navy, 189; as father of cadet at Royal Naval College, 85, 86, 88, 94; on *Halifax Herald* coverage of public inquiry, 137; investigative trip to Halifax, 88, 96; and mission of Edward Martin to London, 14, 16; portrait, *74*; promotion of Frederick Wyatt to CXO, 21; and role and precedence of Rear-Admiral Chambers in Halifax, 22-3; and relocation of Royal Naval College, 106-7; reporting relationships to, 21; request for information of *Galileo* and *Picton* incident, 154; and suspension of Frederick Wyatt, 156, 173; working relationship with George Desbarats, 83; on Wyatt's marital situation, 161

Kingsmill, Walter (Cadet), 93, 94

Kirkwood, Kenneth Porter, 110-11

Kitz, Janet, 4

Knight Templar, HMS, 28, 63

Kronprinz Wilhelm (renamed USS *Von Steuben*), 67

Labour force, limited, due to casualties, 100, 104, 107-8

Lady Evelyn, HMCS: crew at military funerals, 109; history of, 18; patrol duty, 28, 67, 72, 89; photograph, *75*; position during explosion, 28, 29, 31, 52; weather reports, 94, 102

Lansdowne, HMCS, 52

Laurentian, HMCS (formerly SS *King Edward*), 18, 26, 89

Laurie, Mr., 47, 91

Laurier, Wilfrid (Sir), 83

Le Marchant, Evelyn R. (Vice-Admiral, RN), 63, 64

Le Médec, Aimé (Captain of *Mont Blanc*): action before collision of *Mont Blanc* and *Imo*, 35; arrest of, 185, 196; arrival in Halifax Harbour on 5 December, 29; attempts to indict after discharge, 201; blamed for collision at inquiry, 184, 185, 191; discharge of, from manslaughter trial, 198; order to abandon ship after collision with *Imo*, 36; police protection for, 114; testimony at public inquiry, 141

Lindsay (Colonel), 99, 108

Longland, Fred, 44

Longshoremen's Union, 108

Lovett, L.A., 200-1

Luz Blanca, SS, 206

McBride, Richard (Sir), 19, *77*

McGannon, Charles, 163-4

MacGillivray, Dugald, 99, 153, 173-4

McIlraith, R.T., 104

McKay, W. (Lieutenant Commander, USNR), 28, 68

Mackenzie (Cadet), 39, 46

Mackey, Francis (Frank) (Pilot of *Mont Blanc* [TSK]): arrest of, 185, 196; attempts to indict after discharge, 201; blamed for collision, 174-6, 184-5, 191; career, after Halifax explosion, 147; discharge, in manslaughter trial, 198; in Frederick Wyatt's testimony, 146; piloting of *Mont Blanc* into Halifax Harbour, 29; testimony at public inquiry, 123, 163; in William Henry's summation to inquiry, 183

Maclean, A.K., 130

McLennan, Charles A. (Lieutenant, 76th, Colchester and Hants Rifles), 58-60

MacLennan, Hugh, 4, 5

McLeod, Robert A., 196, 197

MacNeil, Robert, 4, 5

MacPhail, Sir Andrew, 4

Maggie, tugboat, 63, 64-5

Maine (state), medical assistance by, 97

Makiny, John L. (Mate, RNCVR): on effects of

explosion on *Nereid*, 49; observation of collision of *Mont Blanc* and *Imo* from deck of *Nereid*, 33-4; testimony at manslaughter trial of Wyatt, Le Médec, and Mackey, 197, 198

Margaret, HMCS, 18, 26, 39, 50, 90

Maritime Command Museum, 14

Martin, Edward H. (Captain, RCN): absence during aftermath of explosion, 136; on arrival of *Mont Blanc*, 157-8; biography, 14; as commander of dockyard, 14; critique of, by Andrew Cluney, 177; exchange of duties with Vice-Admiral Story, 173; exonerated of blame by Louis Demers, 192; initially not called to testify at inquiry, 153; letters from Frederick Wyatt, 149-50, 158, 163, 182-3; 1917 mission to London, 14, 16; on problems with Frederick Wyatt, 160-1; on problems with pilots, 158-60, 193-4; and removal of Royal Naval College to Kingston, 172-3; request for additional testimony, 167-8; as responsible for Halifax Harbour, 131; testimony at public inquiry, 156-62; working relationship with Admiral Kingsmill, 21, 171-2, 173, 205

Martin, P.F. (Mayor of Halifax): concern over lack of precautions regarding *Picton*, 153; critique of, by C.C. Ballantyne, 141; question on authority for Halifax Harbour, 131; request that Captain Hose be removed from inquiry, 137

Massachusetts Medical Unit, Maine (US) National Guard, 96, 97

Mattison, Albert (Acting Boatswain, RCN), 37, 38, 42

Medical assistance: after Halifax explosion, 64, 87-8; American, 55, 68, 96-7, 105; Naval Hospital, 48; nurses, 68; *Old Colony* as hospital ship, 68; prompt arrival of, 96-7; troops, in Halifax at time of explosion, 11

Mellish, Humphrey: attack on Burchell's behaviour during inquiry, 175; on confusing regulations governing munitions ships, 142-3; as counsel for *Mont Blanc*, 122; final summations for public inquiry, 175

Messines, HMCS, 18, 26

Mewburn, S.C. (Major-General), 130

Middleham Castle, SS, 25, 90, 96, 124

Middleton, J.R., 126

Militia. *See* Canadian Militia; Department of Militia and Defence

Militia Department. *See* Department of Militia and Defence

Minesweeping trawlers and tugboats: clean-up of Halifax Harbour after explosion, 136; lack of damage in explosion, 98; role of, in Halifax Harbour, 16-17

Mining catastrophe (Stellarton, Nova Scotia), 153

Mitchell, John (Acting Boatswain, RCN), 37

Mont Blanc, SS: arrival of, on 5 December, 29-30; blamed for collision, 34-5, 113-14, 184, 191; casualties during rescue efforts, 125; collision with *Imo*, 3, 34-5; crew, at public inquiry, 123, 124, 141; crew, manning of lifeboats, after collision with *Imo*, 36-7; dangerous cargo, 3, 30, 36, 62-3, 114, 123; explosion, effects of, 41-52; fire, after collision with *Imo*, 36; minor explosions after collision, 38; movement into Halifax Harbour on 6 December, 5, 32, 144-6; permission to enter Halifax Harbour, 126-7, 128, 132; ruled equally to blame for collision by Privy Council, 187; in William Henry's final summation for inquiry, 178, 179. *See also* Le Médec, Aimé (Captain of *Mont Blanc*)

Morgan, William (Chief Petty Officer [Writer], RCN), 44, 163

Morning Chronicle (Halifax): coverage of public inquiry, 120, 127, 128, 135; on second *Picton* fire, 169-70; on testimony of Edward Martin, 157-8

Morrill, USCG cutter, 29, 55, 68, 105

Morton, Desmond, 4

Moses, Stanford E. (Captain, USN), 67, 70

Moulton, Carl (Private recruit, British Expeditionary Force), 55-6, 56

Munitions ships: in judgment of inquiry, 185; lack of precautions, 142-3, 153; and public traffic regulations, 30. *See also Galileo*, SS; *Mont Blanc*, SS

Murray, T.A. (Lieutenant-Commander, RNCVR), 22, 62, 64, 65, 66

Musquash, tugboat, 16-17, 42, 65, 66, 124

Navy. *See* Royal Canadian Navy (RCN); Royal Navy (RN); US Navy

Nereid, tugboat, 17, 33-4, 49, 147, 197, 198

Newcombe, Percy F. (Acting Commander, RCN), 20, 44, 54

Newspapers: early reports of Halifax explosion, 84, 86; praise for American medical assistance, 96-7; and wartime censorship, during public inquiry, 124. *See also Evening Journal* (Ottawa); *Halifax Herald; Morning Chronicle* (Halifax); *Ottawa Journal*

Newton (Captain of *Calgarian*), 115

Niobe, HMCS: arrest of Stoker Campbell by marines from, 27; casualties, 44, 108; clean-up after explosion, 71-2; crew, as work parties retrieving stores, 92; crew, unauthorized absence after explosion, 53-4; effects of explosion on, 42, 43, 44; hit by tsunami after

explosion, 43-4; loss of communication with
naval headquarters after explosion, 88-9; as
naval accommodation and office space, 20;
photograph, *78, 81*; position, during collision of *Mont Blanc* and *Imo*, 5, 27, 31, 34;
and RCN Examination Service, 20; repairs
required, after explosion, 98; report of collision of *Mont Blanc* and *Imo*, 39, 40; and
rescue efforts, 44, 56-7, 90; as symbol of
"tinpot navy," 23; as training ship, 19-20
Nixon, E.A.E. (Commander, RN): arrival on
Niobe after collision of *Mont Blanc* and *Imo*,
39; commanding officer of Royal Naval
College of Canada, 14; and effects of explosion on Royal Naval College, 45-6; injuries
sustained during explosion, 46-7; replaced
temporarily by Edward Martin, 173
Nolan, Joseph, 122
North Ordnance Magazines, 56-7
Northern King, SS, 94
Northwind, SS, 90

Ocean Terminals, 100, 101, 104, 153, 155
O'Hearn, Walter, 197
Old Colony, USS, 105; as hospital ship, 95, 97;
meals, for hospital staff and patients, 68;
medical assistance provided by, 55, 64, 68,
98, 105; position before explosion on 5
December, 28-9
Orde (Cadet), 46
Orduna, SS, 106, 110
O'Reilly, William (Gunner, RCN), 44, 56-7
Ottawa Journal, on public inquiry into Halifax
explosion, 132

Palmer, William, 14
Pasco, Fred C.C. (Captain, RCN): biography,
16; and clean-up of Halifax Harbour, 136;
command post for ships' orders, after
explosion, 49; concern over testimony of
Frederick Wyatt, 154-5; on fire aboard
Galileo, 139; on *Galileo* shipping incident,
155; injuries, 48, 60, 64, 68, 95; as interim
commander of dockyard, 16; meeting with
William Henry over evidence, 153; ordered
to remove *Picton* after second fire, 169; passing of command to Captain Hose, 60; position during initial fire on *Mont Blanc*, 40;
and regulations for munitions ships, after
Halifax explosion, 138; and rescue efforts
after explosion, 55, 64; on resumption of
dockyard operations, 110; suspension of
Frederick Wyatt, 155, 156; testimony at public
inquiry, 136, 143-4; transfer of, 173
Patrol boats, *78*, 98
Patronage: and Halifax pilotage service, 118-19,

146-7, 192; political, aversion of Admiral
Kingsmill to, 23, 106, 120
Pentelow (Cadet), 46
Petterson, H.C. (Surgeon, USCG), 68
Phillips, Mr. (Stores assistant), 91
Pickford and Black (steamship agents), 99, 152,
156, 164
Picton, SS: crew, at public inquiry, 124; damage
to, 65, 90, 96; fire precautions, lack of, 153;
fires on, 114-16, 169, 177; inspection of safety
measures on, 155; position, before explosion,
25; request by navy for information on, 154;
unloading of ammunition from, 139, 144, 178
Pilotage services: critique of, by Louis Demers,
191, 192; critique of, by media, 130; as issue at
public inquiry, 122, 127-8, 146-7; and movements of *Imo*, 145-6; pilots, alleged ignoring
of regulations, 102, 158-60; pilots, naval
handling of complaints about, 192-5; and
political patronage, 118, 147; reports on ship
movements, ignored by Examination Office,
151-2, 156; royal commission on, 196; and
testimony of Frederick Wyatt, 149-52. *See
also* Halifax Pilotage Commission; Mackey,
Francis (Frank) (Pilot of *Mont Blanc*);
Regulations, shipping
Pilots. *See* Halifax Pilotage Commission;
Pilotage services
Pitts, Arthur C.S. (Lieutenant, RNCVR), 50, 60
Port Convoy Officer, 23
Port of Halifax. *See* Halifax Harbour
Press. *See* Newspapers
Price, Richard (Writer), 163-4
Prince, Samuel Henry, 4
Public Traffic Regulations, 30
PV-I, minesweeping trawler, 16
PV-II, 75
PV-IV, 115
PV-V, 26, 50, 89
PV-VII, 16, 32, 52

Quarantelli, E.L., 4

Radio: news of Halifax explosion, 85-6. *See also*
Fleet Wireless School; Wireless Office
Railways: damage to, 71; telegraph services, 84
RCN. *See* Royal Canadian Navy (RCN)
Read, Joseph, MP, 203
Regulations, shipping: after explosion, 101-2; in
judgment of inquiry, 185; and munitions
ships, 138, 143-4; testimony of Edward
Martin at inquiry, 157, 158; testimony of
Walter Pasco at inquiry, 143-4; in William
Henry's final summation for inquiry, 180
Reid, J.D. (Minister of Railways and Canals),
104, 130, 169

Relief efforts. *See* Halifax Relief Commission; Halifax Relief Committee
Renner, Edward (pilot), 141, 185
Ridges, Robert (Lieutenant, RNCVR), 107
RNCVR. *See* Royal Naval Canadian Volunteer Reserve (RNCVR)
Robertson, Thomas R., 122, 167, 176, 201
Robinson, Bill (Lieutenant), 39, 46
Rockhead General Hospital, 57
Ross, J.K.L. (Jack)(Commander, RNCVR), 76
Rousseau, Joseph A. (Staff Surgeon, RCN), 48, 64
Royal Canadian Navy (RCN): blamed for Halifax explosion, x, 134; budget approval of, 203; chain of command, 136, 195; conflict with British Royal Navy over authority in Halifax Harbour, 22-3; control of munitions ships, after explosion, 128-9; creation of, 9; Examination Service, 20; fleet, antiquated, 9-10; lack of early communication on Halifax explosion, 84-6; morale, after inquiry, 189-90; Patrol Service, in Halifax Harbour, 17-19; personnel changes, after public inquiry, 173; and pilots, non-compliance with regulations, 192-5; poor public opinion of, 23-4, 132, 147-51, 206, 207, 208; and role of harbour-master in Halifax, 142; shipping traffic control, critique in media over, 126-9, 154; underrepresented in military history of Halifax explosion, 5. *See also* Department of the Naval Service; *Niobe*, HMCS; Royal Naval College of Canada
Royal Naval Air Service, 110
Royal Naval Canadian Volunteer Reserve (RNCVR), 22, *73, 77*
Royal Naval College of Canada: activity, before explosion on 6 December, 32; buildings, used for dockyard operations after explosion, 110; description, 14; effects of explosion on, 43, 45-7; injuries to cadets, 93; relocation of, 106-7
Royal Navy (RN): assistance after Halifax explosion, 95; conflicting jurisdictions with Royal Canadian Navy in Halifax Harbour, 22-3; and control of Halifax Harbour, 9; and shipping convoys in Halifax, 128-9
Rudolf, Francis, 142
Ruffles, J.R.R. (Lieutenant, RN), 66
Runic (former name of *Imo*), 30
Russell, Benjamin (Judge), 197-8, 201

Sailors' Memorial, Halifax, 14
St. Julien, HMCS, 18, 26
Saranac, SS, 89-90, *90*, 94, 96
Sarty, Roger F., 4, 14, 172, 206, 207

Saxonia, SS, 106
Scanlon, T. Joseph, 4
Senior Officer of Escorts, 23
Shearwater, HMCS (formerly HMS) , 19
Sherwood, Percy (Sir) (Dominion Police), 85
Silver, Arthur, 14
Smith, George R., 152, 153, 156, 164
Smith, J. Willard, 33
Stadacona, HMCS, 18, 26, 209
Stella Maris, tugboat: attempt to extinguish initial fire on *Mont Blanc*, 37; attempt to tow *Mont Blanc* from Pier 6, 37-8; casualties, 42; crew, at public inquiry, 124; effects of explosion on, 42; movement before explosion on 6 December, 33
Stellarton, Nova Scotia, mining catastrophe, 153
Stevens, R.M.T. (Commander, RCN), 171
Storehouses: damage to, 91; reconstruction of, 102-4, 108; rescue of goods from, 91
Story, Oswald (Vice-Admiral, RN [Ret.]), 172, 173, 174, 197
Stotesbury, Jack (Able Seaman, RNCVR), 56
Stuart, Charles (Commander, RNR), 173, 174
Submarines: anti-submarine defence, 16, 21; attacks on ships by, 28; Canadian, as escorts to ships, 19; Canadian, effects of explosion on, 50; German, attacks on North American ships, 10, 11, 16, 17, 206-7
Symington, Powers (Captain, USN): assistance to ships during storm of 7 December, 90; final report and departure from Halifax, 104-5; on lessons of Halifax explosion, 114; meeting with Rear-Admiral Chambers, 70; offer of medical assistance, 67-8; and search parties, 98; and work parties for repairs, 93

Tacoma, USS, 66-7, 68, 70, 98, 105
Tas DeWolf & Son (steamship agents), 99
Telegraph services: alert to danger before explosion, 62; message to Admiralty after explosion, 66; railway, 84, 88; restoration, after explosion, 71, 95. *See also* Fleet Wireless School
Telephone services, 48
Thompson, E.B. (Lieutenant, RNR), 58
Titanic, RMS, 109
Torpedo Boat Shed, destroyed during explosion, 47
The Town That Died, 4
Trawler 22, 207
Trawler 32, 207
Trawlers, *78*
Triggs, T.K. (Commander, RN), 37-8, 38, 66
Tucker, Gilbert, 4
Turnbull, James (Captain, RNR), 62, 63, 65, 94-5, 111, 117, 155 6

U-156, German submarine, 206-7
United States Coast Guard, 29
United States Naval Reserve (USNR), 28-9
United States Shipping Board Emergency
    Fleet, 141
US Navy: assistance after Halifax explosion, 70,
    93, 95, 98; assistance to Canadian sub-
    marines, 19; medical assistance, after explo-
    sion, 68, 96, 97, 98; presence in Halifax
    Harbour on 5 December, 28-9; and shipping
    convoys in Halifax, 128-9; use of Halifax
    Harbour as port, 10
USNR. *See* United States Naval Reserve
    (USNR)

Vaughan, Miss, 47
Veach, Rev. Captain, 109
Veals, George, (Wireless Learner, RNCVR), 47
Victoria General Hospital, 68
Von Steuben, USS (formerly *Kronprinz
    William*), 67, 70, 90, 98, 105

Wagland, SS, 29
Walker, W.T. (Lieutenant-Commander, RCN),
    50, 197
War Measures Act, 195-6
Wellington Barracks: effects of explosion on,
    42, 57, *80, 81*; magazine, prevention of fire
    at, 58-9; treatment of casualties at, 58
W.H. Lee, motor boat, 17, 38-9, 40, 65, 139
Whitehead, Herbert (Mate, RNCVR): attempt
    to rescue *Mont Blanc* sailors after collision,
    36, 37; injuries, 43; testimony at public
    inquiry, 142, 178; view of collision of *Mont
    Blanc* and *Imo* from *CD-73*, 34-5; view of
    initial fire on *Mont Blanc* from *CD-73*, 36, 38
Wickens, A.H. (Veteran, RNCVR), 53-4
Wilfrid C., tugboat, 17
Wilson, John A. (Director of stores): at 8
    December meeting organized by Rear-
    Admiral Chambers, 99; distinguished service
    of, 207, 208; and reconstruction of store-
    houses, 102-4, 105, 108, 109-10; trip to
    Halifax, 86, 92, 98

Wireless Office, 47
Wireless School. *See* Fleet Wireless School
Woods, A.L. (Lieutenant, RNCVR), 51
Woolams, Richard (Lieutenant, RNR), 33
Woollcombe, Edward (Cadet, Naval College),
    59
Work parties, after explosion, 91-2
Wyatt, Frederick Evan (Acting Commander,
    RCN)(Chief Examining Officer): accommo-
    dation aboard HMCS *Niobe*, 20; acquittal of
    manslaughter, 201; arrest of, 185, 196; biogra-
    phy, 20-1; career after leaving navy, 205;
    comments by William Henry, after
    judgment of inquiry, 187-8; critique of, by
    Andrew Cluney, 176-7; critique of, by Louis
    Demers, 192; critique of, by Thomas
    Robertson, 176; critique of, in media, 154; at
    8 December meeting organized by Rear-
    Admiral Chambers, 99; delay in testimony
    at public inquiry, 143; discharge from RCN,
    154, 193, 202; disloyalty to superior officer,
    150, 168, 204; information on arrival of *Mont
    Blanc* on 5 December, 30; letters to Edward
    Martin, 164-5, 168, 182-3, 184, 187; marital
    problems of, 161, 168; meeting with William
    Henry, 153, 163; and naval chain of com-
    mand, 136; position during initial fire on
    Mont Blanc, 38-9; on problems with pilots,
    149-52, 165-7; relief of duties, 167, 169;
    suspension of, 173, 174; testimony at inquiry,
    144-6, 147-52, 154-5, 164-7; testimony
    regarding *Galileo* incident, 155-6; in William
    Henry's final summation for inquiry, 179-80,
    181

YMCA, destroyed during explosion, 47, *79*
Ypres, HMCS, 18, 26

Zwicker, John (Sergeant, 63rd Regiment)(Hali-
    fax Rifles), 115